The end of overeating.

TAKING CONTROL OF OUR INSATIABLE APPETITE

DAVID A. KESSLER, MD

PENGUIN BOOKS

PENGUIN BOOKS

Published by the Penguin Group
Penguin Books Ltd, 80 Strand, London WC2R ORL, England
Penguin Group (USA) Inc., 375 Hudson Street, New York, New York 10014, USA
Penguin Group (Canada), 90 Eglinton Avenue East, Suite 700, Toronto, Ontario, Canada M4P 2Y3
(a division of Pearson Penguin Canada Inc.)
Penguin Ireland, 25 St Stephen's Green, Dublin 2, Ireland (a division of Penguin Books Ltd)
Penguin Group (Australia), 250 Camberwell Road,
Camberwell, Victoria 3124, Australia (a division of Pearson Australia Group Pty Ltd)
Penguin Books India Pvt Ltd, 11 Community Centre, Panchsheel Park, New Delhi – 110 017, India
Penguin Group (NZ), 67 Apollo Drive, Rosedale, North Shore 0632, New Zealand
(a division of Pearson New Zealand Ltd)
Penguin Books (South Africa) (Pty) Ltd, 24 Sturdee Avenue, Rosebank, Johannesburg 2196, South Africa

Penguin Books Ltd, Registered Offices: 80 Strand, London WC2R ORL, England

www.penguin.com

First published in the United States of America by Rodale Books 2009
First published in Great Britain by Penguin Books 2010

3

Printed in England by Clays Ltd, St Ives plc

978-0-141-04781-2

www.greenpenguin.co.uk

Mixed Sources
Product group from well-managed
forests and other controlled sources
www.fsc.org Cert no. SA-COC-1592
© 1996 Forest Stewardship Council

Penguin Books is committed to a sustainable future
for our business, our readers and our planet.
The book in your hands is made from paper
certified by the Forest Stewardship Council.

For Paulette, through thick and thin
And, as always, for Elise and Ben

CONTENTS

PART ONE
Sugar, Fat, Salt

PART TWO
The Food Industry

PART THREE
Conditioned Hypereating Emerges

PART FOUR
The Theory of Treatment

PART FIVE
Food Rehab

PART SIX
The End of Overeating

INTRODUCTION
TO THE UK EDITION

The struggle against overeating knows no national boundaries.

Although the United States gave birth to the obesity epidemic that began in the late twentieth century, and remains at its epicenter, many European nations are being pulled in the same direction. If current trends in Great Britain continue, some 40 percent of residents will be obese by 2025.

The French are also following that trajectory. Almost 20 million people in France (out of a population of 63 million) are considered overweight, and almost six million of them are obese. The bestselling *Why French Women Don't Get Fat* may be due for an update.

But throughout much of Western Europe, portion sizes are still smaller, fast-food outlets have not achieved the same level of saturation, and there are more constraints on where and when it is appropriate to eat. Far from becoming a norm, the American way of eating remains a source of astonishment to many in the United Kingdom.

When Dr. Leddi Woods, a professor and an expert in obesity and public health, first came to the United States, she recalls "It was an assault on my senses. Food is everywhere. A wide variety of overcoloured, overolfacted, oversized gaudy baubles of sugar hit you, wherever you turn."

She was particularly struck by the contrast in snacks served at professional events. In the United Kingdom, these were always modest —participants at a seminar, for example, would typically be offered biscuits of about 100–120 calories apiece, and small cups of tea or coffee. But in the United States, "I was offered full-sized cans of fizzy drinks and packets of chewy cookies (300 calories apiece), or brightly coloured filled crackers (250 calories), or sweetened granola bars (250 calories). Everywhere in the US things are larger, brighter, sweeter and you are offered more. It is an effort to eat a reasonable portion of non-fried, fresh food."

As long as American food habits continue to seem bizarre, Britain has the chance of putting on the brakes. Unfortunately, that does not seem to be happening. "The way Europe is heading has been made starkly obvious to me now that I have seen what has happened in the United States," said Dr. Woods.

Alan Milburn, the former British Minister of Health, agreed. "Where the US is today, the UK will be tomorrow."

The reasons for obesity are much the same around the world, and the food industry is a major culprit. The modern global food corporation exists to grow its revenues and increase its profit, and it can only do that by selling more product, even when communities are already saturated with food. Portion sizes of cookies, confectionary, fizzy drinks and ready meals have increased 20 to 100 percent in the UK in the last ten years. There is no doubt that Britons are being served more calorie-dense food than healthy alternatives.

But people don't have to buy it, right? It's not quite that easy. As the research in *The End of Overeating* demonstrates, foods rich in sugar, fat and salt promote continued intake, pushing us to keep on eating. The industry dials fat, sugar and salt into just about everything it sells, makes food available on every corner through widening distribution networks, and uses marketing to persuade us that eating any time, day or night, is a socially acceptable form of entertainment.

All of that makes food so stimulating that our brains have literally been hijacked. That is what has not been understood until now. Millions of people have become conditioned and driven to overeat. Our brains have been activated by a neverending bombardment of food cues. We have "encoded" our perception of food in the beckoning realm where reward resides.

Multinational food corporations may not understand the neuroscience, but they know that certain inputs—namely, sugar, fat and salt—achieve their sought-after output—people come back for more. Industry executives are not concerned about our personal struggle to control what we eat. They are more interested in trying to foster the habit of "more."

The fight to alter our behavior, and resist the cues urging us to take another bite, is ours alone. To win, we must first change the way we look at food.

INTRODUCTION:
YOU ARE THE TARGET

I've learned to recognize overeating in restaurants all over America. It's not hard, because people who have been conditioned to overeat behave distinctively. They attack their food with a special kind of gusto. I've seen them lift their forks, readying their next bite before they've swallowed the previous one, and I've watched as they reach across the table to spear a companion's french fries or the last morsel of someone else's dessert. Certain foods seem to exert a magical pull on them, and they rarely leave any on their plates.

As I watch this kind of impulsive behavior, I suspect a battle may be taking place in their heads, the struggle between "I want" and "I shouldn't," between "I'm in charge" and "I can't control this." In this struggle lies one of the most consequential battles we face to protect our health.

The End of Overeating was born as I watched *The Oprah Winfrey Show.* Dr. Phil, the program's former resident psychologist, was talking about why people are obese and what they have to do to lose weight.

When he asked for a volunteer from the audience, a large, well-dressed woman named Sarah came forward. Resting his hand on her shoulder, Dr. Phil asked Sarah to talk candidly about the self-defeating behavior that, he insisted, led to weight gain. He said he wanted to know what made her "do what you know you don't want to do."

At first Sarah was all smiles as she told her story. "I eat all the time," she said with a nervous giggle. "I eat when I'm hungry, I eat when I'm not hungry. I eat to celebrate, I eat when I'm sad. I eat at night. I eat when my husband comes home."

Dr. Phil pressed Sarah to describe how she felt about herself.

The sunny visage began to change as she confessed to feeling like a failure. Sarah called herself "fat" and "ugly" and said her actions often left her disappointed, frustrated, and angry. "I feel that I can't accomplish what I set up my mind to do. I feel that I can't do it, that I don't have the willpower."

Choking back tears, she described how her focus sometimes turned obsessively to her eating behaviors. "My whole thought is about why I eat, what I eat, when I eat, with whom I eat," she said. "I don't like myself."

Turning to the audience, Dr. Phil asked, "How many of you here related to something you heard?" About two-thirds of its members raised their hands.

Sarah's struggle obviously struck a familiar chord in a lot of people. In fact, it struck one in me.

One afternoon, I decided to conduct an experiment that pitted temptation against willpower.

I walked into a bakery in San Francisco and asked for two semi-sweet chocolate-chip cookies. Back home, I pulled the cookies out of their bag and placed them on a paper plate, just beyond my arm's reach. They were thick and gooey—chunks of chocolate filled the craters of the cookies and rose into peaks.

I focused my attention on them, monitoring my own response. I sighed deeply and bit my lower lip. Almost indifferent to the flowers on the table and even to the framed photos of my children on the counter, I was fixated on those cookies until I forced myself to pull away. At some point, I noticed that I had moved my right hand a few inches closer to them, but I had no conscious recollection of my decision to act. I tried to concentrate on reading the newspaper, but I kept glancing back to the plate.

Feeling vaguely uneasy, I headed to my upstairs office, which is about as far away from the kitchen as I can get. But even from that safe distance, I could not fully shake the image of the cookies.

Eventually, I left the house without having eaten them, and I felt triumphant.

Hours later, I headed to Caffè Greco, a North Beach institution where the cappuccino is said to be the best in the city. A large glass jar filled with homemade cookies sat on the counter.

I ordered an orange-chocolate cookie and ate it at once.

I set out to understand what is driving these kinds of behaviors. I wanted to know why Sarah couldn't stop eating, even though doing so made her miserably unhappy and jeopardized her health. I wanted to know why my determination could so easily collapse.

I was intent on learning what could be done to help Sarah, me, and the millions of people just like us.

I began to listen more closely to people struggling with weight problems, listening the way a doctor needs to listen. I watched as well, paying close attention to how they behaved around food. It soon became clear that Sarah was not alone.

My conversation with a journalist, a forty-year-old man I'll call Andrew, reminded me that the struggle respects neither gender, nor socioeconomic class, nor age. Andrew, who is about five feet nine inches tall and weighs about 245 pounds, has written fearlessly from many of the world's battlegrounds. He has spent time with jihadists, suicide bombers, and war-hardened soldiers, and he hasn't flinched. But when I placed M&M's on the table before him, Andrew felt barely able to cope.

"When I'm in a meeting or interviewing someone and there is food on the table, I'll spend half my time thinking about that food," he admitted. His internal dialogue seesaws between "Man, that looks good, I could eat that," and "I'm not going to eat that because I don't need it."

His conflict begins early in the day and never lets up. "I wake up in the morning knowing that food is my enemy and that I am my own enemy," he observed. "It's uncontrollable."

At lunch Andrew is likely to be tempted by a basket of hot, fresh bread served with butter. On city streets Starbucks seems to summon him, and at home his refrigerator beckons irresistibly. "It just goes on and on and on," said Andrew. Like so many people who have difficulty controlling their eating, he sees food as an obstacle course he must navigate.

Andrew finds pharmacies and convenience stores particularly challenging: If he manages to get past the candy aisle without succumbing, he has to stare down more candy at the checkout. In a typical tug-of-war Andrew will pick up candy, put it down, then pick it up again, over and over and over. Sometimes he'll win his battle to get out the door without buying the candy; sometimes he won't. If he does make the purchase, he often feels so disgusted with himself that he'll pour half the contents into the trash—and then polish off the rest.

He described what he calls his "food soundtrack." "When I finished my bowl of Wheaties today, I immediately thought, 'Let me bring a banana and an apple to work so I'm not tempted, so I don't eat that corn muffin downstairs at the office.'"

But any success is momentary and is quickly replaced by further thoughts of food. "I talk to myself," he said. "I'll ask, 'What am I going to eat for lunch?' 'What if I get hungry at three?' 'What are we having for dinner? I hope it's good.'"

On a successful day, using maximum restraint, Andrew will consume about 1,500 calories, which is what he wants to eat in order to lose weight. But the next day he may consume 5,000. He rarely knows when he's full and feels mystified by people who don't share his single-mindedness.

"I can comprehend suicide terrorism more easily than I can comprehend somebody who just doesn't think about food," he said, without a trace of facetiousness.

Pizza is Andrew's favorite food, and when he smells a hot slice, he's completely distracted. "All I'm thinking about is that pizza," he admitted. "Very little holds my attention the way a pizza holds my attention. I'm telling you, food talks. All food talks.

"I bet when an addictive gambler walks into a casino, he will recognize with resignation that he's going to gamble and lose money. I think that recognition makes him upset, but it also makes him exhilarated. Like that gambler, I think that time gets suspended when I walk into a pizza place. Time is suspended, you're not in time anymore, you're not in your own body anymore.

"I pretend that there are no consequences to my actions. All that exists is me and that pizza, me and that pizza. That's the feeling."

I hadn't planned on tormenting Andrew when I put those M&M's before him and asked how they made him feel.

"They are incredibly distracting," he allowed.

"Would eating them make you feel better?" I asked.

Andrew said the first taste would give him a "rush" that was incredibly satisfying. But as he kept popping the candy into his mouth, he knew he would begin to feel ill. "More than ten or fifteen M&M's and it's just too much. It's like the sugar is digging a hole in my stomach."

Despite this, he'll keep on eating them.

I heard a degree of self-loathing in Andrew as he told his story. "The worst thing for me is to be caught in the act of buying M&M's," he admitted. He'll shove the candy into his pocket as soon as he leaves the cashier, hoping no one will see him.

"I'm a fat guy," he said, "and nobody wants to watch a guy who's overweight eat bad food. They just find it repulsive."

"How do you feel about yourself after you eat them?"

"I say to myself, 'There's another loss of control, another 240 calories that I don't need.' But all of the rational thoughts in the world can't compete with the color and expectation of an M&M."

Nothing else has that kind of power over Andrew, a man accustomed to running his own life. "An inanimate object, an inanimate food has power," he said, a hint of disgust in his voice.

Andrew recognized the promise of reward embedded in food. "It adds color to the day," he said, acknowledging that he feels pulled in by its "comfort, stimulation, sedation, happiness, the chance to put fun in the day."

America, he said, has become "a food fun house . . . a carnival of delicious, fatty, salty, sugary, and, more to the point, accessible and cheap delights. How could you expect to go to the carnival and not want to go on the rides? It's bright and colorful and fun and exciting. There are all these pings and noises. Of course you want to go on a ride; of course you want to play the game; of course you want to spend your money on this stimulation."

"Do you feel better when you eat?" I asked.

"The funny thing about eating endless amounts is that it's illogical, because the feeling is momentary," he said. "You can create one more moment of good feeling, but it never lasts."

That is a classic description of the body's reward system. "The good feeling is ephemeral, but it's what makes the behavior reinforcing," I explained. "Because it doesn't last, you want to do it again."

I asked Andrew whether he understood why he lost control.

That was a total mystery to him. "No idea," he answered. He was keen to know why food could hold such power over him.

"You've been conditioned by food and by cues that remind you of that food," I explained. "They focus your attention, promote anticipation, and build desire."

I wanted Andrew to realize that many people are wired for food the same way he is, and they're just as likely to lose control.

The food industry has been remarkably successful at designing foods to capture the attention of people like him. Food manufacturers, food designers, and restaurant owners may not fully understand the science behind the appeal of their foods, but they know that sugar, fat, and salt sell. As surely as if he were wearing a bull's-eye on his chest, Andrew is one of the industry's targets.

———————————

There's no shortage of people who lack control in the face of highly palatable food. And not all of them are overweight. I spoke with a young law student I'll call Samantha. She's twenty-five years old, five feet six inches tall, and 120 pounds, but her words could have come from Sarah or Andrew.

"If food is put in front of me, I find it an eternal struggle not to eat," said Samantha. "I hate going to work because they have bowls of candy everywhere. I'll leave my apartment and go to the library to study because we're not allowed to have food there.

"I keep thinking that it would be so easy just to make healthy choices, so why can't I do it? But instead, I rationalize what I eat in the weirdest ways. I have friends who feel the exact same way, and we marvel at people who are not like this. I don't understand how they do it."

Samantha stays thin because she doesn't always give in to the pull of food, and she exercises vigorously. But her struggle is fever-ish, and she is just as frustrated as the overweight people with whom I spoke.

"As soon as I'm not actively doing something, I'm thinking about what I'm going to eat. These are crazy thoughts to have. When I talk out loud about this, I feel ridiculous. It should not be all-consuming. I'm a smart girl with a lot going on in my life. The fact that I think about food for so many hours every day is madden-ing. I should be thinking about law school, not about how many Hershey's Kisses I've eaten today."

Still another woman, a colleague I'll call Claudia, told a similar tale.

"What happens when you start to eat?" I asked.

"Sometimes I can't stop. It doesn't happen at every meal, but if there's appealing food in front of me, or I've been thinking about food a lot for some reason, I'll keep eating, even to the point of being sick."

I encouraged Claudia to share her food memories.

"There are days when I dream about food," she said. "I think back to delicious meals I once had and long to feel the same sense of anticipation, happiness, and fulfillment they provoked."

Recollections of pleasures past seemed to spill from her. A birthday dinner at the Cheesecake Factory five years ago . . . a perfect late-night slice of New York pizza . . . and something she called Charlie cookies, "a little bar of heaven on earth."

Other favorites on her list: smoothies . . . corn on the cob . . . candy bars . . . potato chips. Some foods were obviously associated with her childhood or happy memories. There was, for example, the pasta sauce she could eat by the spoonful right from the jar, a favorite since age five. "I crave foods that my father used to make for me and dishes I once had in my college dining hall," she said.

Not everything she mentioned would make a nutritionist cringe—fresh fruit and a great salad got her excited, too. But the common thread was a preoccupied focus on the food she liked. "It's what I think about, what I can't wait to get home to," she admitted. "Left to myself, I will usually eat and eat and eat."

"Do you know why you do this?" I asked.

"No," she admitted, "I don't."

Millions of people are like Sarah, Andrew, Samantha, and Claudia. They don't have any of the eating disorders we've learned to recognize and treat, but food is never far from their minds. And once they begin eating, they can't seem to stop. Long after they've ceased to feel hungry, they're still eating. No one has ever explained what's happening to them and how they can control their eating. That's my goal in this book.

PART ONE

Sugar, Fat, Salt

Something Changed . . . America and Britain Gained Weight

For thousands of years human body weight stayed remarkably stable. Throughout adulthood we basically consumed no more than the food we needed to burn. People who were overweight stood apart from the general population. Millions of calories passed through our bodies, yet with rare exceptions our weight neither rose nor fell by any significant amount. A perfect biological system seemed to be at work.

Then, in the 1980s, something changed.

Katherine Flegal was one of the first to recognize the trend, but like many good researchers faced with an unexpected finding, she thought her numbers must be wrong. A senior research scientist at the federal Centers for Disease Control and Prevention, Flegal had been studying data from an enormous federal government survey of the health and nutritional status of American households. Her figures indicated that the number of people who were overweight had spiked dramatically.

Researchers had never seen such extreme numbers. In earlier

decades, American adults typically gained a couple of pounds between the ages of twenty and forty and then lost a couple of pounds in their sixties and seventies.

The shift that riveted Katherine Flegal's attention came from government survey data collected from 1988 to 1991, which revealed that fully one-third of the population aged twenty to seventy-four weighed too much. In fewer than a dozen years, 8 percent more Americans—about 20 million people, roughly the population of New York State—had joined the ranks of the overweight.

Her training and professional experience had taught Flegal to be cautious. In a complex and ambitious survey, errors can creep in at many points, and data often show anomalies that disappear with further scrutiny. She knew her information had to be accurate before she sounded an alarm.

"We checked it to a fare-thee-well," she said, describing her research team's review of regional analyses, time trends, and quality-control techniques. Nothing seemed out of place. The evidence of an abrupt increase in the number of overweight Americans appeared to be valid.

Still, she was nervous, especially since no one else seemed particularly aware that Americans as a group were becoming heavier. Hoping to find studies confirming these provocative data, her team scoured the published literature, but few journal articles were relevant. At professional meetings Flegal casually asked other researchers what they thought was happening with weight in America. Most thought it was the same as it had always been.

Americans were gaining millions of extra pounds, yet at first these pounds remained invisible. The medical community, the scientific community, and the federal government were not quick to notice the trend.

And so Flegal's team wrote up its data and went to press. The study, published in the July 1994 issue of the *Journal of the American Medical Association*, reported that a comparison of current and earlier data on the weight of Americans had revealed "dramatic increases in all race/sex groups." When a respected academic journal calls some-thing dramatic, it's the equivalent of a red alert. The results were consistent virtually across the board—among men and women, young and old, black and white. The rate of obesity in America had evidently exploded.

I asked Katherine Flegal to tell me how average weight had changed over time. Her graphs showed that the population had got-ten bigger over the decades. In 1960, when weight was still relatively stable in America, women ages twenty to twenty-nine averaged about 128 pounds; by 2000, the average weight of women in that age group had reached 157.

A similar trend was apparent in the forty-to-forty-nine-year-old group, where the average weight had jumped from 142 pounds in 1960 to 169 in 2000.

Also striking was the evidence that we were entering our adult years at a significantly higher weight, reflecting the gains that had taken place during childhood and adolescence. And from age twenty to age forty, many of us kept gaining. Rather than a few pounds, the average adult man was gaining more than a dozen pounds in those years.

Flegal observed something else. While on average everyone was getting heavier, the heaviest people in the population were gaining disproportionately more weight than others. The spread between those at the upper end of the weight curve and those at the lower end was widening. Weight gain was primarily about overweight people becoming more overweight.

A shift in Britain, while not quite as dramatic, is equally appar-ent. Three decades ago, fewer than one in ten Britons were obese. One in four is obese today. The number of overweight and obese males has increased 75 percent in the UK in the last decade. And it is projected that by 2050, Britain could be a "mainly obese society."

What had happened in such a short time to add so many mil-lions of pounds to so many millions of people? Many years of research led me to an unexpected answer.

Certainly food had become more readily available in the 1970s and 1980s: We have larger portion sizes, more chain restaurants, more neighborhood food outlets, and a culture that promotes more out-of-home eating. But having food available doesn't mean we have to eat it. What's been driving us to overeat?

It is not a want born of fear that food shortages lie ahead. Once this had been so. In the Bible, seven years of plenty were inevitably followed by seven years of famine, so we needed to build storehouses of fat in preparation. But in America and Britain, where even northern supermarkets are filled with summer fruits much of the year, that logic doesn't apply.

Nor is it a want rooted in hunger or the love of exceptional food. That kind of logic is not what's driving the out-of-control eating we see in Sarah, Andrew, Claudia, and so many others like them.

We know, too, that overeating is not the sole province of those who are overweight. Even people who remain lean, like Samantha, feel embattled by their drive for food. For them, it takes the most determined restraint to resist what feels like an almost overpowering push to eat.

Little help has been available. Family members, friends, and colleagues have not had the knowledge to offer support. Many, including doctors and health care professionals, still think that weight gainers merely lack willpower, or perhaps self-esteem. Few medical personnel or nutritionists, few psychological experts or public health advocates, have recognized the distinctive pattern of overeating that has become widespread in the population. No one has seen loss of control as its most defining characteristic.

Those who have succumbed to the pull of food are spending billions of dollars in search of a cure, determined to rid their bodies of the burden of weight. But they are squandering most of their money, finding only short-term weight loss and a vain hope that it will last.

That is because we have not understood why eating certain foods only makes us want to eat more of them. No one has recognized what's really happening. Let me try to explain.

Overriding the Wisdom of the Body

CHAPTER 2

People get fat because they eat more than people who are lean. I know this seems obvious, but we've spent decades being confused about it. Even now some people question the link between food consumption and weight gain. But we finally have strong evidence that weight gain is primarily due to overeating.

The confusion can be traced, at least in part, to the fact that when people are asked to keep a record of everything they eat, the differences between lean-weight and overweight individuals often appear minor. This observation led to all sorts of theories about the primary role that metabolism, diet composition, and genetics might play in weight gain. It was a long time before we realized that the explanation was much simpler: Most people do a poor job of reporting what they eat, and overweight people are particularly inaccurate reporters. So much of our eating takes place outside our awareness that it's easy to underestimate how much food we actually put into our bodies.

Sharon Pearcey and John de Castro, both behavioral neuro-scientists, compared food intake among a group that had gained more than 5 percent of its current body weight in the previous six months with a group whose weight had not fluctuated significantly during the same period. Participants were armed with a diary and asked to keep comprehensive records of every morsel they ate and every sip of fluid they drank, as well as where, when, and with whom. They also noted how hungry, thirsty, depressed, or anxious they felt before and after each episode of eating. As an added check on accuracy, subjects were given a camera and instructed to photograph their food before and after they ate; a time-and-date stamp appeared on every picture.

The research confirmed that people tend to substantially underestimate their food intake, a finding that was apparent in both groups of study subjects. But it also showed an obvious and dramatic contrast between the two groups—the weight gainers ate an average of almost 400 calories a day more than the comparison group. At that rate, they stood to put on more than two pounds every three weeks.

In another study, scientists monitored the weight gain of a group of children for several years. As it turned out, the weight of their parents and the amount of energy the children burned were less important factors than their caloric intake. The children who ate more weighed more.

While vigorous exercise can help control weight, a body of research shows that physical activity levels do not necessarily predict weight gain. More surprisingly, defects in metabolism are not an explanation either—in fact, most studies show that individuals who are obese (officially defined as having a body-mass index of 30 or above) or overweight (with a body-mass index of 25 or above) burn more energy than their lean counterparts.

How much we eat predicts how much we weigh. Sometimes the most obvious explanation turns out to be the right one.

For nearly a century scientists believed humans had biological mechanisms to balance the calories we consume (our energy intake) with the calories we burn (our energy expenditure). This dynamic process was supposed to allow us to maintain a relatively stable amount of fat on our bodies and limit fluctuations in weight.

We have presumed that the wisdom of the body is maintained through a feedback system known as homeostasis. Like temperature or blood pressure, which the body also tries to keep within relatively narrow ranges, energy is supposed to be regulated by a homeostatic process that keeps the body's energy stores stable. By closely matching food intake and energy expenditure, this biological strategy has allowed us to consume hundreds of thousands of calories every year without losing or gaining much weight.

It's a highly sophisticated system that can be explained simply: Many parts of the body talk to one another.

The brain is the command center of an elaborate communications network essential to energy regulation. This network involves the brain, the central and peripheral nervous systems, the gastrointestinal tract, the hormonal system, fat tissue, and more. The brain's hypothalamus receives signals from all these sources, integrates that information, and decides what needs to be done to maintain the body at a steady weight.

But this homeostatic system, while relevant, turns out to be less powerful than many scientists have assumed. If we could maintain energy balance effectively, we wouldn't be gaining so much weight. Our bodies would compensate, either by burning more calories or by shutting down our appetites. Obviously, that is not happening.

Over the past decade, scientists have tried to explain this failure by searching for defects in the homeostatic system. Their results have been disappointing. While some genetic and chemical defects have been identified, they seem to be rare and don't adequately account for the most common forms of obesity.

Robert De Niro's efforts to gain weight for the movie *Raging Bull*—and then lose it—demonstrate the limits of the homeostatic system. Hollywood celebrities may not seem to have much in common with the average American, but the extremes to which De Niro had to go for his role gave us experimental information it would have been hard to get another way.

First, he gained sixty pounds for the film by loading up on calories, and then he dropped most of that weight.

When I asked how he'd been able to do it, De Niro explained that it had been easy to lose the first thirty-five or forty pounds. "I stretched the rubber band and let it come back," he said.

But the last twenty pounds had been much harder. His body seemed inclined to settle at a weight that was higher than it had been before his gain. Returning to his prefilm weight, De Niro said, had required a vigilant mind-set. He likened the process he'd gone through to that of an alcoholic trying to stay sober.

Without knowing the biological explanation, De Niro had sensed that the homeostatic system was not acting alone.

Despite all the research focused on homeostasis, it is not the only influence on food intake. Researchers have shown that what we eat doesn't depend solely on signals sent by the brain to maintain a stable weight. Another region of the brain, with different circuitry, is also involved, and often it's in charge. This is known as the reward system.

And in America, in the fight between energy balance and reward, the reward system is winning.

Like the homeostatic system, the body's reward system is essential to survival, encouraging us to seek out pleasurable things like sex and food. Powerful biological forces are at play that make us *want* something enough to pursue it and then make us feel momentarily better once we obtain it. The anticipation of reward provides motivation to act.

Motivational pathways in our brains have developed over the millennia to keep us alive. Activated by stimuli in the environment, they generate an emotional response, which then drives our behavior. In other words, we receive information and we act on it. If the message is "This is good," we move closer to gain the benefit; if the message is "This is dangerous," we're likely to withdraw.

It is possible to activate the brain's reward centers by artificially stimulating them with an electrode, which is sometimes done during animal experiments. One study showed that when the far-lateral hypothalamus region was stimulated, animals ate well beyond the point where they would otherwise have stopped.

Another study demonstrated the power of the reward system even more dramatically. Food was placed at the far end of a room with an electrified floor that delivered an unpleasant shock. Animals had to walk across that floor to reach their food. The strength of that shock stopped an animal that hadn't eaten for a while from walking across the floor to obtain food. Under normal circumstances, hunger did not provide enough motive to act, given the consequences. Stimulate the reward centers, though, and the result was just the opposite: Even an animal that wasn't hungry was willing to cross the electrical floor in order to secure a reward.

Outside the laboratory, there are other stimulants, of course. And that raises provocative scientific questions. Can they also stir the reward centers of the brain? Is it possible that eating certain foods can stimulate us to keep eating—and eating and eating?

Sugar, Fat, and Salt Make Us Eat More Sugar, Fat, and Salt

To understand how eating promotes more eating—and why homeostasis is under sustained assault—we must first understand the concept of "palatability" as the term is used scientifically. In everyday language, we call food palatable if it has an agreeable taste. But when scientists say a food is palatable, they are referring primarily to its capacity to stimulate the appetite and prompt us to eat more. Palatability does involve taste, of course, but, crucially, it also involves the motivation to *pursue* that taste. It is the reason we want more.

Palatability is largely based on how food engages the full range of our senses. Usually, the most palatable foods contain some combination of sugar, fat, and salt. The sensory properties of palatable foods—the cold, creamy pleasure of a milkshake, the aroma of chocolate cake, the texture of crispy chicken wings sweetened with a honey-mustard dipping sauce—all stimulate the appetite. And it's that stimulation, or the anticipation of that stimulation, rather than genuine hunger, that makes us put food into our mouths long after our caloric needs are satisfied.

"Palatable foods arouse our appetite," said Peter Rogers, a biological psychologist at the University of Bristol, in England. "They act as an incentive to eat."

Our preference for sweetness is no surprise. Newborns who are given drops of a solution of sucrose and water exhibit pleasure with their facial expressions. And the sweeter the solution the more they prefer it.

Adam Drewnowski, at the University of Washington, in Seattle, has spent thirty years studying human taste, food preferences, and dietary choices. Like many of his colleagues, he initially focused on sugar, but he soon became convinced that sugar itself is not the only reason we're so partial to sweet foods. If nothing else mattered, more of us would just open a packet of sugar and eat it.

No one had looked closely at fat until the 1980s. "The focus was on the pleasure response to sugar, as though sugar were the only sensation in food that people responded to," said Drewnowski. Certain there was more to the story, he set out to prove it. He found that what we like is not sugar alone, but sugar in combination with fat. Fat, he wrote, "is responsible for the characteristic texture, flavor, and aroma of many foods and largely determines the palatability of the diet."

Because fat provokes so many different sensations in the mouth, we can't always tell which foods contain the most fat or why we prefer one sugar-fat mixture to another. But we can certainly point to what we like best.

Drewnowski conducted a study in which he added various amounts of sugar to five different dairy products—skim milk, whole milk, half-and-half, heavy cream, and heavy cream blended with safflower oil. Skim milk had almost no fat, while the cream-and-oil mixture contained more than 50 percent fat. Asked to choose which they liked best, people gave low marks to products with sweetened skim milk (with lots of sugar and little fat) and to unsweetened cream (lots of fat, little sugar). Mix the same amount of sugar into low-fat and high-fat products, however, and people invariably chose the higher-fat mixtures. Fat and sugar levels *both* influence preference.

The Cheesecake Factory knew that, back when they were trying to convince David Overton, the chain's founder, to approve a new menu offering. By glazing a chicken dish so that it would pick up extra sweetness or by cooking food in extra butter, they gave food enough of a "halo effect" to win Overton over, recalled one of the research chefs at the chain.

The combination of sugar and fat is what people prefer, and it's what they'll eat most. The art of pleasing the palate is in large part a matter of combining them in optimal amounts. That can do more than make food palatable. It can make food "hyperpalatable."

It is, however, possible to make a food too sweet, too fatty, or too salty.

Many of us have what's called a "bliss point"—the point at which we get the greatest pleasure from sugar, fat, or salt. Scientists depict this as an inverted U-shaped curve: As more sugar is added, food becomes more pleasurable until we reach the bliss point at the top of the curve, and then the pleasure experience drops off. For sweet beverages, that point is about 10 percent—drinks containing more sucrose than that generally taste too sweet, and we enjoy them less.

The salt curve is similar but steeper, according to food industry expert Dwight Riskey, who worked for Frito-Lay. A smaller change in the salt concentration will have a bigger impact than a comparable change in the concentration of sugar, he explained. That's why it's so easy to oversalt food. The bliss point for salt is determined to some extent by the food it's in—we want less salt in soup than we do in potato chips or crackers, for example. The salt level we enjoy may also be determined by what we've learned from our early encounters with food.

But when the mix is right, food becomes more stimulating. Eating foods high in sugar, fat, and salt makes us eat *more* foods high in sugar, fat, and salt. We see this clearly in both animal and human research.

Barry Levin, a physician and professor at the New Jersey Medical School, demonstrated this principle with rats. He bred one strain to overfeed when a high-calorie diet was available, producing an obesity-prone rat. The other strain did not ordinarily overfeed—an obesity-resistant rat. After a period of eating extra calories, the obesity-resistant rats typically cut back their food consumption much faster than obesity-prone rats.

But when both groups of rats were offered a rich, creamy liquid high in sugar and fat, those patterns changed. All the animals ate without restraint. Levin said that when they are given such a palatable combination, "they will just gorge themselves." Increasing only the fat content of a resistant rat's diet won't make the animal overeat or become obese. But feed it a high-fat, high-sugar diet, and it will grow just as fat as an obesity-prone rat on a high-calorie diet.

Variety and ready availability further amplify overeating. Anthony Sclafani was a graduate student at the University of Chicago in the late 1960s when he started trying to understand what promoted excess consumption. When he fed animals high-fat foods, they gained more weight than those fed chow pellets (the bland food that's typically given to laboratory rats), but his results weren't particularly dramatic.

Then, by chance, he put a rat on a lab bench near some fallen Froot Loops, the high-calorie, high-sugar cereal. He was struck by how fast the animal picked up the cereal and started to eat it.

Sclafani turned that casual observation into a more formal experiment. After familiarizing test animals with the taste of Froot Loops, he let them loose in an open field. Rats prefer to stay in corners and won't readily venture across a field to eat chow pellets, but when Froot Loops were available, they scurried over to them.

Next, Sclafani studied the effect of a "supermarket diet." The mix of foods he fed his animals could be purchased at any grocery store: sweetened condensed milk, chocolate-chip cookies, salami, cheese, bananas, marshmallows, milk chocolate, and peanut butter. After ten days, animals that were fed the supermarket diet weighed significantly more than rats that were fed bland chow. And the rats on the supermarket diet continued to gain weight, eventually becoming twice as heavy as their control counterparts. Sclafani concluded that feeding adult rats "a variety of highly palatable supermarket foods was a particularly effective way of producing dietary obesity."

Why did they keep on eating? What happened to the homeostatic ability to balance energy consumption and expenditure? Why did the rats fail to defend themselves from weight gain?

Sclafani answered those questions in a single sentence: "In the normal rat, free access to palatable foods is a sufficient condition to promote excessive weight."

Coupled with evidence collected by other scientists, Sclafani's results support the idea that the biological system that's designed to maintain energy balance can go awry when animals have easy access to a variety of foods that are high in sugar and fat.

Experiments with humans show much the same thing, especially when they're offered foods they prefer. In one study, participants were asked to keep track of the foods they ate for seven days and to rate their preference for each meal on a scale of 1 to 7. Most people gave higher ratings to foods with higher levels of fat and sugar. Unsurprisingly, they also ate more of them, consuming almost 44 percent more food at meals they rated a 7 than at those rated a 3 or below.

In another study, researchers at the National Institutes of Health confined male subjects to a ward in which their food intake could be monitored. For the first few days the men were fed a diet designed to keep them at their current body weight; since many of them were significantly overweight, that meant an average of just under 3,000 calories a day. (Approximately 50 percent of those calories came from carbohydrates, 30 percent from fat, and 20 percent from protein.)

The participants were then allowed to eat whatever they wished from two free vending machines that contained a variety of entrées and snacks. This gave them twenty-four-hour-a-day access to meats, cheese, and bread; tortillas and pinto beans; cereal, pastry, and desserts; french fries, popcorn, and chips; fruits, vegetables, nuts, and beverages. The men were asked to follow their typical eating patterns as closely as possible.

You've probably guessed the result. Given the opportunity to eat without restriction, participants consumed an average of 4,500 calories daily—150 percent of what they actually needed to maintain a stable weight. One person consumed almost 7,000 calories, the equivalent of about seventeen quarter-pound hamburgers. In general, the study subjects also ate substantially more fat and less protein during the period of unrestricted eating; the typical diet contained 48 percent carbohydrates, 40 percent fat, and 12 percent protein.

All of this demonstrates scientifically what most of us know from experience: When offered a varied selection and large portions of high-sugar, high-fat, high-salt foods, many of us will eat them in excessive amounts.

The Business of Food: Creating Highly Rewarding Stimuli

"Higher sugar, fat, and salt make you want to eat more," a high-level food industry executive told me. I had already read this in the scientific literature, and heard it in conversations with neuroscientists and psychologists. Now, an insider was saying the same thing.

My source was a leading food designer, a Henry Ford of mass-produced food who had agreed to part the curtain for me, at least a bit, to reveal how his industry operates. To protect his business, he did not want to be identified.

But he was remarkably candid, explaining that the food industry creates dishes to hit what he called the "three points of the compass." Sugar, fat, and salt make a food compelling, said the designer. They make it indulgent. They make it high in *hedonic* value, which gives us pleasure.

"Do you design food specifically to be highly hedonic?" I asked.

"Oh, absolutely," he replied without a moment's hesitation. "We try to bring as much of that into the equation as possible."

During the past two decades there has been an explosion in our ability to access and afford highly palatable foods. Restaurants—where Americans spend 50 percent of today's food dollar—sit at the epicenter of this explosion.

Countless new foods have been introduced in restaurants, and most of them hit the three compass points. Sugar, fat, and salt are either loaded onto a core ingredient (such as meat, vegetable, potato, or bread), layered on top of it, or both. Deep-fried tortilla chips are an example of loading—the fat is contained in the chip itself. When a potato is smothered in cheese, sour cream, and sauce, that's layering.

I asked the designer to describe the ingredients in some foods commonly found in popular restaurants today.

The many American fast-food chains that are now so ubiquitous in Europe have introduced techniques for optimizing food that drive more eating. It is not just that they serve food with more fat, sugar, and salt, or that intensive processing virtually eliminates our need to chew before swallowing, or that snacks are now available any time of the day. It is the combination of all that, and more.

I asked the food designer to describe the signature dishes at Kentucky Fried Chicken. He called the fried chicken "a premier, quintessential example" of putting more fat on our plate. "They have optimized the breading system on the chicken."

KFC's "proprietary" approach to battering its food results in "an optimized, fat pick-up system," he explained. With its flour, salt, MSG, maltodextrin, sugar, corn syrup, and spice, the fried coating imparts flavor that touches on all three points of the compass while giving the consumer the perception of a bargain—a big plate of food sold at a good price.

"Strip off all the fried breading on a piece of chicken and put it next to the fried product with all of its coatings and you will see that the size of the chicken suddenly shrinks," said the food designer. "KFC's approach has permeated the quick-service restaurant business because it not only increases the fat, but makes the stuff look bigger."

Initially, KFC meals were built around a whole chicken, with a pick-up surface that contained "an enormous amount of breading, crispiness, and brownness on the surface. That makes the chicken look like more and gives it this wonderful oily flavor."

Over time, the company began to alter the base on which the coating was built. There was less meat in a chicken nugget compared to a whole chicken, and a greater percentage of fried batter. But the real breakthrough was popcorn chicken. "The smaller the piece of meat, the greater the percentage of fat pick-up," the food designer continued. Popcorn chicken is a "home run . . . it takes it way over the top."

For the industry, the menu item also promises a higher margin of profit. "Now, we have lots of pieces of a cheaper part of the chicken. If you get a basket of these things, it looks like 'wow, look at all the food I'm getting,' but by volume, maybe 2/3 of it is batter and breading." The product has been "optimized on every dimension," with the fat, sugar and salt combining with the perception of good value to virtually guarantee consumer appeal.

Mashed potatoes are the usual companion to the chicken at KFC. To save on shipping costs and maintain uniformity, the highly processed product is reconstituted by each restaurant outlet, which simply add water to dried potatoes. But that "leaves it tasting like a mass of fluffy starch," said the food designer. The flavor solution is to "hit it with gravy," which is loaded with starch, sugar, salt, MSG, caramel color, and flavorings (but devoid of protein, fiber, or micronutrients).

"What am I really eating?," he asked rhetorically. "You're eating very easy-to-digest starch that goes right down, you swallow it without chewing. Before you know it, you have eaten enormous amounts of starch and carbohydrates with very little satiety feedback."

He walked me through some offerings at other popular food chains. Burger King's Whopper was a good example of a food that touched on the three points of the compass – and then was altered for further effect. In its first, stripped-down form, the burger was explosively rich in fat, sugar, and salt. When the chain began adding more beef, extra cheese, or a layer of bacon, it became "an ICBM."

McDonald's broke new ground in another way – by making food available on a whim. "Food is very accessible, you can eat between meals. The great growth at McDonalds has been the snacking occasion," said the food designer. "That took down the barrier. You get hungry, you want something, your mind pushes off the reality of what you ought to eat, and you end up picking up a hamburger and a giant soda or French fries."

Restaurant executives also discovered how to capitalize on success with a high-fat, high-salt morning meal. "They took what they learned from the core lunch and dinner menu and applied it to breakfast. The sausage McMuffin and the egg McMuffin are stand-ins for the hamburger. In effect, you are eating a morning hamburger."

Pushing Up Our Settling Points

CHAPTER 5

For years I wondered why I was fat. Science seemed to suggest it was my destiny.

"Set point theory" says that adult weight is destined to remain at a predetermined level and that we will adjust our energy intake and output to keep it there. According to set point theory, I was fat because my body's "thermostat" was set high. The capacity to compensate for either inadequate or excess food intake reflects the homeostatic system in action. The theory is that if I lose weight, my body tries to get it back, slowing down my metabolism until I return to my predetermined set point. That made homeostasis a useful way to explain the failure of diets.

But if the set point worked, it should not only defend me against weight loss, it should protect me from weight gain. When I eat more, my body should theoretically be compensating by speeding up my metabolism to burn more energy, but it does not. To understand what has pushed up weight curves over the past few years, it is more useful today to think instead about the body's "settling point."

The settling point theory goes beyond homeostatic mechanisms to make room for a number of independent influences on weight. A somewhat more nuanced model, it is built on the idea that weight is not set at a predetermined level, but is determined by a balance of many factors. On the appetite side, the drive to eat and the capacity to be satisfied are primary. On the expenditure side, the major factors are the ability to oxidize fat and burn calories, along with the level of physical activity. The settling point is the place where all of this comes to equilibrium.

I hypothesize that the point where our weight settles is primarily the result of motivation and availability—how much we want to seek out food and how readily we can obtain and eat it. In the short term, we may be able to restrict our eating, lose weight, and reach a new settling point. But if we return to earlier patterns and familiar environments, we will pursue reward with renewed vigor, gain weight, and return to the old settling point. That's why diets fail.

Constant access to sugar plus fat, salt plus fat, and sugar plus fat plus salt pushes up the settling point. We move along the weight curve because the body's furnace is not burning quite enough fuel to keep pace with our energy intake. Eventually the upward spiral ends as we reach our capacity to increase consumption in response to sensory stimuli—but by then our weight has settled in a very different zone.

This is by no means a universal response. Food loaded with fat and sugar asserts its hold—its capture—on each of us with varying intensity. Some respond with indifference; others are able to eat just a little and then stop. But for the millions of people whose attention it grabs, the drive for reward aggressively asserts dominance over the drive for balance. It is not our biological destiny to return to a set point.

That reward drive can become an obsession, although it's one that many people keep private. Take, for example, my colleague Claudia's response to frozen chocolate peanut-butter cookies. She calls them Charlie cookies, and they're one of her favorite desserts. In addition to chocolate chips and peanut butter, they contain relatively few ingredients: just oats, corn syrup, brown sugar, butter or margarine, vanilla, and salt. In effect, the oats serve as the binder for what is otherwise nothing more than three kinds of sweeteners, plus fat and salt, topped with a frosting of semisweet chocolate chips and peanut butter.

One day I spotted Claudia walking down the hallway with a plate of them, and I asked her to describe their appeal. "The chocolate smell is very distracting," she said. "I keep looking at them and thinking how good it would taste to have a bite. My stomach is starting to react. The back of my tongue tingles."

Claudia knows from the past exactly how she'll experience the first bite of that frozen cookie. "It takes only a few chews for the chocolate–peanut butter layer to melt. As it does, the flavor goes from a cold, concentrated spot on my tongue to very warm and mushy, a salty-sweet, liquidy mush that seems to fill my entire mouth."

That combination of texture and taste works its magic. Claudia knows it takes about fifteen bites to consume most of the cookie and another half-dozen chews to swallow the lingering bits of oats and chocolate. "I'm very conscious of the complexity of the chewing process," she says. "As more pieces of the cookie melt, all the flavors combine, and more and more flavor is released at the back of my mouth."

Claudia ate two of the cookies as she continued her vivid, sensual description. "The flavor is actually most potent after I've already swallowed the bite. It just makes me want to eat more to combine the pleasure of the flavor with the pleasure of the act of chewing and eating and swallowing."

The sight, the smell, the taste, and the texture of those cookies all captivated Claudia. Only her auditory sense was not engaged. It was a mere cookie, but to Claudia and others like her, it emitted a strong emotional charge.

I brought together a cross-section of colleagues to talk about their reactions to fats and sugars. Claudia and Maria, who are both over-weight, were willing to join. Rosalita and Jacob, who are thin, also came along. Earlier I'd asked them to name their favorite snacks; now I opened up the packages they had identified—Little Debbie's Swiss Rolls, peanut butter M&M's, and a Snickers bar—and displayed them on the table.

I asked them to share the thoughts running through their heads as they sat around that table.

Maria, who was partial to the cake rolls, began to describe them in the language of the senses. "Creaminess and moistness," she said. "I see their contours—the shape is perfect for a bite. I imagine how they'll feel in my mouth. Sweet, but not too sweet." The aroma of the chocolate-and-cream blend appealed to her as well. "I just want to reach over, grab them, and take a bite," she sighed. As she talked, I could almost see her desire.

Before I unwrapped the snacks, Maria said she had not been thinking about food, and she hadn't felt hungry. But now she felt compelled to stare at the cake and to imagine it in her mouth. She knew she wouldn't be able to resist for long. "I keep looking at it," she admitted. "The outside coating is delicious. I'm fooling myself by thinking that I'll eat only one."

Suddenly Maria became angry. "I do not want them," she said. "But I cannot control my desire to eat them.

"I'm obsessing. I feel totally out of control."

The struggle taking place in Maria's brain is one familiar to many of us. I felt that a scientific understanding of what Maria and others like her were experiencing emotionally might begin to make a difference to millions of Americans.

Claudia had much the same emotional response. Her obsession with Charlie cookies was rivaled only by her full-tilt focus on the Snickers bar. She kept thinking about that candy. Like Maria, she wasn't hungry, but she felt completely distracted by the chocolate bar and couldn't stop looking at it.

"I feel very wanton, as if I don't have control over myself, my impulses," she told us. "If I were alone, I'd eat it in a flash."

Only our presence in the room held her back. "I'm not going to eat this in front of any of you," she said. "But I know I'm going to eat it, even though I don't want to. It's a done deal. I'll eat the whole thing."

With those words, Claudia's anxiety about deciding whether to eat the candy bar had passed. She told me she had felt jittery as I unwrapped it, and indeed I noticed she had nervously tapped her fingers on the table. She said she expected to feel disgusted after eating the candy, but right now she was calm.

"I'm not anxious, because it's only a matter of time before I eat it," she explained. "The hard part of arguing with myself is over. Before and after is when I feel awful, tormented."

Rosalita spoke next. Although thin, she obsesses about food as much as the others. She told me she had already eaten some chocolate earlier in the day and four cookies the previous evening. She commented on the appealing aroma of the M&M's and explained how she usually approached the candy. "First I'll eat just a few, not a lot. Then I'll have a few more. And I'll keep doing that until I feel sick."

Trying to compensate, Rosalita drinks plenty of water and makes it a point to eat a vegetable. She's an old hand at that sort of strategy. The Snickers bar didn't appeal to her because it looked too big, and she knew eating it would make her feel guilty. Instead, she tends to reach for small sweets, like bite-sized pieces of candy. And when a colleague brings in cookies? "I'll eat one, go to my desk, and think about them. Then I'll go back for another one. And I'll do that for the rest of the afternoon."

Rosalita almost never feels physically full. She never leaves food on her plate. When food is around, she thinks about it constantly, but she has developed techniques that allow her to keep her weight in check.

Although Jacob is also partial to peanut butter M&M's, he doesn't necessarily need to eat them. "I'm full," he said, looking at the open bag. "I already had a cookie about an hour and a half ago. They don't interest me." He liked sweets, he explained, but had no desire to eat them when he wasn't hungry. "They just don't seem appealing."

Jacob eats mostly for fuel. "I just want to get eating out of the way," he says. He rarely gives much thought to food. Claudia and Maria couldn't understand his attitude.

Seeing the strong response that highly palatable foods can generate helped me understand why the settling point gets pushed up in the face of reward. No one in the group had even eaten the snacks on the table, yet their presence was enough to make some people feel less in control.

Claudia, Maria, and Rosalita do not fit any of the formal criteria for disordered eating. They don't, for example, behave like a woman who could not pass by a pastry shop without devouring fifteen cakes, one of the first cases of binge eating to be described in research papers. They are not binge eaters who will eat huge quantities of food in short periods of time. They don't purge after they eat excessively. They don't exhibit the psychological problems, such as depression, that are often associated with eating disorders.

But they feel powerless in the face of certain foods. This may be the primary characteristic of what is sometimes referred to as emotional or compulsive eating, although there are no formal definitions of these terms. Their behavior is best understood as a reward-driven response to the sensory stimuli associated with food.

This response isn't exclusive to overweight people. Many thin people have the same impulse—it's just that, like Rosalita, they have found ways to maintain control. The capacity of food to acquire a powerful salience, or prominence, in the human mind is strong. How do inanimate objects—M&M's, Charlie cookies, cake rolls—acquire such power over us? What allows them to so thoroughly dominate our attention?

How do these foods spin so many of us out of control?

Sugar, Fat, and Salt
Are Reinforcing

CHAPTER 6

Rewarding foods tend to be reinforcing, meaning that they keep us coming back for more. I put an M&M in my mouth, it tastes good, and I return for another. The sugar and fat in the candy reinforce my desire to keep eating it.

Scientists ask two questions to determine whether animals find a substance reinforcing:

- Are they willing to work to obtain it?
- Do they respond to other stimuli they've learned to associate with the substance?

By these criteria, sugar, fat, and salt are clearly reinforcing.

One decisive piece of evidence is exquisitely simple. French researchers first allowed one group of animals to eat freely while restricting the diet of another group. Next they measured the speed at which each group ran for chow compared to Choc and Crisp, a German chocolate-flavored cereal high in sugar and fat.

It was no surprise that the hungry animals ran faster toward chow than animals that had been allowed to feed freely. But hunger did not influence the appeal of Choc and Crisp—both groups headed toward the cereal at almost the same speed.

We once thought that in the absence of hunger, food could not serve as an effective reward. That idea proved to be wrong. As the French experiment demonstrates, animals will work for foods that are high in sugar and fat even if they are not hungry. They'll also work for salt solutions, especially if they've ever been salt depleted. Another persuasive study demonstrated that animals will work for high-sugar foods. That research, conducted at Carleton University in Ottawa, Ontario, used a progressive ratio technique that forces rats to work harder and harder to obtain their next reward.

At the beginning of the study, getting a reward was easy. When an animal pressed a lever once, it earned its first reward. The second reward came after three presses of the lever. Next, six lever presses were required. A fourth reward took ten lever presses, a fifth took sixteen, and a sixth took twenty-three presses of the lever.

Researchers look for the breaking point, the point beyond which the animal will not keep pressing the lever in search of a reward. In the Canadian study, rats generally worked harder—that is, they pressed the lever more—to get higher concentrations of sucrose. On average they pressed enough to earn five rewards of a solution without sucrose, about six rewards of a 10 percent sucrose solution, and about eight rewards of the 20 percent solution. To get that eighth reward of 20 percent sucrose, a rat had to press the lever forty-four times.

Interestingly, this study also showed that there's a limit to how sweet animals like their solutions. They worked less at a sucrose concentration of 30 percent, pressing the lever only enough to earn, on average, just under seven rewards. Like people, they have a sucrose bliss point (although, at least in this study, it seemed to be higher than ours).

That's still plenty of work in pursuit of reward, and a clear demonstration of the reinforcing qualities of sugar.

Foods high in fat get similar results. Using mice as test animals when she was at the University of North Carolina at Chapel Hill, Sara Ward would measure the willingness of animals to work for a corn-oil solution even when they were not hungry. She also used a progressive ratio, allowing an animal to earn a reward after poking its nose into a hole a certain number of times. A 10 percent corn-oil solution had the greatest reinforcing properties, with the breaking point occurring after slightly more than twelve rewards. It took her animals just over fifty nose pokes to earn that reward. Fat, too, is a reinforcer, with a reward value that stimulates an animal to work.

Animals are willing to work even harder for foods that are high in sugar *and* fat. Ward used Ensure, a liquid nutritional drink that contains both, to conduct another nose-poke experiment. Adopting the same progressive ratio she'd applied to corn oil, she found that mice worked enough in an hour to earn approximately fourteen rewards, the last one requiring seventy-seven nose pokes.

This is scientific confirmation that the combination of fat and sugar is a strong reinforcer. In a conversation with Ward, I asked her how strong it really was. The breaking point at which the animals will no longer work for the reward, she told me, is slightly lower than the breaking point for cocaine. Animals are willing to work almost as hard to get either one.

My own look at a vanilla milkshake confirmed the reinforcing value of sugar and fat and helped me better understand what matters most. Working with colleagues at the University of Washington and Western Washington University who are experts at determining which qualities in a substance motivate us to pursue it, we were able to determine that in products combining sugar, fat, and flavoring, sugar exerts the greatest influence. Fat is also reinforcing, but calorie for calorie, sucrose is the dominant factor.

The power of the vanilla milkshake and other high-sugar, high-fat foods is further amplified as cues become associated with them.

Along with taste and other sensory characteristics, the location where the food has previously been available and the events associated with past consumption can also become reinforcers. In time, these cues become as important in food-seeking behavior as the food itself.

A bowl of M&M's, for example, can be reinforcing before I touch a single one. If I've eaten the candy in the past, I'm stimulated by the sight of it because I know it will be rewarding. I reach for an M&M, eat it, and experience that reward. The visual cue gains power.

Cues associated with the pleasure response demand our attention, motivate our behavior, and stimulate the urge we call "wanting." When those cues are present, we learn to pursue food with greater vigor to secure the expected reward. With experience, the association between cues and food becomes even stronger, and we become more single-minded in our focus and our pursuit. That increases consumption. We pursue the food more frequently, and the resulting pleasure leads us to repeat the behavior. A continuous cycle of cue-urge-reward is set in motion and eventually becomes a habit.

The "conditioned place paradigm" is a time-tested scientific technique for assessing the reinforcing properties of one particular cue: location. The stage is set when a desired substance is given to an animal in a certain location. We then compare the animal's preference for being in that location after the desired substance is removed to its preference for being someplace similar where the substance has never appeared.

A substantial body of scientific literature has accumulated over the years to show that animals become conditioned to prefer environments where opiates, amphetamines, morphine, and other drugs were previously available. More recently, some scientists have turned their attention to the question of whether certain foods can also generate a conditioned place preference.

One study examined how animals learn to associate snack foods with location. The experiment began with a test to determine which of two chambers of a cage a rat preferred, measured by how much time it spent there. No food was provided in either chamber.

The animals, which were not hungry at the time of the experiments, were then divided into two groups. The first was given Froot Loops in its less-favored chamber. The second group was fed standard chow in the chamber it preferred. Next, the second group was offered Cheetos, a high-calorie, high-fat snack food, in its less-preferred chamber, while the first group got standard chow in its preferred locale. Both groups of animals spent more time in their less-preferred chamber, presumably motivated by the opportunity to consume either Froot Loops or Cheetos.

Then the initial chamber preference test was repeated. Again the rats were free to choose their locale, and again there was no food in either chamber. The findings were clear: Regardless of their previous choices, both groups of rats had learned to prefer the chamber where they had eaten either Froot Loops or Cheetos. Their exposure to foods high in sugar or fat had conditioned them to prefer the place where that exposure had occurred.

For humans, too, location is one of the most potent cues. Pass the mall where you know you'll find a Ruby Tuesday or the neighborhood where your town's best pizza is available, and you'll experience a desire that you didn't have a moment before.

Evidence that high-sugar, high-fat foods are reinforcing, then, comes from two key findings in animal studies: Animals are willing to work harder for those foods, and the foods intensify the power of cues, such as where the animal once encountered the stimuli.

Three other features of food also exert a powerful influence on our desire for more.

First, *quantity*. Give a rat two pellets of food rather than one, give a person two scoops of ice cream rather than one, and they'll eat more. Portion size matters.

Second is the *concentration* of rewarding ingredients. Adding more sugar or fat to a given portion boosts its desirability (although only up to a point; in excess, either one can lessen its appeal).

Finally, *variety* plays an important role. We saw this when Anthony Sclafani demonstrated that a supermarket diet can throw off the body's system of energy balance, but providing access to different kinds of foods is only one way to increase stimulation. We can also add features to the environment in which a food is served—associating it with an external signal, such as light or sound. Or we can load in sensory inputs, such as adding chocolate chips to ice cream. Another way to achieve variety is with what's called *dynamic contrast*. The Oreo cookie, with its combination of flavors and textures (bitter chocolate wafer, sweet cream filling), is a classic example of a food with dynamic contrast.

Sugar and fat are reinforcing, and cues, quantity, concentration, and variety all increase that reinforcement value. That still doesn't mean everyone will go after these foods with equal effort. Some people are likelier than others to find food more reinforcing and are thus willing to work harder to obtain it. What the evidence tells us is that sugar and fat, as well as the cues predicting that sugar and fat are available, can condition the behavior of those who are vulnerable.

Amping Up the Neurons

CHAPTER 7

When we put food rich in sugar, fat, and salt in our mouths, we stimulate neurons, which are the basic cells of the brain. Neurons are connected in circuits and communicate with one another to create feelings, store information, and control behavior. They respond to rewarding foods by firing electrical signals and releasing brain chemicals that then travel to interconnected neurons. We say those neurons are "encoded" for palatability.

"What does it mean for a neuron to encode?" I asked Howard Fields, a professor of neurology and physiology at the University of California, San Francisco.

"If a neuron encodes the color red, it will fire more when a red light is showing than when any other color is showing," said Fields. "Encoding means that the neuron shows a preference by firing more."

A small proportion of neurons are uniquely encoded to respond to a single sensory characteristic of food. For example, one neuron may respond only to taste, another only to texture. Others may be stimulated exclusively by the sight, smell, or temperature of food. Certain neurons are even more specific; some are particularly responsive to sweet, salty, sour, or bitter tastes.

Neurons encoded for sucrose respond vigorously to sweeter foods. "The sweeter the sucrose solution, the more those neurons fire," Fields explained. "The more these neurons fire, the more sucrose the rat will consume." We also know that artificial sweeteners can generate the same effect.

There are, in addition, neurons that respond to specific combinations of sensory inputs. "A single cell can be tuned to a whole set of different sensory-oral attributes," said Edmund Rolls, professor of experimental psychology at Oxford University, in England. Using functional magnetic resonance imaging (fMRI) technology, Rolls has created images of how the brain responds when it's stimulated. His work allows us to see specific neural circuits in action. For example, a neuron stimulated by a sweet taste that has been coupled with a fatty texture would be active when we eat, say, an éclair.

A single food can also stimulate many different neurons simultaneously. One set of neurons may fire at its sugary taste, while another fires in response to its creamy texture, and still another is provoked by its aroma.

The cumulative effect of all this is that sensory stimuli amp up the neurons, getting them to fire more. The message to eat becomes stronger, motivating the eater to act more vigorously in pursuit of the stimulus.

The most dominant source of the power of highly palatable foods comes from just one of the senses: taste. Although the sight and smell of food, as well as other sensory stimulants, enhance food's appeal and motivate us to eat, taste has by far the most direct connection to the body's reward system. Alone among the senses, taste is hardwired to brain cells that respond to pleasure. It prompts the strongest emotional response.

Gerard Smith, a pioneer in the study of ingestive behavior at New York–Presbyterian Hospital, coined the term "orosensory self-stimulation" to refer to a cyclical process in which eating delicious foods tells the brain to make us want more of those foods.

The reinforcing properties of food are lodged primarily in their capacity to stimulate the taste apparatus. Whatever we say about preference or liking or salience refers primarily to food's orosensory properties, said Smith. "If you're talking about the things that drive eating or make food more appetizing, you're always talking about orosensory effects."

The neurons in the brain that are stimulated by taste and other properties of highly palatable food are part of the opioid circuitry, which is the body's primary pleasure system. The "opioids," also known as endorphins, are chemicals produced in the brain that have rewarding effects similar to drugs such as morphine and heroin. Stimulating the opioid circuitry with food drives us to eat.

When we first put a highly palatable food into our mouths, taste buds in the tongue respond by sending a signal to an area of the lower brain responsible for controlling many of our involuntary activities, such as breathing and digestion.

When the lower brain receives that signal, it activates the neural circuitry that contains natural opioid molecules. Whether the opioid circuits are activated by highly palatable foods or by drugs, they enable the body to perceive a rewarding experience. Responding unconsciously, an animal may move its jaw and tongue, and an infant may smile.

Awareness of pleasure is a higher brain function, as is the record of the experiences associated with it. From the lower brain, the sensory experience of taste travels through the midbrain, reaching regions where the sensory signals of food are integrated. Those signals are ultimately relayed to the "nucleus accumbens," an area of the brain that is a center of reward.

In addition to their stimulating effects, the opioids produced by eating high-sugar, high-fat foods can relieve pain or stress and

calm us down. At least in the short run, they make us feel better—
we see this in infants who cry less when given sugar water. We can
also observe that animals feel less pain when they're administered
opioid-like drugs and even less when they're allowed unrestricted
access to sucrose at the same time.

In a cyclical process, eating highly palatable food activates the
opioid circuits, and activating these circuits increases consumption
of highly palatable food. This is evident in studies demonstrating
that animals eat more high-sugar, high-fat foods after receiving an
opioid injection. We also know that after using drugs that stimulate
the opioid circuitry, people report that palatable food is more pleasant, and they eat more of it.

The power of opioids to stimulate us, calm us down, and give
us pleasure has been made concrete by scientific advances that
allow us to detect associated molecular changes in the circuits of
the brain. For example, we can see that the molecular machinery
that produces opioids within the body changes after chronic exposure to chocolate Ensure.

Engaging the opioid mechanisms can also interfere with a phenomenon known as "taste-specific satiety." After eating a certain
amount of one food, animals typically become satisfied with its taste
and stop eating it—but they'll keep on eating if something else is
available.

When palatable foods stimulate the opioid circuits, that pattern
changes. Josh Wooley, a neuroscientist at the University of California, San Francisco, demonstrated this with chocolate- and banana-
flavored food pellets called Supreme Mini-Treats, which consist
primarily of sucrose and fat.

He first allowed his test animals to eat as much chocolate as
they wanted for an hour. Then he gave them ninety minutes of
unrestricted access to both banana and chocolate, and he observed
that the animals chose to eat significantly more banana. Apparently
their initial exposure to chocolate had reduced but not eliminated
further interest in that flavor, but left them enough appetite for the

novel taste of banana. The same thing happened in reverse: When exposed first to banana, an animal later ate more chocolate when given a choice of flavors.

Something very different happened in the next phase, when Wooley injected opioids into the brains of his animals after exposing them to either the chocolate or banana pellets. Now the initial flavor was the one they continued to prefer. Stimulating the opioid circuitry overcame the natural tendency for taste-specific satiety. They didn't grow tired of it.

Another way to demonstrate the role of the opioid circuitry is to block the production of opioids and watch the results. One set of experiments is done with a class of drugs known as opioid antagonists, such as naltrexone and naloxone. Typically, these are used to treat human dependence on morphine and heroin because they negate the pleasure that people otherwise derive from those substances.

Scientists also use opioid antagonists to learn more about the influence of the body's opioids on eating behavior. For example, Josh Wooley found that animals ate less chocolate after they were injected with naltrexone, presumably because blocking the opioid signals took away its reward value.

Other researchers have demonstrated that opioid antagonists shorten the length of a meal. In one study, animals that were fed a high-sucrose meal initially ate for a longer period of time than those fed a cornstarch diet. No surprise there. But the picture changed when naloxone was administered. Both groups of animals ate less, but the effect was more dramatic among the sucrose-fed rats. Interfering with opioids had the strongest effect on the food the animals preferred.

For all its influence over our behavior, the wellspring of pleasure in the brain is not very large. Scientists have mapped the web of opioid circuits that make up the pleasure center and can take pictures as it lights up in response to the taste of sugar, fat, and salt.

One small region lies at the center of all that pleasure. Kent Berridge, at the University of Michigan, has called this the "hedonic hot spot." He believes that stimulating that hot spot—just one cubic millimeter, about the size of the head of a pin, in the nucleus accumbens—causes us to like something, *really* like something. The hot spot "seems to actually magnify, to causally enhance, the pleasure of the taste," said Berridge. "It lays an extra pleasure gloss onto the taste sensation."

We Are Wired to Focus Attention on the Most Salient Stimuli

Eating and the desire to eat need to be understood as separate activities involving separate mechanisms in the brain. Their distinct roles help us understand another brain chemical: dopamine.

If opioids give food its pleasure and help keep us eating, dopamine motivates our behavior and impels us toward food. By strengthening our sense of anticipation, dopamine gets us to engage in a complex set of pursuit-and-acquisition behaviors so we can recapture the remembered pleasure of a favored food. Dopamine drives desire through a survival-based capacity known as "attentional bias." Defined as "the exaggerated amount of attention that is paid to highly rewarding stimuli at the expense of other (neutral) stimuli," attentional bias allows us to pick out what matters most so we can pursue it. It gives rewarding foods their prominence in our minds. The more rewarding the food, the greater the attention we direct toward it and the more vigorously we pursue it.

John Salamone, a professor in the Department of Psychology at the University of Connecticut, was a graduate student when he first noticed that hungry animals became extremely hyperactive when offered food pellets. In fact, they behaved like animals that had been treated with amphetamines. Salamone also noticed that blocking dopamine with an antagonist drug damped down that frenzied activity considerably.

He went on to study how hard animals with normal levels of dopamine will work to obtain food rewards, compared to those with depleted dopamine levels. Salamone's research team placed four tasty food pellets at one end of the top of a T-shaped maze and two pellets at the other end. The rats learned where the larger portion of food was available, and when they reached the T intersection, they consistently turned toward the larger food portion. When investigators depleted the rats' dopamine levels, the animals slowed their movement toward food but still maneuvered their way to the four pellets.

Salamone's next step was to erect an eighteen-inch barrier that made access to the four-pellet side harder. A lot of training was required before animals with normal levels of dopamine were able to do the considerable work necessary to overcome that obstacle and reach the food. Watching them scale the barrier was a bit like watching Richard Gere master the obstacle course in *An Officer and a Gentleman*, Salamone said. "The rats get a running start, they leap to the top of the barrier, they grab it and fling themselves over, and then they go down the other side and they eat their four pellets."

From an evolutionary perspective, that effort made sense. "Dopamine is involved in the activational aspects of foraging behavior," Salamone explained. "And this is very important for survival, because a part of survival is being able to expend enough energy and be active enough to gain access to the stimuli that are necessary."

Dopamine-depleted animals behaved differently. They were unwilling to work hard enough to overcome the barrier. Instead, they settled for the easier option, turning to the unobstructed side of the maze to reach the two pellets.

While dopamine increases an animal's ability to work, its activities are carefully targeted. The release of dopamine in the presence of the most salient stimuli guides an animal to act with appropriate vigor to pursue the greatest reward. The capacity to filter out lesser background "noise" is essential to that process.

Howard Fields described a study in which animals chose between two chambers, each holding a sweet solution. The study animals were first given the option of licking either plain water or a 3 percent sucrose solution; then they had a choice between that 3 percent sucrose mixture in one chamber and a more concentrated, 10 percent sucrose solution in the other. In both instances, they preferred the relatively sweeter option, showing that a 3 percent solution was good enough when the alternative wasn't sweet at all but was less attractive if something even sweeter was available. The neurons in the brain's nucleus accumbens encoded that preference, firing more dopamine for the most highly concentrated solution.

Animals, humans included, seem to have a built-in preference for features larger than those that occur naturally. Ethologists, scientists who study animal behavior, have tried to understand the attraction of "supernormal stimuli."

Consider the oystercatcher, a shorebird with black-and-white plumage, a red bill, and brightly colored legs. Back in the 1950s, Dutch ethologist Nikolaas Tinbergen conducted now-classic studies of the bird's incubation behavior and discovered something astonishing: When presented with a choice between brooding its own small egg and the giant egg of a much larger bird, the oystercatcher invariably chose to sit on the giant one.

Research with the herring gull and the greylag goose uncovered much the same thing. Both of these birds prefer an egg that is biologically impossible for them to have laid.

We also see this with butterflies. When a male is courting, he'll be drawn to the female by the rate at which she flickers her wings. But when a butterfly is presented with some kind of artificial stimuli that flickers even faster, that's what he'll prefer.

Most of the relevant research about supernormal stimuli was conducted decades ago, although some contemporary writers and scientists have taken on the topic as it relates to food in recent years as well. I wanted to talk to one of the original researchers in the field. John Staddon, now a professor of biology and neurobiology at Duke University, seemed startled to be tracked down as an expert on the subject. "I wrote some stuff on this years and years ago," he told me, surprised that I had uncovered his work.

His early findings seemed to deserve new scrutiny as I considered the possible analogies to food.

Staddon and I talked about the concept of "asymmetrical selection pressure." From the standpoint of evolution, a bird's preference for a larger egg over a smaller one makes sense. Smaller eggs are more likely to be nonviable, so birds that consistently choose them would not have been likely to survive as a species. Their preference for a giant egg is a logical extension of a preference for the egg that seems most likely to be viable.

I asked Staddon about the kind of food we eat today. "Now I'm eating very energy-dense sugar and fat," I said. "And I've artificially created it. It didn't exist in the wild. Is it a supernormal stimulus?"

It would be, said Staddon. "It is not only exaggerated, it also has never been seen in nature." Those features define the term.

"Why do I prefer an exaggerated stimulus?" I asked.

"Your ancestors were punished for preferring a smaller-than-normal stimulus but not punished for preferring a larger-than-normal stimulus," explained Staddon, harkening back to asymmetrical selection pressure. He talked about the "gradient of preference" established by evolution—whether it's a gigantic egg or a hyperpalatable food, a lot seems to be more desirable than a little. An entertainment spectacle, such as Disneyland or Las Vegas, attracts us in much the same way.

Today's choices only push us farther along that gradient. "In the selection pressures acting on the species, more sugar was always better than less," said Staddon. The amount of sugar in food today goes beyond the level we could have experienced naturally—and that just means we desire it all the more.

Rewarding Foods Become
Hot Stimuli

CHAPTER 9

On a scientific level, I already understood that salient foods focus our attention and that dopamine promotes the approach behavior that brings us to them. I also understood this on a personal level, through my enthusiasm for chocolate frozen yogurt with sprinkles and cookie dough.

Not so many decades ago a single flavor of store-bought ice cream was a special treat. Our options ran to vanilla, chocolate, and strawberry—and when we could buy all three flavors in a single carton, we saw that as a great innovation. Over time, many more flavors became available, and then specialty ice cream stores opened, serving premium, higher-fat ice cream. In the 1970s, Steve's Ice Cream was the most famous ice cream parlor in the Boston area, earning its reputation for long lines of fans by mixing "smoosh-ins"—Heath bars, Reese's peanut butter cups, and other confections—into a scoop of ice cream. Then a novelty, now it's entirely commonplace. The food industry has certainly figured out what captures consumer awareness.

Today, of course, ice cream has countless flavors and varieties, and so do most other foods. Once there were just a few kinds of hot, fresh bagels—we could buy a plain bagel, or one with sesame or poppy seeds. Now bagels come flavored with onions, garlic, cinnamon and raisins, blueberries, and chocolate. The Panera Bread chain goes further, offering the cherry vanilla bagel, the Asiago cheese bagel, the French toast bagel, and the Dutch apple and raisin bagel. Each one comes loaded with sugar on fat on salt.

Mike McCloud of Uptown Bakers, an artisanal wholesale bakery based in Maryland, called these "tricked-out" bagels. "You take a basic concept like a bagel, which is a very clean bakery item. To appeal to a different market segment, you 'trick it out,'" McCloud said. "You add ingredients to change the mouthfeel and the texture. You put jalapeños and corn kernels in it and call it a southwestern bagel."

My son says that Panera's cinnamon crunch bagel is the best he's ever eaten. It's the restaurant's top seller, so that's what I decided to try.

I read the list of ingredients first. After unbleached flour and water, the bagel contained both vanilla drops (which include sugar and partially hydrogenated palm kernel oil) and cinnamon drops (with sugar and palm oil). Other ingredients included brown sugar, honey, vanilla, salt, molasses, and more palm oil, topped with sugar, cinnamon, and soybean oil.

Taking my first bite, I concentrated on the sensory hits it provided. The topping gave the bagel a crunchy sweetness, which contrasts nicely with the soft interior. The aroma of cinnamon was pleasant and persistent, and the vanilla chips offered appealing bursts of flavor.

As I chewed, the bagel was quickly transformed into a moist wad in my mouth, with the crunch becoming finer as it dissolved. It was easy to chew and to swallow, and its sweetness lingered yet didn't overwhelm the other flavors. Well lubricated by its fat content and mixed with my saliva, the wad of bagel melted perfectly in my mouth, disappearing after only a few chews.

The cinnamon crunch bagel was manufactured to perfection. Panera had figured out how to put fat, sugar, and other flavor enhancements together to provide exactly the sensory experience I wanted.

Armed with a deeper understanding of how the human brain is wired to focus attention on the most salient stimuli, you may listen differently to the following television advertisement sponsored by T.G.I. Friday's, the chain restaurant designed to be the ultimate food carnival.

> This isn't about grabbing a bite. It's about a bite grabbing you. 'Cause when Friday's gets hold of your appetite, we're not letting go. We are going to bring on the flavor 'til your taste buds explode like fireworks. We are going to dribble glazes and pour on smoky sauces. We are going to pan-fry, sauté, and dream up new dishes that have never been created before. Three courses. New tastes.

This is an apt description of how a food becomes salient and how we respond. One appetizer, the Parmesan-Crusted Sicilian Quesadilla, is described on the menu as follows: "Packed with sautéed chicken, sausage, bruschetta marinara, [and] bacon and oozing with Monterey Jack cheese. We coat it with Parmesan and pan-fry it to a crispy, golden brown, then drizzle it with balsamic glaze."

Dessert is equally multisensory: Chocolate Peanut Butter Pie topped with whipped cream and a Reese's peanut butter cup, or Chips Ahoy! Ice Cream Sundae topped with Chips Ahoy! cookie crumbles, hot fudge, caramel sauce, and whipped cream.

No one has studied the effects of the T.G.I. Friday's quesadilla or Panera's cinnamon crunch bagel on dopamine, but it's not a drastic leap to suggest that they have the same effect as other combinations of stimulating ingredients. Chocolate, with its high fat content, and sucrose increase dopamine levels in animals that have eaten recently enough not to be hungry. Combine sucrose and alcohol and we see the same multisensory effect. And there is even more arousal when we combine all three stimulants—an animal that eats a combination of sucrose, chocolate, and alcohol releases the greatest levels of dopamine.

When layer upon layer of complexity is built into food, the effect becomes more powerful. Sweetness alone does not account for the full impact of a soda—its temperature and tingle, which results from the stimulation of the trigeminal nerve by carbonation and acid, are essential contributors as well.

"The complexity of the stimulus increases its association to a reward," said Gaetano Di Chiara, an expert in neuroscience and pharmacology at the University of Cagliari, in Italy. Elements of that complexity include tastes that are familiar and well liked, especially if they aren't always readily available; a multitude of sensory inputs; and the learning associated with having had a pleasurable experience with the same food in the past.

We have discovered that increasing the multisensory aspects of a stimulus, or adding other compatible stimuli, can strengthen the reinforcing effect. The more potent and multisensory foods become, the greater the rewards they may offer and the more we learn to work for them. Much of the excitement takes place in the orbitofrontal cortex, the brain region where neurons fire in response to rewarding foods. The more someone wants to eat highly palatable food, the more activity we see in the orbitofrontal cortex. The excitement in the brain generated by these multimodal stimuli increases our desire for further stimulation.

This is not the kind of language the food industry likes to use in its advertisements. But the science helps us understand what happens when we walk into many of America's most popular restaurants. It explains how foods become hot stimuli.

Cues Activate Brain Circuits That Guide Behavior

Activity in the brain is stimulated not only by food itself, but also by cues suggesting that food is nearby. First, we have to learn through experience that a cue is linked to a specific food. Once this happens, the signal that predicts the food, rather than the food itself, generates the dopamine response. This signal then becomes the trigger of desire. We call this a "conditioned stimulus." The cues grip us, arousing us to act.

Every high school student knows the story of Pavlov and his dogs. In the late nineteenth century, Russian scientist Ivan Petrovich Pavlov began studying the reflexive responses of his animals. His enduring contribution was to demonstrate that if he rang a bell at the same time he fed his dogs, the animals would learn to associate the sound of that bell with food. Eventually the animals would secrete saliva and drool at the sound of the bell, even when it wasn't accompanied by food.

The bell became a conditioned stimulus, generating a predictable response.

Conditioning can happen quickly. In one study, people were given a high-sugar, high-fat snack for five consecutive mornings. For days afterward, they wanted something sweet at about the same time each morning that they had been fed the snack, even though they had not previously snacked at that time. Desire had already taken hold.

Wolfram Schultz, a professor of neuroscience at the University of Cambridge, is among contemporary scientists who have built on Pavlov's seminal finding in their studies of dopamine. Schultz is interested in the cause and timing of spikes in dopamine activity.

An animal releases dopamine in a steady and fairly consistent pattern when it is not being stimulated. But give an animal a reward, and transient bursts of increased dopamine can be detected in its brain.

By implanting electrodes in the nucleus accumbens of an animal, Schultz was able to record the timing and level of that dopamine release. In an experiment, he looked at what happened when monkeys were given a reward they didn't expect—a taste of sweet juice. There was an upward spike in their dopamine levels.

Next he gave the monkeys a visual or auditory cue, followed almost immediately by the same juice. Once they became familiar with that sequence of events, their patterns of dopamine firing changed. Based on learned experience, the animals began to recognize the cue as a signal that the juice was coming and responded with elevated dopamine activity. Rather than firing at the reward itself, dopamine fired in response to the stimulus that predicted the reward.

Given dopamine's role in focusing attention, the pairing of a cue with a reward had a potent effect on behavior.

When Regina Carelli, a professor of psychology at the University of North Carolina at Chapel Hill, measured electrical activity in the brain of a rat, she saw something similar. Milliseconds after the animal received a cue it had learned to associate with palatable food, several subsets of neurons responded to the conditioned stimulus by firing robustly. When the cue did not predict a food reward, the brain responded very differently, with some neurons exhibiting a much smaller response and others showing almost no activity at all.

The contrast was clear: Cues that are associated with rewards turn on electrical activity in the brain.

"Incentive salience," a term coined by Kent Berridge, helps explain what's going on. Simply put, incentive salience is the desire, activated by cues, for something that predicts reward. It's a learned association—we learn to *want* a food or some other substance we once *liked*. We may no longer like that food (although often we do). But it's the wanting, not the liking, that drives us to do the work necessary to obtain that food.

Cue-induced wanting, said Berridge, is "triggered by the sight of a cookie or someone lighting up a cigarette nearby or clinking the ice cubes in the glass of alcohol. . . . Those kinds of cues have the power to evoke the desire to take that thing again." Experience imbues the cue with incentive salience. Positive emotions become embedded in cues, which then develop a force of their own.

We've already seen some kinds of cues. Animal studies often use a light or a tone. For humans, visual cues include not only the sight of food, but the sight of a restaurant where we once ate that food, the street corner we pass en route, or a billboard advertising that restaurant. Sounds and smells, as well as attributes such as time of day and location, can assume the same stimulating power. So, too, can the people and the moods, both positive and negative, that were once associated with a stimulus. The aroma of a cherry pie can evoke your grandmother's home-cooked meals, creating desire.

Driven by dopamine, these cues motivate the reward-seeking behavior that is a basic survival tool. Once a cue gains incentive salience, dopamine pushes us to pursue the object of our desire and doesn't readily allow us to be thrown off course.

"The pursuit of rewards tends to proceed to completion despite obstacles and distractions," commented Steven Hyman, professor of neurobiology, as well as provost, at Harvard University. "If I were heading up to my study to find a neuroanatomy paper, any distraction might derail my intention to go and read it. But if I'm going in pursuit of something rewarding, especially something intensely rewarding, I'll tend to complete the task."

Over time, the pairing of a cue and a reward may intensify further. The association can increase in strength as a result of repeated experience, or sensitization. A classic drug effect, sensitization is the mechanism by which the same dose of a drug produces a larger effect with repeated use. "We can talk about the motivational power of cues if they are evoking something like incentive salience," said Berridge. "And that can build over time, either through learning or if sensitization kicks in to magnify the cue-triggered neuronal process."

In my conversation with Berridge, he theorized that only a subset of the population has heightened incentive salience, and that rewarding foods trigger overeating primarily in that group. Whether or not these people actually like the food more, Berridge suspects they will respond to the presence of food cues more intensely and are more likely to be overpowered by them.

Schultz's monkeys and Carelli's rats, like Pavlov's dogs, have been conditioned to expect that a cue will be followed by a reward, and because of that learned association, they release dopamine in the presence of a cue. John Salamone and others have demonstrated that dopamine then leads us to eat rewarding foods, which in turn stimulates the pleasure-enhancing opioid circuitry.

Putting together the various lines of study, we gain a fuller picture of the cycle: A cue triggers a dopamine-fueled urge . . . dopamine leads us to food . . . eating food leads to opioid release . . . and the production of both dopamine and opioids stimulates further eating.

The cue stimulates arousal, we pursue the reward and we experience release, and the arousal eases.

Cues ensure that we will work hard to obtain the reward. That concept is well known in the food industry, where the most important goal of food design is to create anticipation.

Emotions Make Food Memorable

CHAPTER 11

Given the sensory power of sugar, fat, and salt, we might expect everyone to be drawn to much the same foods. But we're not, in part because our preferences are strongly influenced by what has happened to us in the past. A history of personal experience gives particular foods an emotional charge, and those emotions become lodged in our memory.

Andrew, the journalist we met in the opening of this book, recalls being taken as a young boy to Carvel, the legendary ice cream chain in New York, to celebrate every Little League victory. The childhood memory still holds enough power that whenever he goes back to New York, his desire to head to Carvel battles with his determination not to do it. It takes his wife, whom he jokingly calls his "AA sponsor," to hold him back.

For me, it's chocolate-covered pretzels that have become imbued with emotional resonance. Walking past the hotel where I bought those pretzels years earlier jogs my memory of the pleasure associated with them and makes me want more. The circumstances that once surrounded the act of eating a rewarding food become the core of an emotional experience, and that feeling gets stored in working memory, where it can be readily recalled. A cue triggers that recall, and recall stimulates desire.

As those positive associations become ingrained, they can motivate our behavior even when we're not aware of them. Food becomes what Walter Mischel has called a "hot stimulus," lighting up the emotional centers of the brain, getting us to think, feel, and respond to our desire. Memories interact with the reward pathways that drive our behavior.

We can see the potency of memory and reward illustrated in a study in which subjects were shown pictures of various items, some linked to an opportunity to earn a monetary reward and some not. Unsurprisingly, MRI scans showed that when people looked at pictures signaling a monetary reward, the dopamine-rich areas of their brains were activated.

Three weeks later the researchers asked the same study participants what they remembered about the pictures—and discovered that participants had a significantly sharper memory of the pictures that predicted rewards.

"These results provide evidence for a relationship between activation of dopaminergic areas and . . . long-term memory formation," wrote the study investigators.

Or, in the arguably more poetic words of two Stanford scientists, "Reward circuits can whisper in the ear of memory circuits."

One clear weekend afternoon I drove across the Golden Gate Bridge and up to Sonoma County with Bill Schultz, a close friend visiting from the East Coast. We were on a quest for a restaurant where he had eaten a unique dessert fifteen years before—a strawberry milkshake inside a chocolate bag. (It was made by filling a paper bag with chocolate, then freezing it so it became a container for the shake.) Both the presentation and the combination of tastes still loomed large in his mind, and we went from restaurant to restaurant searching for the chef who had created the unforgettable concoction.

"When people conjure up a memory of a food that they really like a lot and it is not available to them for some reason, they feel desire," said Marcia Pelchat, an expert in physiological psychology who works at Monell Chemical Senses Center. "A memory of pleasure leads to desire."

Bill remembered both the taste and the unique look of the milkshake, but it was the setting and his emotions at the time that intensified his longing. The day he encountered the dessert had been a special one. Nearing the end of an adventurous, cross-country road trip, he was celebrating with an outdoor meal among friends in a California vineyard. Marriage was on his horizon.

That sensory pleasure and personal history had become embedded in the idea of the milkshake, and Bill recalled it all in our afternoon's odyssey through northern California in search of a taste, and a memory.

The power of such memories is undeniable. Ask people what they were doing on November 21, 1963, or September 10, 2001, and they're unlikely to recall. But mundane details about the days that followed are seared into the memories of most Americans alive at the time. This common experience is supported by a substantial body of research suggesting that we're better at remembering details when they're associated with emotionally charged events.

That's the food industry's goal in its television advertising. We aren't being sold nutrition or satisfaction. We are being sold emotions. That's what the Applebee's campaigns "Eatin' Good in the Neighborhood" and "The Flavors That Bring People Together" are all about.

Rewarding Foods
Rewire the Brain

CHAPTER 12

In theory there's a limit to how much stimulation rewarding foods can generate. The biological value of dopamine lies in its power to activate an animal's pursuit of food. When food is not immediately necessary, the brain is built to release less dopamine. We are supposed to habituate—to neuroadapt—by reducing the neural response that otherwise drives us toward a stimulus. That's part of the drive for balance. "Homeostasis does not tolerate excesses," said Andras Hajnal, associate professor of neural and behavioral sciences at Pennsylvania State University.

Sometimes that's indeed what happens, as a study by the Italian researcher Gaetano Di Chiara showed. When he first gave animals a cheese-flavored snack food called Fonzies, the levels of dopamine in their brains increased. Over time, habituation set in, dopamine levels declined, and the food lost its capacity to activate their behavior.

But there's more to the story. It turns out that if the stimulus is powerful enough, novel enough, or administered intermittently enough, the brain may not curb its dopamine response after all. Desire remains high. We see this with cocaine use, which does not result in habituation. A person who uses drugs of abuse will continue to release dopamine, generally at the same level as occurred with the initial use.

Hyperpalatable foods alter the landscape of the brain in much the same way. I asked Di Chiara to study what happens after an animal is repeatedly exposed to a high-sugar, high-fat chocolate drink. When he'd completed his experiment, he sent me an e-mail with "Important results!!!!" typed in the subject line. He had demonstrated that the dopamine response did *not* diminish after an animal was exposed to the chocolate drink for a prolonged period of time. There was no habituation.

Novelty also impedes habituation: Dopamine levels remained elevated when the opportunity to feed on Fonzies was followed by access to chocolate. Habituating to one rewarding food does not habituate us to another.

Intermittency is another driver. Give an animal enough sugar-laden food, withdraw that food for the right amount of time, and then provide it again in sufficient quantities, and dopamine levels may not diminish.

Andras Hajnal and I decided to study the effect of both continued and intermittent exposure to a high-fat, high-sugar vanilla drink on the brain's dopamine system. When we exposed animals to the highly palatable food daily for eight weeks, the brain was stimulated to keep on releasing dopamine—we saw no evidence of habituation. And when we limited exposure to just two days a week, the stimulating effect was even greater, with more dopamine being released.

The trick to overcoming habituation, Hajnal told me, was to keep the food "relevant" to the animal. That can be achieved by offering a tantalizingly small amount of stimulating food, providing access to that food at the same, predictable time, or using other strategies that create a sense of anticipation. The effect is to undermine the brain's capacity to habituate to a persistent stimulus.

There's still a lot we don't know about the relationship between the dopamine-driven motivational system and our behavior in the presence of rewarding foods. But we do know that foods high in sugar, fat, and salt are altering the biological circuitry of our brains. We have scientific techniques that demonstrate how highly rewarding and reinforcing foods—and the cues associated with them—change those circuits. Craig Schiltz, who conducted research at the University of Wisconsin–Madison, has shown that there are shifts in what he calls the "functional connectivity" among important brain regions: After repeated exposure to stimuli and cues, the connections among the neural circuits change, and so do their response patterns.

Rewarding foods are rewiring our brains. As they do, we become more sensitive to the cues that lead us to anticipate rewarding foods. In that self-perpetuating circularity lies a trap into which Sarah, Andrew, Samantha, and Claudia, whose stories began this book, have fallen. They cannot control their responses to highly palatable foods because their brains have been changed by the foods they eat.

Eating Behavior
Becomes a Habit

CHAPTER 13

Habits develop when familiar stimuli activate well-established neural pathways that produce repetitive behavior. The same cues prompt us to react the same way.

Over time, the act of eating highly rewarding food creates an automatic response. We build "action schemata," mental imprints of the actions we take and the specific sequence in which we take them. Action schemata develop more quickly and become stronger when the stimulus driving our behavior is reinforcing.

Once a script becomes imprinted in the brain, the behavior it dictates becomes so routine that we can respond before we're even conscious of a stimulus. A substantial body of scientific literature attests to this: Researchers have been able to measure movement before subjects know they're going to move. Brain activity stimulates a motor response in advance of awareness.

I called Joshua Berke at the University of Michigan in Ann Arbor to learn more about how repeat experience strengthens the circuits in the brain. He helped me understand the somewhat fuzzy but useful distinction between goal-directed and habit-driven behavior.

An example of goal-directed behavior is the process of thinking about ice cream, desiring ice cream, and then taking deliberate steps to obtain ice cream. All of this involves a specific set of motivational neural circuits. If I walk into my house intent on taking a carton from the freezer, my activity is goal directed and consciously reward driven. I want that ice cream and I'm going to act to obtain it.

But if I do that often enough, the mental process changes. It becomes habit-driven behavior—less deliberate and more repetitive—and engages different neural circuitry. No longer motivated by a conscious desire for food, I head straight to the refrigerator when I get home because it's a habit. My motor behavior has become automatic.

Dopamine influences both types of behavior, revving up the motivational circuits of the brain and strengthening the power of habit. The circuitry operates in roughly parallel loops, with one loop acting as the processing center for motivational information and another focusing on the motor activity associated with habits.

The implications for someone trying to control food intake are obvious. As habits are learned, the brain "comes to code whole sequences of behavior as performance units that can be triggered by specific contexts," explained scientists who study neural representations of habits. Cues in the environment become the triggers of predictable and automatic actions.

When it comes to food, we are, in essence, following an eating script that has been written into the circuits of our brains.

Habits permit living creatures—both those with highly developed brains and those with less-developed brains—to act quickly in response to routine events. This can be convenient, allowing us to do something without the need to pay close attention; we can tie our shoelaces and still hold a conversation. But that convenience comes at a price. The brain architecture making it possible allows us to act without awareness, not fully in control of our actions. In fact, that loss of control is the whole point.

"Loss of control is the effective strengthening of this habitual system," Joshua Berke said. "A habit is a way of saving cognitive effort. It makes sense to have a system that, when faced with the same situation over and over, allows a fixed response without having to think about it."

Habits are learned slowly, but once they are in place, they are by their very nature difficult to break. "One defining feature of habits is that they are resistant to extinction," said Berke. "Habits are very inflexible. . . . They're very unresponsive when a situation changes."

The distinction between behavior driven by a goal and behavior driven by habit is demonstrated well by another study of high-sugar food. For a week researchers placed sucrose pellets at the end of a runway, and a group of animals ran to eat them at the first opportunity. The animals were then moved to another room where they again ate sucrose pellets in large quantities, but this time they were deliberately made ill when their meal was over. When they returned to the runway the next day, their behavior looked markedly different; instead of running toward the food, they ambled in that direction and showed little interest in eating it.

Contrast that with the results after a longer exposure. In the next round of experiments, animals had three weeks, rather than one, in which to eat the sucrose pellets at the end of the runway. Everything else stayed the same—after the three-week test period, they were again offered large quantities of sucrose pellets and again made ill. Back on the runway the next day, their behavior was no different than it had been before they became sick. The animals again ran vigorously toward the food and put it in their mouths.

"It is a nice illustration of the difference between motivational behavior and habit," said Berke. After a single week's exposure, the association of the food with illness had stripped away the animals' motivation to eat more. But after three weeks, habit set in and the animals acted without awareness. The outcome—eating food that had once made them ill—was no longer a deterrent to repeated motor activity. That's an experience familiar to people as well, including me. In the past, eating too much pizza has made me feel ill, but that did not prevent me from eating it again.

The more rewarding the food, the stronger the learning experience that creates the automatic behavior. That's the danger of habit. But habit formation has the potential for good as well. If we can learn to turn all of this around, we can eventually create new habits, ones that motivate us to pursue other, healthier sources of reward.

PART TWO

The Food Industry

A Visit to Chili's

CHAPTER 14

Years of research had educated me about how sugar, fat, and salt change the brain. I understood some of the parallels between hyperpalatable foods and drugs of abuse, and about the links among sensory stimulation, cues, and memory. I'd met enough people like Claudia and Maria to understand how even the thought of food could cause them to lose control.

But I wasn't fully prepared for the discoveries I made about irresistibility and whoosh, the Monster Thickburger and Baked! Cheetos Flamin' Hot, about indulgence and purple cows. Without necessarily understanding the underlying science, the food industry has discovered what sells.

I was sitting at Chili's Grill & Bar in Chicago's O'Hare Airport waiting for a late-night flight. At a nearby table a couple in their early forties was deep into a meal. The woman was overweight, with about 180 pounds on her five-foot-four-inch frame. The Southwestern Eggrolls she had ordered were listed as a starter course, but the enormous platter in front of her had been heaped with food. The dish was described on the menu as "smoked chicken, black beans, corn, jalapeño Jack cheese, red peppers, and spinach wrapped inside a crispy flour tortilla," and it was served with a creamy avocado-ranch dipping sauce. Despite its name, the dish looked more like a burrito than an egg roll, an only-in-America fusion approach.

I watched as the woman attacked her food with vigor and speed. She held the egg roll in one hand, dunked it into the sauce, and brought it to her mouth while using the fork in her other hand to scoop up more sauce. Occasionally she reached over and speared some of her companion's french fries. The woman ate steadily, working her way around the plate with scant pause for conversation or rest. When she finally paused, only a little lettuce was left.

Had she known someone was watching her, I'm sure she would have eaten differently. Had she been asked to describe what she had just eaten, she probably would have substantially underestimated her consumption. And she would probably have been surprised to learn what the ingredients in her meal really were.

The woman might have been interested in how my industry source, who had called sugar, fat, and salt the three points of the compass, described her entrée. Deep-frying the tortilla drives down its water content from 40 percent to about 5 percent and replaces the rest with fat. "The tortilla is really going to absorb a lot of fat," he said. "It looks like an egg roll is supposed to look, which is crispy and brown on the outside."

The food consultant read through other ingredients on the label, keeping up a running commentary as he did. "Cooked white meat chicken, binder added, smoke flavor. People like smoky flavor—it's the caveman in them."

"There's green stuff in there," he said, noting the spinach. "That makes me feel like I'm eating something healthy."

"Shredded Monterey Jack cheese. . . . The increase in per-capita consumption of cheese is off the chart."

The hot peppers, he said, "add a little spice, but not too much to kill everything else off."

He believed the chicken had been chopped and formed much like a meat loaf, with binders added, which makes those calories easy to swallow. Ingredients that hold moisture, including autolyzed yeast extract, sodium phosphate, and soy protein concentrate, further soften the food. I noticed that salt appeared eight times on the label and that sweeteners were there five times, in the form of corn-syrup solids, molasses, honey, brown sugar, and sugar.

"This is highly processed?" I asked.

"Absolutely, yes. All of this has been processed such that you can wolf it down fast . . . chopped up and made ultrapalatable. . . . Very appealing looking, very high pleasure in the food, very high caloric density. Rules out all that stuff you have to chew."

By eliminating the need to chew, modern food processing techniques allow us to eat faster. "When you're eating these things, you've had 500, 600, 800, 900 calories before you know it," said the consultant. "Literally before you know it." Refined food simply melts in the mouth.

With more than 1,400 locations and $3.2 million in sales per restaurant in 2007, Chili's has been immensely popular. I visited the chain's restaurants in perhaps twelve different settings, many of them more than once. Often the restaurant was full, and sometimes crowds clustered at the front door waiting for tables.

At a Chili's north of the Golden Gate Bridge, I ordered Kickin' Jack Nachos, which were a featured appetizer, and two entrées—Boneless Shanghai Wings and Margarita Grilled Chicken—for myself and a colleague.

First, the Kickin' Jack Nachos. The plate was artfully presented, with the chips arranged in a circle surrounding a colorful chopped salad topped with a mound of pico de gallo salsa and another mound of sour cream. A slice of jalapeño pepper rested in the center of every chip. Marketed with the tagline "Live a little," the Kickin' Jacks are a variation on the chain's classic nachos. The fried corn chip serves as the carrier for a layer of mashed black beans and a layer of zesty Monterey Jack cheese (there's more cheese in the Kickin' Jack nachos than in the classic version). A margarita spice mix gives them "extra kick."

Next, Boneless Shanghai Wings. As described on the menu, these were "crispy breaded chicken breast topped with sweet and spicy ginger-citrus sauce and sesame seeds. Served with spicy-cool wasabi-ranch dressing for dipping." A dozen fat and textured chicken nuggets were set down in front of me—they looked great and had flavor to match.

Finally, Margarita Grilled Chicken. "We start with tender, juicy chicken breast, marinate it with our classic Margarita flavoring, and grill it to perfection," according to the menu. The dish is served with rice, black beans, strips of fried tortilla, and salsa. My dinner companion seemed to think it was relatively healthy.

Like the other dishes, it's artistically presented—a crosshatch of grill marks blackens both sides of the large, boneless breast, which sits atop accompaniments of contrasting colors and textures. The uncooked chicken had been in a marinade that combined orange juice, tequila, triple sec, sweet-and-sour mix, and artificial color, thereby including sugar, two kinds of oil, and salt. It was shipped frozen in twenty-five-pound bags, each containing about fifty pieces of meat, plus whey protein concentrate and modified tapioca starch.

Nick Nickelson, a chief scientist at the Dallas-based Standard Meat, a supplier to Chili's, said that the chicken and marinade were tumbled together in a piece of equipment that resembled a cement mixer. "It pulls the marinade into the muscle," said Nickelson, breaking down the cellular structure of the meat and tenderizing it in the process.

Another common way to get marinade into meat is through needle injection. Hundreds of needles are used to pierce the meat, tearing up the connective tissue. "It's been prechewed," said Billy Rosenthal, former president of Standard Meat.

For all that, very little in the appearance or flavor of Chili's food suggests how much sugar, fat, or salt it contains, or how easily it goes down. A woman sitting near me eating nachos finished about two-thirds of her portion and then pushed her plate to the far side of her table. A few seconds later, she reached over and began to nibble again.

Every time I ordered food at a Chili's I casually asked the server, "What's in this?" Sometimes I asked the same question of the manager. I never asked for the recipe—I knew that was proprietary information. I didn't care what spices and seasonings were used, but I did want to know the major ingredients in the food I was ordering. As a consumer, I thought it was reasonable to find out what I was going to eat.

Staff were generally reluctant to answer my question.

"We can't tell you," one manager said flatly.

"What are you concerned about?" asked a server. "What are your allergies?"

"I'm not sure I'm allowed to say," someone else said hesitantly.

Whatever the ingredients, my food consultant contact seemed to understand why some foods just slide down the throat. About the Boneless Shanghai Wings, he said, "Taking it off the bone is like taking the husk off the nut." That processing step reduces the need for chewing, making the food faster to consume.

Those wings contain a solution of up to 25 percent water, hydrolyzed soy protein, salt, and sodium phosphate. The water is in there for several reasons. First, it bulks up the chicken—the industry calls this "reducing shrinkage." Second, water is cheaper than chicken breast, so it's less costly to produce. And finally, water makes the food softer and chewing easier.

Before the chicken is shipped from the manufacturing plant, it's battered, breaded, predusted, and frozen. This creates a salty coating that becomes crispy when fried in fat. "All this stuff absorbs fat, dries out this batter and breading, and replaces water with oil. So now you've got batter and breading that is probably 40 percent fat," according to the food consultant. The crispy coating, which also contains corn-syrup solids, dried yeast, and soybean oil, may represent up to half the volume of the nuggets on the plate.

Boxes containing eight four-pound bags of ginger-citrus sauce, each with a refrigerated shelf life of about four months, are shipped to Chili's restaurants to accompany the chicken. The ingredients in the sauce sound relatively benign: sugar, hoisin sauce, vinegar, soy sauce, garlic, chili paste, modified food starch, and orange juice concentrate. But sugar is the dominant nutrient, and salt is listed three times.

The ginger-citrus sauce "introduces syrupy, sweet, clingy stuff," said the consultant. "Sugar on sugar, really just different sugars. And lots of salt. And lots of intense flavor." The hoisin sauce contributes saltiness and a browning effect, while the orange juice concentrate adds a tangy fruit flavor.

Apparently Chili's considers all of this insufficiently enticing. Accompanying the fried and sweetened chicken concoction is a wasabi ranch dressing, which is made from mayonnaise, buttermilk, spices, and wasabi powder and has a pleasantly sharp bite. "Wasabi has kind of a cool, green look to it, and people love creamy," said the consultant. "The most popular salad dressings are creamy," he added. "The most popular soups are creamy."

The wings are served in a basket lined with waxed paper and bits of strange-looking crispy noodles that absorb excess fat.

"How sensory is the meal?" I asked.

"It's the quintessential example of how to cram as much hedonics as you can into one dish," he answered. The needle on his three-point compass must have been gyrating wildly.

Like most chain restaurants in America, Chili's serves hyper-palatable food that requires little chewing and goes down easily.

Cinnabon: A Lesson in Irresistibility

CHAPTER 15

The Cinnabon story began in a farmhouse in Snohomish, Washington, thirty-five miles outside Seattle, where family and friends once gathered for legendary Sunday dinners of fried chicken, baked beans, and cinnamon rolls. A woman named Jerilyn Brusseau recalled the spirit of those occasions vividly; this was her grandmother's house, and she remembered the love her grandmother poured into those cinnamon rolls and the eager delight in the eyes of guests who were about to eat them.

An avid cook herself, Brusseau eventually opened her own French-style bakery and café. She had envisioned a sophisticated place that would serve handcrafted croissants, quiches, and pastries, but her family insisted that her grandmother's country-style cinnamon rolls be included on the menu, as well. The café quickly gained renown for its luscious cinnamon rolls, and people traveled great distances to sample them. The *New York Times* wrote about those irresistible cinnamon rolls. And then, one day in 1985, the phone rang.

Rich Komen was on the line. Komen is the founder of Restaurants Unlimited, which today owns about thirty American-style restaurants, including steakhouses, grills, and fish houses.

"Jerilyn, I have an idea," he said. "How would you like to make the world's greatest cinnamon rolls?"

"You bet," Brusseau replied.

Cinnabon was a marriage of Brusseau's culinary prowess and Komen's vision of small bakeries selling fresh, warm cinnamon rolls in shopping malls, airports, and other easy-to-find places around the country.

The signature product was developed in a test kitchen where Brusseau and Komen worked obsessively on every detail. "We began to create together the language for the quality and characteristics we wanted," said Brusseau. "We started from the outside in. We wanted it to look this certain way. We wanted it to be voluptuous and full and round and have many, many, many wraps. We wanted it to be aromatic in a certain way, pungent and so appealing that people couldn't resist it.

"We wanted a dough that had a quality like a pillow, a dough that would be soft. . . . And then the syrup—the cinnamon caramel in the center would be very soft and syrupy so there would be this contrast of textures." They also envisioned a creamy topping. "We wanted this creaminess . . . a cream that would actually be spooned over the top of the rolls that would just add to this indulgent quality."

Brusseau and Komen were consumed by the quest for the finest and freshest ingredients available. They consulted with spice experts, who schooled them in the qualities of cinnamons grown all over the world, before settling on a bark from Sumatra. (Later Cinnabon used cinnamon from Vietnam, as well.)

For months the partners baked and sampled hundreds of cinnamon rolls, testing and cross-testing for different properties. Their special challenge was to design something that could be cooked in a convection oven so the rolls could be served warm within thirty minutes.

They eventually succeeded in their quest to develop the roll they wanted—the one Brusseau said was "very indulgent" and "absolutely irresistible." Cinnabon celebrated its twentieth anniversary in 2005 with 600 bakeries worldwide.

I wanted to identify the properties that make "the world's greatest cinnamon rolls" so irresistible. Brusseau warned that the answer did not lie only in the ingredients list. That, she said, didn't begin to convey the artistry or enticement of a Cinnabon.

"What creates irresistibility is caring, attention, visual appeal, and the appeal of aroma, texture, and consistency," she explained. "The taste is so fulfilling. It just has something that is *yum*." The cinnamon's fragrance and flavor, and the memories it evokes, are also important, she said. "Cinnamon is a real carrier. There's something about it, an intrinsic warmth."

I pushed her on the impact of some key ingredients. "Wheat and yeast are the basics that will give me bread," I said. "What's the next enhancement?"

"Salt brings up the flavor," said Brusseau.

"What's next?"

"Sugar." She explained why three different kinds are used. Granulated white sugar sweetens the dough and helps create its soft texture. Brown sugar in the sticky filling that runs to the center of the wrap gives a caramel flavoring, and powdered sugar in the frosting melts easily and adds a light, creamy consistency.

Brusseau said fat was a further enhancement, giving the dough "a certain elasticity and richness," and enriching the "luscious brown sugar, cinnamon syrupy, caramely gooey stuff inside." The cream cheese in the frosting "gives it that really nice, creamy texture" and contributes to the aroma that draws people in.

Cinnamon, vanilla, and lemon add other flavor notes, and Brusseau said the warmth of the rolls is yet another essential element. "Temperature creates this appeal. It heightens the aroma, it heightens the flavor, it heightens the whole sensory experience."

"What happens in my mouth when I eat this?" I asked.

First comes the "cinnamon hit," she explained. Then a series of flavors and textures unfold as I bite into the pillowy dough and taste the sweet, slippery filling and the creamy frosting. "It melts in your mouth. It disappears easily. The swallow is very nice," Brusseau said. "It's amazing to me how much people love Cinnabon."

Given her professional interests and the extraordinary success of her signature product, I was somewhat surprised to learn how concerned Jerilyn Brusseau is about childhood obesity.

"If someone today asked me to create the world's greatest cinnamon roll, I'd probably think differently about it," she said candidly. "Twenty years ago, it was a once-in-a-while indulgence. I wasn't so worried about obesity among kids. Now I am. . . . I'm very concerned that kids are growing up eating too many things like Cinnabon every day of their lives."

But she felt no need to apologize for her success. "I make cinnamon rolls for my family for special events. I make Cinnabons for friends. I love to teach people about the lineage of cinnamon rolls, about this ordinary food made extraordinarily well so that you can really have a wonderful sensory experience. But I don't teach them to eat it four times a day. It's all a matter of balance."

Balance was something Brusseau once lacked in her own life. In her twenties, thirties, and forties, she battled bulimia and anorexia. A chef and restaurant operator who lived her days surrounded by tempting indulgences, there had been a time in her life when Brusseau lost all sense of when she was hungry and when she was full.

That's Entertainment

CHAPTER 16

Pink's is a hot-dog stand. Since its inception as a pushcart, it has been in the same Los Angeles location for more than sixty-five years, at the corner of Melrose and La Brea Streets. The food is legendary—the family-owned restaurant boasts photographs of hot dog–eating celebrities on its Web site, and it's earned a place of honor on "Best of Los Angeles" lists. When Pink's celebrated its sixtieth anniversary by selling hot dogs for sixty cents apiece, customers waited in line for four hours to get them. Among the twenty-one varieties available at Pink's are the Bacon Chili Cheese Dog, the Brooklyn Pastrami Swiss Cheese Dog, and the Three Dog Night Dog (three hot dogs wrapped in a giant tortilla and served with bacon, cheese, chili, and onions).

I talked with Gloria Pink, whose in-laws, Paul and Betty, founded the operation, and asked how the business had changed over the years. "It is all about entertaining people," she explained, emphasizing the importance of offering variety and special tastes. "That's what the food business has become."

Food as entertainment? I hadn't quite thought in those terms. Later I learned that a more colloquial word is used in the food industry: "eatertainment."

A framed photograph of a cheese-and-pepperoni pizza reinforced the idea that the industry has evolved to provide mass entertainment. I noticed the photo on my food-industry source's office wall and asked him about it.

"It's visually very appealing . . . great taste, great texture and mouthfeel," he said of the pizza's crispy crust, sauce, and savory toppings. "Mentally, your mouth waters."

I understood what he meant. I could almost smell the aroma of a pizza fresh from the oven as I looked at the photo. I could almost taste it. Most chain restaurants feature similar photographs—often prominently displayed on the menu, on table cards, or near the order counter, along with enticing written descriptions.

The food industry understands exactly what it's doing when it markets foods with such compelling imagery, said my source. In the face of the pleasure that pizza promises, consumers "suspend more rational thought and are drawn to the indulgence of it." The pleasure becomes a distraction, directing attention away from thoughts of a food's fat or caloric content.

"It's a very indulgent pizza," he said. "Indulgent is a growing thing."

The food consultant explained that Americans spend a relatively low percentage of their personal income on food, which makes it easy for them to upgrade to premium products—those that are most palatable, most indulgent, and, not incidentally, the most profitable for the industry. "Indulgence is the primary driver in premium products," he said. "Generally, they're higher in flavor and often higher in fat, and a lot of imagery goes with them. It's a very profitable place for the food and beverage industry."

Purchasing indulgent food is an inexpensive form of entertainment, the consultant continued. "You can indulge at any level, from the lowliest fast-food emporium to the fanciest white-tablecloth, table-service restaurant."

In marketing indulgence, the industry knows something about us that we don't fully know about ourselves. It knows that when we walk into a restaurant, we're seeking much more than a satisfying meal. We are hoping for a respite from daily pressures, and restaurants cater to that with food, imagery, and atmosphere that keep us entertained. In a world where people often feel under stress, "Food is escape, more and more," the consultant said. "The more the food industry behaves like the entertainment industry, the more profitable it is."

When everyone is competing for what the industry calls "share of wallet," that's a powerful motivation.

I turned to a venture capitalist who knows the food business intimately—and has put a lot of money on the table to help it grow. He, too, talked about stress in contemporary society. Starbucks, he said, has recognized and responded brilliantly to a cultural need. The caffeine and sugar in the coffee, with their energizing effects, are certainly part of the equation, but the chain also offers something much more primal.

"It's about warm milk and a bottle," he told me. "One of my colleagues said, 'If I could put a nipple on it, I'd be a multimillionaire.'"

By encouraging us to consider any occasion for food an opportunity for pleasure and reward, the industry invites us to indulge a lot more often. That theme populates the marketing reports and conferences that drive food-service decision making.

"Self-indulgent treating fulfills a very important psychological function," declares one report. "Indulging in a premium snack is a self-centered activity, a small moment of relaxation, of 'me-time.'"

Another industry report, "Premium Indulgence: Capitalizing on the Growing Trend for Premium Treating," which sells for about $6,000, expands on this theme. "Growing levels of stress create a need for indulgence and relaxation," declare the authors, who estimate that consumers spend billions of dollars on "premium treating occasions." Other highlights from the report: "Consumers are indulging themselves more often. . . . A growing proportion of snacking occasions are premium. . . . Self-rewarding encourages premium snacking. . . . There is a growing feeling that people need to reward themselves. . . . There is a blurring of distinction between needs and desires." The report went on to offer numerous ideas for exploiting these trends.

Similar themes were sounded at a Chicago conference on restaurant trends sponsored by six food-industry leaders—among them Heinz, PepsiCo, the National Pork Board, Smucker's, and Tyson. Here, too, the discussion focused on catering to consumers whose lives are increasingly harried. According to a survey conducted by the restaurant research firm Technomics, consumers are working longer hours and feeling more stress, and almost half of them say "their personal responsibilities can be overwhelming" and "they deserve to eat out at restaurants as often as they like."

But as eating out becomes more routine, the restaurant experience risks becoming something less special. That means restaurateurs need to develop creative, new approaches if they are to gain what a Technomics speaker called a larger "share of stomach." Conference speakers proposed a number of ways to do that. One was to expand takeout offerings—consider "takeout as an *experience*—not a transaction," advised one Technomics representative. That's why Boston Market advertises its ready-to-eat supermarket line made from "craveable chef-inspired recipes." It also explains Applebee's Carside To Go service, with a special parking space and a dedicated server to hand-deliver each order, and Outback's Curbside Take-Away, which maintains in each of its more than 800 stores a staff of three workers who are dedicated exclusively to delivering food to waiting cars. "I don't even have to put on shoes," one satisfied Outback customer told a reporter.

Another suggested strategy for gaining stomach share was creating a child-friendly environment. Among the tips for achieving that: "'Dippables' put fun back in food"; desserts offer an "opportunity for creativity"; and "upgrades and add-ons provide increased check opportunities."

The goal in each example is clear: Consumers feel compelled to indulge, and entitled to do so; the key to a successful food business is to offer them the best opportunities for that.

The Era of the Monster Thickburger

CHAPTER 17

During the course of my research, food had begun to look different to me. I used to assume that when I ordered green beans at my neighborhood Japanese restaurant in San Francisco, I'd be getting a healthy plate of green vegetables. Now I realized I was more likely to be served beans that had been deep-fried in an oil-filled wok.

United States Department of Agriculture data show that today we're eating more of everything. By far the largest increase has been in the consumption of fats and oils, with a 63 percent jump over a thirty-three-year period, from per capita annual consumption of about fifty-three pounds to about eighty-six pounds.

The use of sugars and sweeteners is also up—by a modest 19 percent—and in that same period we ate 43 percent more grain and 7 percent more meat, eggs, and nuts. USDA data also report that we're eating 24 percent more vegetables, which seems like good news until you learn that a large component of those vegetables are deep-fried potatoes, in the form of french fries.

The ready availability of formerly scarce fats and sugars reflects centuries of change in agriculture and more recent developments in manufacturing, distribution, and government regulations. W. Philip T. James, an expert nutrition researcher and chairman of the International Obesity Task Force, offers an intriguing evolutionary perspective on the transformation of our food supply and our eating patterns over time. Early human diets contained only about 10 percent fat. Sugar intake, primarily from ripe fruit, was also modest. But these commodities were essential sources of the energy needed for survival, and we developed the biological tools to appreciate them when we could get them. That may be why we have three hundred or more olfactory receptors to sense the odors associated with fats, as well as an innate preference for sweetness.

An industrial and agricultural transformation after World War II "led to a remarkable increase in animal protein and crop production, and substantial increases in the availability of butter and vegetable oils," wrote James. The levels of fat and sugar in food today illustrate the industry's enthusiastic response "to biological drives and commercial opportunities," he continued. "It is little wonder that food manufacturers, responding to taste panels and sales returns, have focused, particularly in the last two decades, on providing this evolutionarily rare but highly prized sensory mix as a routine in an increasingly varied number of foods made for convenient consumption."

Foods rich in combinations of sugar and fat are not entirely recent innovations—the grilled cheese sandwich and the milkshake are American standards. But hyperpalatable foods are much more the norm today than they were in the past.

Take the creamy rock shrimp tempura at an upmarket Japanese restaurant in Manhattan. The shrimp was rolled in mayonnaise, fried in a sweetened tempura batter, then rolled again in spicy mayonnaise. That's fat on sugar on fat on fat.

When I ordered dumplings with shrimp in a Peruvian restaurant, what arrived was more like a fried doughnut with fried cream cheese inside. Fat on sugar on fat.

The sizzling calamari salad served as a starter at Chinois on Main, Wolfgang Puck's inventive Santa Monica restaurant, was a revelation. I sat at the counter where I could see into the open kitchen as it was prepared. "Sizzling" should have been my clue that the healthy-sounding dish was anything but. The chef threw breaded seafood into an enormous wok and deep-fried it in rice oil. I thought back to the food consultant's comment about salads that are really "fat with a little lettuce."

I ordered the innocent-sounding entrée "Shanghai Lobster with spicy ginger curry sauce and crispy spinach." After the chef opened the body of the lobster, I watched him pan-fry it facedown in peanut oil while the spinach sizzled in an oily wok. After the lobster was fried, it was baked in the oven, and when it arrived at my table, nothing about its appearance revealed the amount of fat it contained. Little wonder that one contributor to *Zagat* wrote, "I will die happy if Shanghai Lobster is my last meal."

In Amherst, Massachusetts, a college crowd seeks out Antonio's pizzas, which are offered with toppings like beef taco, potato and bacon, chicken quesadilla, and a blend of ground beef, pepperoni, sausage, bacon, and extra cheese. The barbecue steak burrito contains black beans, rice, sour cream, and cheddar cheese.

Another student favorite was Fatzo's, which featured an entrée named "Mac the Knife"—a hamburger special topped with macaroni and cheese—and eight different kinds of fries, including baked potato fries with ranch dressing, cheese, bacon, and onions. Sugar didn't dominate, although the food certainly had some, but all of the dishes were filled with salt on fat on salt on fat on salt on fat.

The high-end dessert market is equally impressive in its commitment to sensory stimulation. Take Otis Spunkmeyer, which markets raw cookie dough that can be used by restaurants and cafés to make "supreme indulgence cookies." Its Double Chunky Chocolate Dream uses both white and dark chocolate chunks; the Cranberry White

Chocolate Duo combines white chocolate chunks, sweetened dried cranberry halves, and molasses. Buttery Pecan Decadence and Oatmeal CinnaRaisin Cravin' are two other choices that engage multiple senses.

And of course at the traditional fast-food chains, which account for a sizable majority of the nation's $333 billion restaurant food industry, combinations of sugar, fat, and salt are ubiquitous.

The bun of a McDonald's Big Mac contains not only the flour, water, and salt we expect in bread, but also high-fructose corn syrup, sugar, soybean oil and/or "partially hydrogenated soybean oil". There are plans to remove the partially hydrogenated oil, in line with a broader movement away from trans fats, but that won't transform the bun into health food. A breakfast sandwich from Burger King contains four eggs, four strips of bacon, and four slices of cheese. Pizza Hut offers a pizza with cheese baked into the crust.

And consider these examples:

At the Grand Lux Café in Las Vegas, double-baked mashed potatoes are wrapped in fried spring rolls and served with cheese and bacon. Listed as an appetizer, they come eight to a serving. That's a simple carbohydrate loaded with fat, then surrounded by layers of salt on fat on salt on fat.

One of the signature hamburgers at Hardee's is called the Monster Thickburger, which famously contains 1,420 calories and 108 grams of fat. Bacon, cheese, and mayonnaise are layered on the burger, and the bun is buttered. The Monster Thickburger is little more than fat on fat on salt on fat on salt on fat, all on a refined carbohydrate.

The International House of Pancakes recently put a stuffed French toast combo on its menu. Cinnamon raisin French toast (made with eggs and milk) is stuffed with sweet cream cheese; smothered with powdered sugar, fruit topping, and whipped topping; and served with two eggs, hash brown potatoes, and a choice of two strips of bacon or two sausage links. Breaking it down, the French toast is a load of fat on fat on fat and sugar that's then layered with fat on sugar on sugar and served with fat, salt, and fat.

Food need not be fried to be high in fat, of course. Targeting the children's market, T.G.I. Friday's invented the Cup of Dirt—chocolate pudding, crumbled Oreo cookies, and gummy worms. Fat on sugar on fat on sugar on sugar.

And Starbucks offers a Strawberries & Crème Frappuccino with whipped cream and eighteen teaspoons of sugar: All in all, this "drink" contains more calories than a personal-size pepperoni pizza, and more sweetness than six scoops of ice cream. Yet even that pales in comparison to a slice of Claim Jumper's Chocolate Motherlode Cake, six rich layers that have been featured on the Food Network as one of the most decadent desserts in the country. The man behind the counter told me it had 2,150 calories a slice.

At a convention in New Orleans, a representative of Ellison Bakery helped me understand some of the broader industrial shifts that have occurred over time. Ellison started in a family garage in Fort Wayne, Indiana, as a one-man producer of baked goods that were resold to restaurants and grocers. In the early 1980s the company took a step toward greater complexity, producing cookies for ice cream sandwiches and toppings designed to add a crunchier surface to cookies.

The concept of "add-ins" grew in popularity over the next decade, and Ellison rode that trend. Today it produces a full range of so-called crunch and inclusion products—such as mini fudge cookies, mini-chocolate chips, gingersnap pieces, and cinnamon graham squares—that can be mixed into ice creams and candy for added texture and flavor. "People are looking for indulgence," said the Ellison representative, repeating a theme that was becoming familiar to me. The company responds with products designed for, to use its own words, a special "kick-it-up-a-notch" effect.

Knowing that it's not enough to simply hand customers a packet of sugar or a pat of butter, the restaurant industry has spent a great deal of time learning the most effective ways to incorporate the core ingredients of sugar, fat, and salt into its products.

But the art of designing foods consumers prefer is much more complicated than simply combining three key ingredients. Gail Vance Civille, founder and president of Sensory Spectrum, probably knows as much as anyone in America about what consumers like to eat and why. I traveled to the suburbs of New Jersey to meet this food industry consultant at her company's headquarters.

Until our first meeting I'd never thought much about what occurs from the moment I put a forkful of food into my mouth until that bite is gone—from the first chew through the manipulation to the swallow. Civille has spent a lifetime thinking about every nuance of that process.

Historically, food companies have worried about design deficits, the "off notes" that might turn a consumer away from a product. More recently their focus has shifted to what draws people in. That's what Civille tries to understand as she works on what she refers to as the "fuzzy front end" of consumer desire.

Her expertise is sensory stimulation and food—the multitude of ways all five human senses become engaged before, during, and after eating. Consumers like products that combine the right stimuli in an optimal fashion. Civille believes that understanding the discrete sensory properties of a food and how those properties work together in the mouth is critical to designing a food that will succeed in the marketplace.

The sensory stimulation provoked by sugar, salt, and fat begins before we put food into our mouths and lasts after the food is gone, she said. It can begin with cues, such as a food's package or its presentation on the plate. An appealing smell invariably stimulates desire. Other sensory properties emerge with the first bite and continue as we manipulate the food in our mouths. The second and third bites can stimulate other senses, as does compressing the mass and eventually swallowing it.

Civille told me we perceive some sensory characteristics with our eyes. "You can look at a product and you can see the texture. . . . You see if the surface is smooth or rough . . . whether or not it is grainy. . . . Those visual texture attributes are indicators often of wholesomeness, freshness."

"What else produces the sensory hits we like?" I asked.

Caramelizing food—the process of browning starches, sugars, and proteins—helps do this, she said. Caramelization generates sweeter aromatics and gives food "more impact, more volatiles." It's a flavor found in many of the foods we produce in this country.

"It's a key driver of liking?"

"Absolutely. On a sweet product it's often the number one driver."

"Tell me how fat engages the senses. Why does the industry add so much of it to food?"

One reason, she responded, is that fat contributes to texture in many ways, giving food body, crunch, creaminess, or contrast. Fat makes food feel thicker and richer and "will contribute to a sense of fullness in the mouth."

It also promotes the release of flavor-enhancing chemicals. Civille learned this in Paris, where she noticed that people were routinely buttering their brie cheese sandwiches. Her initial surprise quickly gave way to appreciation. "It tastes great," she said. "Butter helps the cheese actually develop in the mouth. It releases more flavor."

Also, fat helps flavors merge and meld, creating a smooth sensation as it brings disparate ingredients together in a symphonic whole. Civille suggested the same simple experiment that Adam Drewnowski had conducted to illustrate the impact of fat on flavor. Add a teaspoon of high-quality vanilla extract to a cup of heavy cream and another to a cup of skim milk. The first concoction tastes rich and delicious, but the second tastes terrible. Without fat, explained Civille, "the flavor notes do not develop in the same way. The physical chemistry is such that the volatiles are not released in the way that they are released in the fat."

The lubricating properties of fat are also essential, because with them "the product disappears much more rapidly. It absorbs saliva better . . . and it disappears, you have a 'quick getaway,' a quick melt," she explained. Fat contributes to a smooth, even bolus (the wad that forms as you chew food) in the mouth. If fat is removed from a product, it won't break down the same way. Rather than melting, "You get little tiny globs of stuff suspended in saliva," she said. Civille didn't have to add that this would make for an unpleasant sensory experience.

"If it's meant to melt, it better melt," said Civille. "That is critical to the nature of the product. It is critical to the pleasure of the product."

Fat also lingers after we swallow food, leaving flavor behind in the mouth. "Unlike bad wine that just falls off, the volatility is still there, so you still have pleasurable aftertaste."

By the end of my day with Civille, I understood that a vast number of sensory stimuli can be associated with a food: flavor . . . aroma . . . oral texture . . . visual texture . . . manual texture . . . creaminess . . . firmness . . . ease of pour . . . crumbliness . . . melt . . . viscosity . . . tooth stick . . . mouth coating . . . particle size . . . springiness . . . compression . . . adhesiveness . . . moisture absorption . . . chalky film . . . gloss.

Each of these qualities alone has an impact on the pleasure we derive from food, and combining particular attributes in an almost infinite number of possibilities has an even greater effect. My discussions with Gail Civille about sensory stimuli alerted me to what all that loading and layering really does. Those fat-on-sugar-on-fat-on-salt-on-fat combinations generate multiple sensory effects. Which is just what the industry wants.

Consider battered french fries, whose sensory properties include what Civille describes as a "crystalline outer coating that makes them extra crispy."

"And when bacon and cheese are added to those fries?" I asked. "Does that generate more sensory cues?"

Without a doubt, she confirmed. "Adding more fat gives me more flavor. It gives me more salt. And that bacon gives me a lot more lubricity."

That's where the appeal lies. We're eating for sensation.

I was curious about which sensory properties make marketplace winners. The Snickers bar, according to Civille, is "extraordinarily well engineered." While its flavor characteristics are appealing, she said, the real key to its success lies in its even disappearance and clean getaway. "When you eat a Snickers bar, the chocolate, the caramel, the nougat, and the peanuts all disappear at the same time. You're not getting all this buildup of stuff in your mouth."

That contrasts with many products whose nuts become annoyingly lodged between your teeth and your cheek. The genius of Snickers, explained Civille, is that as we chew, the sugar dissolves, the fat melts, and the caramel picks up the peanut pieces so the entire candy is carried out of the mouth at the same time.

The Kettle chip is another success story. Made from sugar-rich russet potatoes, Kettles have a slightly bitter background note, and they brown irregularly, which gives them a complex flavor. High levels of fat generate easy mouth-melt, and surface variations add a level of interest beyond what we typically find in mass-produced chips.

Heightened complexity is the key to modern food design. French fries were once merely french fries, before they were enhanced with bacon or cheese. A hamburger was once a hamburger, and eating it was what Civille called a single event: "You didn't have it loaded up with twenty levels of stimulation creating this multilayered event." We've shifted radically from the food norms of the past.

Supermarket foods have changed, too. Instead of buying potatoes in the produce section, we buy potato au gratin in a package.

Some brands of pasta sauce are loaded with sugar. Foods from around the world are sold breaded, battered, and fried, appearing in the frozen-foods section as chicken tacos and jalapeño poppers, calamari rings and fish sticks, stuffed pierogi and dumplings. And we don't have to buy plain frozen vegetables if we prefer to have them glazed or smothered in cheese and butter sauces.

"Take a look at cereal," said Civille. "You used to get one thing. I mean, raisin bran was a big deal, with two things in a box." She guessed that half of today's cereals have multiple ingredients added to the base flakes or nuggets. When I wandered the cereal aisle of my local supermarket, past Lucky Charms and Cocoa Puffs and Honey Nut Cheerios, I wondered whether that figure isn't higher.

All of this has changed the nature of food. Simplicity has given way to elaborately structured products that give us "more layers, more sensory cues, more sensory stimuli," Civille pointed out.

"And more sugar, fat, and salt?" I asked.

"I'm sure of that."

Scientists were as intrigued as industry about the multisensory effects of food.

In the summer of 2006, I was in Naples, Florida, attending a scientific meeting sponsored by the Society for the Study of Ingestive Behavior. Early one morning I heard a presentation by Richard Foltin, of Columbia University's Department of Psychiatry, who was participating in a symposium entitled "Basic and Clinical Science of Ingestion and Reward."

I was at full attention as Foltin started talking about "positive reinforcement or reward." Although the subject of the morning's session was the pleasure we derive from food, he angled into that conversation by describing another set of stimuli—the combination of cocaine and heroin known colloquially as "speedball."

Foltin spoke of the "real rush" people achieve, the "roller-coaster ride" induced by ingesting substances with differing stimulating and sedating effects. "You're going up, you're going down, it goes away, and then it comes back. It's just great."

People who experience the complex pleasures of these alternating effects learn to manipulate them for the sensations they want, Foltin said. They like each component and they like the mixtures they can achieve. They might use one stimulus several times, and then top off that experience by consuming something else.

"The self-administration of two drugs in close proximity may increase the desired effect of one drug or both drugs or decrease an undesired effect," Foltin explained. Using a combination of drugs could also increase the duration of a desired effect or decrease the duration of an undesired one. Or, he added, the combination could "produce an effect not available with either drug alone."

I did not have to stretch to understand the analogy he was making to food. We top off an excessive meal with an indulgent dessert and seek the additive effects of an agreeable flavor combination, such as hot and sour, or sweet and salty. We find pleasure in a mix of attributes, such as mouthfeel, temperature, texture, and viscosity. When we eat more ice cream because it has added chocolate chips, add creamy blue cheese dressing to fried chicken, or expect entertainment with a restaurant meal, we are in search of multisensory effects.

No Satisfaction

CHAPTER 18

When we talk about the complexity of American foods, we aren't referring to the kind of complexity traditionally associated with fine cuisine or regional or ethnic cooking. The American concept of complexity is built on layering and loading, rather than an intricate and subtle use of quality ingredients. Visitors from other cultures often remark on the difference. Yoshiyuki Fujishima, an executive at Ajinomoto, one of Japan's largest food companies, believes that American food is fundamentally less satisfying than Japanese food.

"The food I used to eat in Japan has complex flavor, and I can get satisfaction with less quantity," he said. By contrast, with American food "you have to have a lot to be satiated."

Europeans say much the same thing. To more sophisticated palates, our cuisine lacks finesse—"There is no curiosity in it. . . . You are swamped with very strong tastes," one source told me. He called American food "over the top."

Where traditional cuisine is meant to satisfy, American industrial food is meant to stimulate.

Our diet today is mostly made up of "easy calories." According to Gail Civille, in the past Americans typically chewed a mouthful of food as many as twenty-five times before it was ready to be swallowed; now the average American chews only ten times.

In part this is because fat, which has become ubiquitous, is a lubricant. We don't eat as much lean meat, which requires more saliva to ready it for swallowing. "We want something that's higher in fat, marbled, and so when you eat it, it melts in your mouth," said Civille. Food is easier to eat when it breaks down more quickly in the mouth. "If I have fat in there, I just chew it up and whoosh! Away it goes."

John Haywood, a prominent restaurant concept designer, agreed. Processing, he said, creates a sort of "adult baby food." By "processing" he means removing the elements in whole food—like fiber and gristle—that are harder to chew and swallow. What results is food that doesn't require much effort to eat. "It goes down very easy; you don't even think much about eating it," said Haywood.

The food consultant who told me about his industry's secrets had much the same perspective. "We've gone through some kind of a metamorphosis over the years. We've made food very easy to get calories from." He talked about the greater degree to which we refine foods now; an example is how we mill away the bran from brown rice and whole wheat flour. As a result the food is "light, it's white, it's very easy to swallow. It doesn't obstruct you in any way. It's easy to get a lot of calories without a lot of chewing."

Because this kind of food disappears down our throats so quickly after the first bite, it readily overrides the body's signals that should tell us "I'm full." He offered coleslaw as an example. When its ingredients are chopped roughly, it requires time and energy to chew. But when cabbage and carrots are softened in a high-fat dressing, coleslaw ceases to be "something with a lot of innate ability to satisfy."

Contrast apples with applesauce and we can see the same phenomenon. When the peel is removed, much of the fiber is lost.

"Then we add sugar to it; we make it so you can practically drink the thing. It doesn't ever provide the satiation of a fresh apple that you have to chew on."

This isn't to say that the food industry wants us to stop chewing altogether. It knows we want to eat a doughnut, not drink it. "What are you going to do with the sugar, put it on your tongue?" asked the food consultant. "I want to chew. I want to feel it in my mouth. The key for the food industry is to create foods with just enough chew— but not too much."

Foods that go "whoosh" don't leave us with a sense of being well fed. By stripping food of fiber, we also strip it of its capacity to satisfy. In making food disappear so swiftly, fat and sugar only leave us wanting more.

Instead of paying attention to what goes into our mouths, we're engaged in a "shoveling process," said Nancy Rodriguez. An expert on the sensory properties of food and head of the product development firm Food Marketing Support Services, Rodriguez asserts, "We eat to be belly filled."

Giving Them What They Like

CHAPTER 19

Like most industries, the food industry doesn't merely design products and send them forth hoping consumers will buy them. It engages in an elaborate process of "reverse engineering" to figure out exactly what we'll like. "They do the mathematics necessary to deconstruct the key drivers" of liking, Gail Civille observed.

The stakes are higher with food than with most other commercial products. Intentionally or not, industry activities take advantage of the biology of the brain, selling us products that alter our bodies.

Success depends on creating a blueprint for producing foods with the right combination of sensory properties. Since some consumers prefer, say, sweeter or saltier foods, the mix of stimulating ingredients will depend to some degree on the target market. But in general, Civille said, industry is "trying to find the formulation that is going to make the greatest number of people want it."

This approach has been honed to a fine science.

By the time he retired as vice president for research and development at Nabisco, Robert Smith had established unassailable credentials in the food industry. On his watch two enduring cookie success stories—Oreos and Chips Ahoy!—had brought the company remarkable profits. Smith helped me see why. His message was that no single aspect of food—neither one ingredient nor one sensory property—gets us to like something. The quest in the industry is to find the combination of qualities that will do that. "The key drivers are multisensory," said Smith. "It's not just one thing."

To identify a desirable mix of attributes, the industry assembles taste panels that allow consumers and professionals to dissect a given product's pleasing qualities. The industry calls this "fingerprinting," and the technique is used to figure out what proportion of which elements will be acceptable to a consumer. "We look at this model to determine what turns consumers on," he acknowledged.

Smith had played a pivotal role in bringing fat-free SnackWell's cookies to market, which is what made me so eager to talk to him. I wanted to know why SnackWell's would not relinquish their grip on me. Time and again I'd eat one, walk away from the box, and return a few minutes later for another. And another. And another one after that. I didn't like my behavior, but I kept doing it anyway. Often I didn't even realize how many cookies I'd eaten until they were all gone.

Nabisco had encountered obstacles en route to getting a no-fat cookie onto supermarket shelves. Before it finally hit on the formula for commercial success, the company had to solve the problem of texture. Without fat, the cookie initially seemed harsh and dry. SnackWell's were ready for the big time only after Nabisco discovered that a small amount of the fatty acid diglyceride was an adequate substitute. That discovery, along with a winning mix of ingredients and flavor notes, gave Nabisco a product that kept many of us coming back for more.

"You need to optimize the right combination," said Smith, again emphasizing the futility of focusing on isolated drivers of taste. "If you simply maximize any one driver, you'll kill the product. It has to have all things together to make it a cookie."

One necessary feature is consistency—the product has to taste the same every time a consumer buys it. A cookie also needs to look like a cookie. When Smith assembled his panels during the Snack-Well's design process, he asked participants to make drawings of how they saw a cookie, knowing that a successful product would have to conform to conventional ideas about appropriate structure. "How the mind sees it is very important," he said. "It's the balance of all factors that drives hedonics."

Providing contrast in a product is another way to maximize multisensory impact, as Oreo cookies demonstrate. Their appealing texture and mouthfeel are popular features, but it's the unique, bitter taste of the chocolate wafer combined with the sweetness of the cream filling that really gives the product so much appeal. That kind of contrast creates what the industry calls "dynamic novelty."

You can't isolate one component of most successful foods to explain why they work. It isn't just sugar, fat, or salt, but the right proportion of each. It isn't just one flavor note, but many. Not one sensory stimulus, but multiple effects.

Now more than ever there's an array of industrial techniques to make it easier to design all of this. As an example, Dwight Riskey, a food industry expert retired from Frito-Lay, told me how the salting of potato chips had evolved. "If you saw the way we applied salt in the old days, it was extremely rough. It was just like somebody standing over the potato chips with a salt shaker," he said. "We have much better scientific tools now. It's a much more mediated and measured process, and a much more uniform kind of delivery."

The goal is to add the right amount of salt in combination with other ingredients. "Optimizing one variable at a time is a terrible mistake, because the optimum salt level is only going to be optimum if you simultaneously optimize chip thickness and sugar content," Riskey said. "The more variables that you can simultaneously optimize, the better you're going to be able to do."

The appeal of food lies in the interaction of its variables. "Mixtures," said Riskey, "are where the magic happens."

What Consumers
Don't Know

CHAPTER 20

There's a certain irony to the emphasis food companies place on tasting panels, as well as on focus groups and other avenues of feedback. Consumers don't really know much about what they're eating. They say they try to avoid certain ingredients—fat, for example— but in blind taste tests they usually prefer foods with more fat. They're likely to underestimate the amount of sugar and salt in a product and aren't even sure when a beverage has truly quenched their thirst.

At Gail Civille's tasting panels, participants tend to make non-specific comments such as, "I like it because it tastes good."

When she presses them to explain what they mean, they use vague phrases like "it's yummy." They know what they like, but typically they don't know why.

The food industry has done a masterful job exploiting that uncertainty. In Civille's experience, consumer judgment is sometimes clouded by advertising and sometimes by a sense of what is supposed to be the "right" choice. Aware that eating excessive salt is frowned upon, a person may say, "I like these potato chips because they're not too salty," even though the chips may actually contain a lot of salt.

Likewise, a consumer's stated preference is often clouded by the knowledge that something is high in fat. When consumers think, "I shouldn't be eating that," they're likely to report, "I don't like it." But in fact, says Civille, blind tests generally show the opposite: "They like the ones that are more salty and more fatty."

Consumers are also misled by the layering and loading of foods. They may say they like broccoli, but what really appeals to them is the version that's fried and has a cheese topping. They may claim to like the look of a crispy potato chip, but what really draws them in is the fat and salt.

Sometimes sugar, fat, and salt are so masked by other flavors that we don't realize these ingredients are there. I asked Civille to identify some of those products. "What's salty that I don't think of as salty? What's sweet that I don't think of as sweet?"

Most bread is highly salted, she said, because salt takes away the bitter taste of flour and brings up the flavor—to 10 on a consumer rating scale of 1 to 15. Some bread also has a lot of sugar—Civille rated the sweetness of a McDonald's hamburger bun at 7 or 8. Ketchup earns an 8 or 9 for sweetness, while the sauce on a Pizza Hut pizza climbs into the 10-to-12 range. Crackers are another revelation. Consumers generally know they're salty but are often surprised to learn how much sugar and fat many of them contain.

And then we have the widespread popularity of ranch dressing. With mayonnaise and buttermilk as its primary ingredients, the fat content may be predictable, but its sweetness is not. Depending on the brand, ranch dressing is likely to have a sweetness level somewhere between 7.5 and 10, according to Civille. "Parents say, 'My children won't eat any other dressing except ranch,' and I want to tell them, 'Yes, and I know why. Because it's sweet.'"

Food product developers seem perfectly willing to exploit this lack of consumer awareness.

If a food contains more sugar than any other ingredient, federal regulations dictate that sugar be listed first on the label. But if a food contains several different kinds of sweeteners, they can be listed separately, which pushes each one farther down the list. Gail Civille thinks this requirement has led the industry to "put in three different sources of sugar so that they don't have to say it has that much sugar. So sugar doesn't appear first."

"Where else do you see four or five different kinds of sugar?" I asked.

"Breakfast cereals," Civille answered. Cereals often include some combination of sugar, brown sugar, fructose, high-fructose corn syrup, honey, and molasses.

"This is all so you don't have to list sugar first?" I asked.

"Right, that's what I think. They hide it from the mothers."

Whatever the true motive, ingredient labeling still does not fully convey the amount of sugar and fat being added to food, certainly not in a language that's easy for consumers to understand. The Kellogg's Frosted Flakes label, for example, indicates that the cereal has 11 grams of sugar per serving. But nowhere does it tell consumers that more than one-third of the box contains added sugar.

The Ladder of Irresistibility

CHAPTER 21

To explore the extent of the food industry's quest to make food irresistible, I asked a colleague to attend the international Pangborn Sensory Science Symposium at Harrogate, a small English town about 200 miles north of London. The gathering brought together experts in academia and industry to talk about their field and its relevance to consumer products.

My interest had been piqued by a workshop entitled "Can the Sensory Profession Provide Industry with Irresistible Products?" I was particularly curious about what Michele Foley would say. Foley is a food scientist at Frito-Lay and was giving a talk called "Simply irresistible—understanding high levels of satisfaction and what it means."

Packages of flavored chips were placed on the seats of the seminar room where she was making her presentation. "Would you say that they're irresistible?" Foley asked as she began her talk. Most people in the audience nodded.

Foley put up her first slide, which displayed a formula for food pleasure: sensory stimulation + caloric stimulation. Then she began describing the study she'd designed to tease apart the components of foods that consumers consider irresistible. Her key research question had been, "What are the kinds of attributes that increase craveability for the product?"

For that study, Foley had gathered 2,000 people who frequently ate one or more of thirty-one different Frito-Lay products, primarily crackers and chips in various flavors and forms. The distinctive feature of her research was its use of people who knew and loved the snack foods and ate them regularly. Based on their recent memories, participants chose from a battery of attributes, including the adjective "irresistible," to describe them. Anywhere from 35 to 70 percent of people who ate a given product identified it as irresistible. The two that earned the most votes for irresistibility were Nacho Cheese Doritos and Cheetos Flamin' Hot.

Next, Foley tried to discern exactly what in those products made them so irresistible. A consumer panel helped her analyze some of the factors that influence this quality. Among them were "texture dynamics," which is the way the sample feels in your mouth as you chew (hard or crisp? tending to fracture or melt?), and "flavor dynamics," which is the variety and complexity of the flavor. (The industry talks about six flavor families in the United States—dairy, grilled, herbs, tangy-spicy, fruity sweet, and seafood.) The timing of a flavor's release during the chewing process is also part of flavor dynamics. Other characteristics of interest are "flavor intensity," scored on a scale of 1 to 15, and "mass dynamics," which is the way in which the sample is transformed in the mouth—for example, whether it forms a doughy mass or melts completely away. Foley also looked for information about how easy a product is to eat, as determined by the amount of work it takes to chew, which is usually a reflection of the size and hardness of a chip.

Foley further analyzed the panel's findings and ultimately pinpointed five key influences on irresistibility. In order of importance, they are: calories, flavor hits, ease of eating, meltdown, and early hit.

"Those are the attributes that drive cravings for you to eat," she said.

Each one of those properties engages the senses in multiple ways, Foley reported. Taken together, "it's about creating a lot of fun in your mouth, a lot of novelty in your mouth."

Within this framework, the appeal of Nacho Cheese Doritos became obvious, especially when Foley emphasized the power of cheese and other dairy flavors to contribute to irresistibility. These Doritos have many sought-after attributes—multiple flavor hits from three different cheese notes and various milks and creams, with salt and oil adding to the pleasure. There's also a crunch and hardness with the first bite, followed by a meltdown that turns the chips into a sauce in the mouth.

The impact of Cheetos Flamin' Hot in the mouth also changes during the act of eating them. "Kids describe the experience as a 'roller-coaster ride,'" Foley said. "They're cheesy and then they're hot and they're spicy." Along the way, they also get crunchy, exciting, and fun, she explained.

These chips are a totally processed product. "You have base cheese and then you spike it with hot or you spike it with tangy. It just makes it more interesting and more complex."

"Spike it?" This was the first time I'd heard that phrase used by the food industry.

Foley was clear about the business imperative driving her research: "It's not about predicting" what consumers will like, she said. "It's about being sure."

To succeed, the industry has to achieve a high degree of "repeat," a measure of how many people buy snack food more than once. Foley measured repeat at six-month intervals for two years. Among her findings: A product that is liked at first taste is not necessarily one that will demonstrate superior marketplace performance. The key to "market repeat," she said, is that after eating, say, six or seven potato chips, the consumer thinks they taste at least as good as the first two did.

"The goal is to leave people with a pleasant experience and a pleasant aftertaste," she explained. "The difference between the first impression and the last impression is what I found to be related to repeat. It's all about the product and whether they get the sensory experience they wanted."

At the Pangborn symposium, Foley asked: "How do we really engineer this stuff into our products?" Her answer: Use flavor notes, texture, and other sensory attributes to incorporate more stimulation in a base product.

Bacon-cheese fries are a good example. Along with dairy and grilled flavors, Foley said, they have a lot of textural components. "You've got some pieces that are crispy on the outside, soft on the inside. It's warm. It's probably gooey, stringy, so you have to use your fingers a lot to eat it, and you have to lick your fingers. It's all multisensory."

In one of her studies, Foley asked experienced eaters of Lay's potato chips to vote on the relative irresistibility of different chips. Consumers rated Baked Lay's, which have a simple flavor and don't melt away in the mouth, as the easiest to resist. Not coincidentally, they're the lowest in fat. Next came Classic Lay's, which are a bit more complex, with caramelized notes from the frying oil that gives them a better melt and more salt. Then barbecue potato chips, followed by sour-cream-and-onion chips, which each have additional flavor hits.

Most irresistible of all, according to consumers, were Kettle Cooked chips. They have a slightly lower fat content and flavors similar to Classic Lay's, but they're more complex, require a bit more work to consume, and have a hard, crunchy texture and a non-uniform appearance that makes every bite unique.

The techniques of layering and loading are essential to the multiple sensory experiences in many of these potato chip varieties. Beginning with a baked product, "You add fat, so you've added calories and a different kind of mouthfeel," Foley said. "Then you add flavors, and then you add texture, and that takes you up the irresistibility ladder."

Dipping is another strategy for adding irresistibility. Dips and sauces add layers of enhancement to the flavors loaded into a chip. "Dipping is a way to add pleasure to the base chips," she explained. There's a lot of sensory stimulation going on "when you dip a chip into a sauce, like sour cream and onion."

Not every product can be made irresistible. "I can train myself to like Lay's baked potato chips, but I can't find them irresistible," said Foley. Extra flavors and other sensory attributes can't adequately compensate for the chips' lack of fat—an intrinsic component of most chips' appeal. But all the other add-ons serve their intended goal of boosting impact, said Foley, so the product at least becomes "more pleasurable, more interesting, more stimulating."

"Basically we're making food more convenient, more fun. That's what we're all about."

"So you take sensory experiences, cuisines, and you make them into snack food?" I later asked Foley.

"And we make it available to you easily."

"And the ability to select different sensory attributes?" I asked. "That's the basis of food science, right?"

"That's really what our job is."

———

Howard Moskowitz, an expert on consumer behavior, also spoke at the Pangborn conference. He argued that the key sensory characteristics of a product need to be assessed concurrently, in many possible combinations, to determine what consumers like. This contrasts with the more traditional one-at-a-time approach to evaluation, in which food consultants first identify the right level of sweetness, then the right level of salt, and so forth. That, says Moskowitz, "is not necessarily the way to create irresistible or highly acceptable products."

His approach requires complex mathematical models, and it's costly. But the investment is worthwhile when he scores a winner. Moskowitz tested six independent variables in forty-four prototype combinations before Prego tomato sauce was ready to hit supermarket shelves. Grovestand orange juice was not ready for market until he had tested sixty-five product prototypes. And it took eighty-seven prototypes before Maxwell House coffee tasted right. That's a lot of coffee. "It certainly would have been easier to do two prototypes and go sequentially," said Moskowitz. "Except we never would have arrived at the answer."

In the competitive and lucrative world of food design, the payoff can be huge—a food people want to buy. "If you can find that optimal point in a set of ingredients," he continued, "you may be well on your way to converting that array of chemicals and physical substrates into a successful product."

There was at least one other reason I was glad to have collected material from the sensory science symposium in Harrogate—the poster I found by Wilma den Hoed and E. H. Zandstra that asked, "What makes a food desirable?" Both scientists work in the Consumer Perception and Behavior Division of Unilever, the European Union's largest consumer products company, and they were clear about the purpose of their study: "For product developers, it is of interest to add elements to a food that make a food highly desired and liked, both initially and over repeated consumption."

Adding elements to drive desire? That certainly spoke to industry intent.

In their study, den Hoed and Zandstra asked Dutch consumers to complete questionnaires immediately after they experienced a strong desire for a particular product. The consumers also joined focus groups in which they identified the sensory properties of foods they liked.

Not surprisingly, consumers preferred products that were high in both calories and fat. They also typically had unique sensory characteristics, such as dual textures (think of a piece of chocolate candy that's firm on the outside, with a soft fruity center); a specific taste (a strongly flavored sauce, for example); or a dual taste (say, one that's both sweet and spicy). Consumers also said the foods they desired had a positive effect on mood, making them feel less tense and more energetic.

The study concluded that over the long term, consumers continue to buy foods that are associated with two features: "Unique sensory attributes . . . and learned characteristics related to positive mood change."

The World's Cuisine Becomes Americanized

CHAPTER 22

Asian cuisine has become hugely popular in the United States—but what we're eating here is not what has traditionally been eaten across the Pacific. The Japanese have built their diet around fish, soy, miso, rice, and vegetables, with protein and salt as the dominant elements. Our approach is a little different.

Bottled teriyaki sauce, for example, combines soy sauce and rice wine to mimic Japanese flavorings, putting an American spin on a classic Japanese cooking technique. The amount of added sugar makes it far sweeter than anything found in Japan. We've also invented new approaches to sushi classics—for example, mayonnaise-topped tempura shrimp now comes wrapped in rice as a sushi roll.

In China, dishes like orange-flavored chicken and sweet-and-sour chicken are widely available, but again, all the sugar is an American contribution. The dish we call "General Tso's Chicken" is loaded with sugar, much to the consternation of the Taiwanese chef who created it. "The dish can't be sweet," he insisted. "The taste of Hunan cuisine is not sweet."

Traditional Chinese cuisine also makes use of a lot more vegetables than are included in our versions. When restaurant owners in this country hand different menus to Chinese and American patrons, it's partly because they're offering their countrymen foods with less fat and sugar. "When I look at American Chinese food, I think it is not Chinese," the owner of Royal Palace in New Haven, Connecticut, told me.

Other traditional Asian cuisines are built around distinctive and contrasting properties that blend harmoniously: the counterpoint of hot and sour flavorings in Vietnamese food, for instance. In the United States we've adopted some of the same combinations, but we typically add other elements—more sugar and more fat.

To get a sense of what happens to Chinese food when it's prepared in America, I started spending time at Panda Express (the nation's largest Chinese restaurant chain, with sales in 2007 of more than $1 billion). The company's offerings provided a remarkable example of the explosion of high-sugar, high-fat, and high-salt foods in the United States.

The Orange Chicken is described on the menu as "tender, juicy chicken pieces lightly battered and fried, sautéed in a sweet and mildly spicy chili sauce with scallions." Preparation of the dish begins in the factory, where the meat is processed, battered, fried, and frozen. Like many processed meats, the dark chicken chunks contain as much as 19 percent of a water-based solution; oil and salt are added as well.

More salt and other spices are added before the battered chicken nuggets are prebrowned in soybean oil, frozen, then shipped out to Panda Express outlets around the country. At the restaurants, the meat is deep-fried in oil for at least five minutes just before it's served. The accompanying chili sauce strikes all three points of the food consultant's compass, with sugar, salt, and soybean oil complementing the vinegar and spices.

The Sweet and Sour Pork at Panda Express has a similar provenance. The menu describes it as "large cubes of pork battered and fried to a crisp, golden brown. Served with sweet and sour sauce with onions, green bell peppers, and pineapple chunks." When I asked, a worker gave me a copy of the label on the "ready-to-cook pork fritters" that are the base of Sweet and Sour Pork. This meat, which contains a 12 percent solution of water, salt, sodium phosphate, and spices, is breaded and battered in a mixture that includes more salt. Before they leave the plant, the pork fritters are fried in canola and/or cottonseed oils. Then they're shipped frozen to the restaurants, where they're fried again—for about eight minutes—before being served in a sweet, sour, and salty sauce. Yet the average consumer has no idea how much fat the typical Panda Express meal contains.

The chain's vegetable spring rolls have also been Americanized. That's why we see sugar twice in the filling—added to the vegetables and to the chicken base that seasons them. Salt is listed two times in the filling and again in the wrapper. Fat makes an appearance in four places—three times in the filling, where it's added to the vegetables, the chicken base (in the form of powdered chicken fat), and the natural stir-fry flavoring (which blends cottonseed, garlic, and ginger oils), as well as once in the wrapper. Those frozen spring rolls arrive at Panda Express outlets with instructions to deep-fry them in oil for five to six minutes.

At the same time we're taking the products of other cuisines and making them distinctly American, we're also taking American foods and sharing them with the world. American franchised food outlets have, of course, become commonplace across the globe. I witnessed the unfortunate effect of this firsthand, when I visited clinics in South Africa that were providing HIV-related care. My assignment took me to some desperately poor townships, yet I kept meeting obese health care workers. I asked a medical colleague to explain the seeming paradox.

Simple, she said. Kentucky Fried Chicken had come to town.

Nothing Is Real

CHAPTER 23

Chemical flavorings are another essential weapon in the arsenal the food industry uses to make food hyperpalatable.

When I strolled the convention center floor at the annual meeting of the Institute of Food Technologists in New Orleans, I wandered past the booth of a company that specializes in making some of those flavor chemicals. A staff person handed me a frozen chocolate drink, and from the first rich, flavorful sip I knew it was something special. The taste seemed to explode on my tongue. It reminded me of a Frozen Hot Chocolate I drank years before and remember to this day. The signature beverage of the Manhattan restaurant Serendipity, it is said to contain a secret blend of fourteen gourmet cocoas.

The ingredients in the frozen drink at the food technology convention told a different story. That product contained chocolate fudge caramel flavor, granulated sugar, cocoa powder, nonfat dry milk, dextrose, heavy cream, and salt—key drivers of palatability, blended together with artificial flavor.

"How much cocoa powder is in here?" I asked the food scientist at the booth.

"Very little," she answered. The manufacturer could list cocoa powder on the label because the drink did contain some, though not enough to contribute a lot to the flavor. Much more is generated through modern chemistry.

"Our business is to make something taste like something, even if it is not," the food scientist added.

I had just encountered another fundamental tool of the modern food business. Along with sugar, fat, and salt, much of the processed food we eat today relies heavily on chemical flavor.

Once I was sensitized to this I began to notice it everywhere. Take the traditional Oreo cookie. Among its primary ingredients are sweeteners, in the form of sugar and corn syrup, oil, and artificial vanilla flavoring. A café near my house sells a mocha drink that combines coffee and milk with a processed mix that has similar ingredients—sugar, coconut oil, corn syrup solids, and a host of flavor additives.

And then there's gelato. In Italy, this rich dessert is traditionally made from whole milk, eggs, sugar, and flavorings, but with its growing popularity in this country, gelato has become something very different. Most commercial gelato sold here begins with a processed base. For example, Ragazzo Gelato, marketed by a company called Frosty Boy, is a dry mix containing milk powder, sugar and glucose solids, milk solids, and a gum-and-emulsifier combination. A restaurant or food manufacturer can then add cream and an endless number of flavors and colors, along with what the industry calls "inclusions," such as candy, fruit, nuts, chips, and crunchy flavorings.

David Michael & Company, a century-old flavor innovator based in Philadelphia, creates some of the packaged and mostly artificial flavors that can be added to the gelato base. The firm prides itself on unusual pairings: apple chervil, blueberry lavender, chocolate espresso chipotle, coconut pineapple Thai basil, and pear apricot ginger. "Let us help you hit your flavor target faster," urges its marketing material.

Postconvention surfing of food industry Web sites made me even more aware that little in food is really what it seems. It's possible to create virtually anything with chemicals. David Michael can overlay grilled, braised, seared, or roasted nuances on a basic beef flavor. The company can replace fruit with a manufactured fruit taste for fillings and juices, and it produces a liquid substitute for butter that's known as Butter Plus, a pound of which replaces fifty pounds of the real thing.

There are many such companies. Savoury Systems markets ready-to-use flavor bases, relying especially on yeast extracts and hydrolyzed vegetable protein, which mimics meat flavoring. It sells chicken, beef, pork, turkey, and bacon flavors, as well as meat enhancers that include hickory smoke flavor base, roast turkey flavor, fire-roasted garlic, and roast chicken base. Its array of chemical-rich shellfish flavorings include lobster and shrimp extract powder, crab powder, and scallop flavor.

Then there are the cheese flavorings sold by Kraft, which include blue cheese, American cheese, and cream cheese. Kraft's powders and dairy flavors, according to the company, are designed "to deliver cheese flavor in any product application," making it possible to reduce "the cheese and dairy content of your products without sacrificing flavor." Many processed foods get their "cheese notes" from powders containing whey or nonfat dry milk solids.

These kinds of imitative goods can be put together in numerous combinations to create almost any known flavor. In the process, the industry transforms a food entirely. Meat that hasn't been grilled can taste like meat that has been. A topping that covers tortilla chips can look like cheese but contains mostly oil and flavoring. "Flavor chemists can develop any type of flavor, from anchovy to wok oil to hummus, using chemical compounds, organic acids, fatty acids, spices, extracts, oils, and a variety of other ingredients," explained one industry trade magazine writer.

Adding artificial chemicals to the basic ingredients of sugar, fat, and salt gives manufacturers remarkable freedom to create novel and stimulating food products.

Chemical-intensive food processing evolved to extend the shelf life of products and to lower food costs. More recently, however, the industry has directed its creative chemistry toward increasing sensation and consumer satisfaction. It's all about impact.

Manufacturers today have the capacity to add almost any sensory effect imaginable to their foods—and, in particular, to incorporate multiple sensations in a single product.

That's the explicit intention of a company called SensoryEffects, which creates nuggets and flakes that are added to baked goods such as breads, muffins, cookies, and cereals to impart flavor, aroma, color, and texture. The company's motto is "every sense in every piece," and its products, which require no refrigeration, cost less than the fruits, vegetables, cheese, and spices they replace. As the firm's literature explains, these products have "the goal of providing the baking industry with everything it needs to enhance the sensory experience on all levels."

At the New Orleans conference I saw many other products designed to do something similar. Foran Spice Company offers a bread seasoning that blends sugar, cinnamon, and oil of cassia, a spice extract. That novel seasoning was the dominant flavor in the creamy icing that topped a deliciously aromatic breadstick. Wild Flavors sells "flavor systems" for baked goods, such as white chocolate almond, chocolate Chambord, creamy caramel, and piña colada. The quest for indulgence is an explicit marketing theme. "Consumers want products that are indulgent and create a mood of experience," declares the company's literature. "Indulgent flavors and creamy textures are important in bringing a decadent experience."

Other manufacturers focus on building sensory effects into meat and dairy products. At its exhibit, Bell Flavors and Fragrances offered samples of pulled pork cooked in cola-flavored barbecue sauce; it might have been the best barbecue I've ever tasted. The company representative praised its "top notes," which are the stand-out flavors.

At the Comax Flavors booth, I drank a white peach tea made from high-fructose corn syrup, white tea powder, citric acid, and flavorings. This tasty beverage was created almost exclusively from artificial ingredients. Comax also sells a butter flavor to replace real butter "with a similarly satisfying flavor, taste, and mouth-feel." The company was explicit about how such products work on the senses: "We transform technology into good taste. Tastes to excite, stimulate, comfort, and linger."

Few consumers understand the extent to which the industry has in recent years used sensation to generate consumer satisfaction, yet the intent is clear in corporate promotional literature. For example, Food Marketing Support Services boasts, "FMSS identifies sensory space to target product development and maximize consumer acceptance" and "FMSS artists excite the senses and create remarkable foods."

McCormick, a spice conglomerate that employs an army of researchers, trend experts, chefs, food technologists, and sensory analysts, is equally explicit. "Satisfying the senses" is a key trend, according to the company. McCormick predicts a growth in meals that "feature flavors, colors, aromas, and textures" and "deliver a true multisensory experience."

Two days on the floor of the Institute of Food Technologists convention were enough to show me that the food industry is not content with the impact it can get from selling layers of sugar on fat on salt. Increasingly, it's also looking to chemical flavoring to drive consumer desire.

Optimize It!

CHAPTER 24

There's more to processing food than using chemical additives to bolster its sensory appeal. Modern manufacturing techniques also make food more uniform, less expensive, and more readily available. They give us infinitely more options to choose from and a lot more opportunities to get pleasure from the foods we eat.

John Haywood is a restaurant designer who helps clients develop novel products and new menu ideas. We met at the Outback Steakhouse on 23rd Street in Manhattan to talk about how food that originates on the farm is increasingly being optimized in the factory.

Contemporary food technology, Haywood said, "gives us the tools to deliver the product." And that product can be anything we want it to be. Processing "smooths out the flavor," stripping away any quality a consumer might find even vaguely offensive, he said. "All of this refined stuff is built for the broad market. It's not polarizing. Food science allows us to appeal to the greatest number of people."

Because every step of the manufacturing process is controlled, a completely consistent product rolls off the assembly line. There's another control advantage, as well. "Processed foods give you more freedom," said Haywood. "You can add anything you want. You can turn the dials to get the fat right, to get the sugar right, to get the salt right."

Dialing in the sugar, fat, and salt. I hadn't thought of food manufacturing in quite those terms before, but that's exactly what's going on.

I returned to my industry source to learn more about how that sort of thing is done. He had a lot to say about the processing techniques that make food much more hedonic today than it was in the past.

Hedonics, in the food consultant's view, involves five factors: anticipation; visual appeal; aroma; taste and flavor; and texture and mouthfeel. Many of the strategies for optimizing hedonics on a mass scale involve partial processing at the manufacturing plant, which allows food to reach restaurants and supermarket shelves in a convenient, easy-to-prepare form. A few decades ago such palatability-enhancing, preprocessing options didn't exist.

The use of "individually quick-frozen" foods—or IQF, in industry parlance—is one novel approach. Traditionally, quantities of food were frozen in a single block. The problem with that method was that when a package thawed, it retained a lot of extra water, making the food inside deteriorate faster. With IQF, foods like shrimp, potatoes, and chicken nuggets are blasted with cold air, cold nitrogen, or cold carbon dioxide as they travel along a conveyor belt, so they freeze in discrete pieces.

Before they're individually quick-frozen, these foods are often partially fried. This allows them to be plunged, straight from the package and still frozen, back into fat for a second frying. Many chain restaurants produce their french fries and, increasingly, other offerings as well, with par-frying techniques. This makes the food taste fresher and more palatable, and the layer of fat added during the par-frying stage makes the food impervious to moisture and gives it a golden sheen.

Par-fried IQF foods are also convenient for home cooking. IQF shrimp, for example, is widely available and has all the qualities the food consultant identified as hedonic. The element of anticipation is there, he said, because shrimp has traditionally been served mostly in high-end restaurants and feels "special." It also has visual and aromatic appeal and "a nice chewy texture and mouthfeel—not too tough; it doesn't involve tiring your mouth." And packaged shrimp is often breaded and fried before it's frozen, giving it what my source called "that crunchy outer thing with a lot of fat in it" that adds to sensory appeal.

From french fries to shrimp, buffalo wings to egg rolls, chicken nuggets to nachos, food is increasingly being assembled, not actually cooked, in chain restaurant kitchens. Many restaurants are no longer showcases for real cooking and creativity but rather are little more than construction sites.

One reason to automate the preparation process is to keep labor costs low. Otherwise, a venture capitalist told me, "you'll die from the chopping disease." Expenses associated with on-site preparation—such as chopping vegetables—cut deeply into profits. That's also why it's so hard to run a business that sells fresh and healthy foods on a mass scale.

Another benefit of preprocessing is that it takes the guesswork out of food preparation. Buffalo wings, for example, are typically seasoned, battered, breaded, and par-fried, then individually quick-frozen at the plant and shipped off to be fried again before serving. The creamy, high-fat dipping sauce they're served with most likely comes out of a jar. "The whole thing is preprocessed except for the final frying off," my source told me.

Even a plate of nachos has largely been processed in advance, using prefried tortilla chips, frozen or canned jalapeño peppers, and packaged cheese mixes. And the avocado that accompanies it has likely arrived in frozen chunks or slices. Likewise, meats are usually trimmed, precut, and sealed in a vacuum package to preserve color and flavoring. That also improves the hedonics, because the meat "hasn't developed an off flavor, it stays 'fresh' longer, and it is always consistent," said the food consultant. "All you have to do is open the package and put it on the grill."

Processed condiments offer another industry shortcut. Instead of whole garlic or fresh onion, the industry uses powdered garlic, powdered onion, or extracts of garlic and onion oils. Powdered tomato, dehydrated and concentrated, is a sweeter substitute for the real thing. Numerous oil extracts—such as rosemary oil, oregano oil, and black pepper oil—are used instead of fresh herbs and spices. These substances eliminate contaminants and enhance consistency. "It's all processed so you don't have quite as much variability in your source," said the food consultant. "Every time you make it in your production facility, it's going to have precisely the same kind of characteristics."

By giving food producers greater control over their products, preprocessing helps them optimize every element in the hedonic equation: anticipation, appearance, aroma, flavor, and texture. No doubt that was why I liked McDonald's Southern Style Chicken Breast—at least until I read the ingredients list, which included sugar, salt, modified tapioca starch, maltodextrin, and artificial flavors, even before it was battered, breaded, and fried.

Food processing is also essential to ensuring uniformity, so that an egg roll at a Chili's in Des Moines tastes the same as one in San Diego. Economies of scale kick in as well, driving down prices so consumers can afford indulgence on a daily basis, not merely as a special treat. The ability to optimize, the food consultant explained, "has helped the availability of more hedonically pleasing food. . . . Every element that can be optimized has been optimized—for hedonics and price and availability and consistency. The industry has a very good ability to figure out what turns consumers on and then to provide it for them in an economical, widely available, highly consistent form."

Frito-Lay's Michele Foley had convinced me that the industry knows how to make an irresistible product. Now another insider was pulling back the curtain on the processing techniques that make certain foods not only easy to find, economical to purchase, and fast to prepare, but a lot more pleasurable to eat, as well.

The Science of Selling

CHAPTER 25

It's hardly news that the food we eat, and the way it's presented, are the handiwork of an industry whose goal is to make a profit. What's striking is the many ingenious ways in which the industry succeeds. One venture capitalist did not mince words when he talked about its intent.

"The goal is to get you hooked," he said bluntly.

Michele Foley had used the term "craveability." Even more revealing than "irresistibility," this seems to be a ubiquitous characteristic of the foods being marketed today. Typically, craveable foods in America are layered with sauces, cheese, and breading. "When in doubt, throw cheese and bacon on it" is a standard joke in the world of chain restaurants, according to food industry consultant John Haywood.

Along with enhancing melt and making food easy to eat, these layers are cheaper to produce than the central ingredient (such as meat or fish) they flavor. They're also visually appealing, straightforward, and familiar. "Craveable takes me to a basic comfort place," said Haywood. "I don't have to work very hard to understand it. I'm not being asked to accept a lot of flavors or things I haven't had before. And I can probably take half of it home with me in a to-go container."

The industry's Crave It! study, sponsored by McCormick, was one attempt to find out what gets people excited about certain foods. Using an Internet-based survey, researchers asked questions about twenty-one categories of food—from chips, cheesecake, and ice cream to hamburgers, pizza, and olives. Ultimately they got responses from several thousand people. "My intention was to unlock the code of craveability," according to Jacqueline Beckley, who heads a product development group and helped design the Crave It! study.

Based on its collected data, the Crave It! study sorted respondents into three groups: the classics, the variety seekers, and the imaginers. Later they added a fourth group, those who focus on good nutrition.

People with a classic mind-set crave highly familiar standards, while variety seekers look for novelty (this is the population for whom the industry designs new flavors of potato chips). The imaginers, said Beckley, "are driven by ambience or romance or emotionality. It is not about the food but about the concept of food."

Food manufacturers and restaurants can design foods that each of these groups find craveable. Take the basic hamburger as an example. Serve it on a bun with a little ketchup, and it suits the classics. Add onions, bacon, and three layers of cheese, and variety seekers are happy. Market it with images of a summer barbecue, and imaginers can't get enough. Eliminate the bun and label it a low-carbohydrate burger, and you'll satisfy those thinking about nutrition.

I asked Beckley what else made a hamburger craveable. "A hamburger has all the required flavors, all the texture. It gets you excited, gets your juices running. You begin to chew through it, you feel alive. It suspends time for a brief moment."

Understanding what makes a food craveable, and to whom, means understanding many characteristics of food that go beyond flavor. Whether it's texture, aroma, or other sensory properties that generate the excitement, Beckley says craveability is "about the body. . . . Your body is trying to modulate its happiness. It is trying to get to a state of bliss."

Providing a comfortable and stimulating eating environment is part of that. People also want to feel they're getting a good deal. "If you make plates bigger and fill them more, everyone makes more money," the venture capitalist said. For a marginal added cost, a restaurant can serve portions large enough to allow customers to eat plenty and still leave with leftovers.

The industry also gives a great deal of thought to the context in which food is presented. It takes full advantage of a substantial body of research showing how sensory cues—variety on our plates, food packaging, lighting, noise level, and other aspects of restaurant ambience, along with social setting—can stimulate intake. Even the name of the food has an effect. In one study, researchers found that menu descriptions ("succulent Italian seafood filet" rather than "seafood filet"; "traditional Cajun red beans with rice" rather than "red beans with rice"; and "satin chocolate pudding" rather than "chocolate pudding") affect sensory perception. People say that foods with more descriptive names look better, taste better, and leave them feeling more satisfied.

Thinking creatively about how to attract more consumers led Starbucks to the Frappuccino, the venture capitalist told me. Although its stores were crowded early in the day, by afternoon "they were so empty you could roll a bowling ball through them," he said. The creation of a rich, sweet, and comforting milkshakelike concoction utterly transformed the business.

Starbucks learned a basic lesson: Make enticing food easily and constantly available, keep it novel, and people will come back for more. With food available in just about any setting, "the number of cues, the number of opportunities" to eat have increased while the barriers to consumption have fallen, said David Mela, senior scientist of weight management at the Unilever Health Institute. "The environmental stimulus has changed."

Call it the taco chip challenge—the challenge of controlled eating in the face of constant food availability. "Forty years ago, you might face the social equivalent of that taco chip challenge once a month. Now you face it every single day," said Mela. "Every single day and every single place you go, those foods are there, those foods are cheap, those foods are readily available for you to engage in. There is constant, constant opportunity."

Portion size is another potent selling tool. Supersize options and all-you-can-eat specials give consumers access to a bottomless well of food for a fractional increase in cost. People eat more when there's more on their plates. Food consultant John Haywood helped me understand why big portions work so well in the restaurant business. When we met at Outback, I ordered Aussie Fries, which came smothered with cheese and topped with bacon bits. Haywood looked at the enormous plate of food as it was set down in front of me and called it a "cheap filler." Then he explained the restaurant's intent with that dish.

"That 20 cents' worth of product gets me $5 of wow," he said.

"It's all about 'How can I make one more penny or one more nickel on that sale?'" explained Mike McCloud, a former Coca-Cola executive. Thirty years ago, he said, a triple chocolate muffin was made with real eggs, real chocolate, and real butter. It was rich and flavorful, but it was also small.

Then "greed took over," said McCloud, explaining a shift in attitude among food companies. Their new mind-set: "I don't want to sell a 2-ounce muffin that's made with real butter. I want to make a 5-ounce muffin for pennies more and make more profit on it."

As a result, today's muffins are much bigger, but most of the real ingredients are gone. Instead of butter they're likely to contain some blend of shortening and oil. Often the ingredient label will list "palm or coconut oil," a clue that the manufacturer is buying the ingredient that's cheapest at a given moment. Powdered egg substitutes replace whole eggs, and an array of inexpensive, processed sweeteners are used. In lieu of real food, the industry is baking with "a chemical mix of preservatives and oil," McCloud said.

In his view, it's the low cost of readily available fats and sugars that drives their use. "If McDonald's could sell anything and make money at the same rate that they're doing now, they couldn't care less whether it was fat- or sugar-laden. It just happens to be that fats and sugars and flours are some of the least expensive food items we have in the world."

McCloud also sees the profit motive behind the push to increase standard beverage sizes. When he worked at Coca-Cola headquarters in Atlanta, "one of our main areas of focus was 'How do we get McDonald's, Burger King, the big customers, to increase their average cup size?'" A small cup of soda measured 8 ounces, but McCloud and his colleagues tried to shift the norm to 12 ounces. They also worked to double the size of the large drink from 16 to 32 ounces.

Since soft drinks sold in chain restaurants are little more than syrup and carbonated tap water, they can provide a profit margin of about 90 percent. It wasn't hard to make their case to McDonald's. McCloud said, "We had to convince everybody that 90 percent of $1 is good, but wouldn't it be great if we could get you 90 percent of $1.50 by adding another 3 cents' worth of product?"

Along with encouraging bigger cup sizes, McCloud said Coca-Cola aimed to boost sales by diverting consumers from water to soft drinks. Part of its strategy was to calculate how much liquid the average person could consume in a year—and then try to increase the percentage of the total represented by soft drinks.

"Our job was to sell more syrup. We would say, 'How can we get the consumer to drink more soft drinks and less water?' We discouraged water giveaways at these places because there was no profit in it" and encouraged consumers to view those enormous cups of soda as good value for the money.

When the beverage companies throw their weight behind a change in norms, they're often successful, McCloud noted. "Coke and Pepsi are so big and strong, they have the horsepower to change people's habits."

There's a contradiction in all of this. At the same time manufacturers are making so much stimulating, high-fat, high-sugar food so readily available, they're also responding to consumer concerns about health. Indeed, this is a substantial area of activity and profit for the industry.

Many food producers and restaurants now provide nutrition calculators on their Web sites, allowing consumers to add up the calories in their foods and find out how much fat, sodium, carbohydrates, and sugar they're eating. And some surprising alliances have been formed in the name of health. T.G.I. Friday's partnered with Atkins Nutritionals to create a menu that appeals to people on the low-carbohydrate Atkins diet. Wendy's is working with the American Dietetic Association to offer consumers educational tools about nutrition.

That kind of paradox reflects broader industry trends, according to Datamonitor, a leading supplier of "business intelligence." In one of its consumer-trends reports, the company declares that "the desire for health and indulgence represents a trend clash." Consumers looking to satisfy seemingly contradictory desires represent an important market opening, according to the report, which proclaims: "Healthy indulgence is a vast opportunity that is underdeveloped by the food and drinks industry."

Increasingly, the industry is supplementing its products with chemicals to persuade consumers that the food is good for them. It's all about grabbing "the consumer's attention" by making "compelling" claims that sometimes "seem to be an exercise in creative writing," admit industry experts.

Apparently, it's working. What used to be the domain of small, specialty health-food stores has attracted national competitors. Kellogg's, for example, introduced candy bars containing the chemical DHA (a fatty acid), labeled them "Live Bright brain health bars," and made bold claims about their value in sustaining brain health. Whatever the merits and potential health benefits of DHA, if any, the other ingredients are no surprise—mostly sugar and fat.

Most restaurants don't make those kinds of claims for their meals, but those who sell the most indulgent sugar-on-fat-on-salt combinations often market low-fat meals as well. Hardee's, home of the Monster Thickburger, proudly announces that its health-conscious customers need not "leave taste behind," and offers up a charbroiled BBQ chicken sandwich, with 340 calories and 4 grams of fat. Chili's includes Guiltless Grill listings on its menu, with "more choices for your healthy lifestyle." McDonald's is marketing its fruit-and-walnut salad aggressively, with photos of the new dish prominently displayed in drive-through lanes and near in-store order counters.

But are those products selling? One food industry executive shrugged off the question. "Who cares?" he asked. "You're going to build your image."

Purple Cows

CHAPTER 26

In industry shorthand, it all comes down to the difference between brown cows and purple cows, according to marketing expert Seth Godin. Brown cows are products that, while perfectly adequate, are fundamentally boring. But a product that's a purple cow—now, that's something that stands out. "The essence of the Purple Cow," writes Godin, "is that it would be remarkable. Something remarkable is worth talking about, worth paying attention to."

And that's what the food industry is trying to develop.

I first learned about purple cows at the New Orleans food technology convention, where Nancy Rodriguez, of Food Marketing Support Services, described the influence of Godin's work, which in turn drew on a nineteenth-century reference. It's a perspective she keeps in mind as she walks the supermarket aisles to see what's on the shelves. Rodriguez says she wants to know who has succeeded in putting purple cows out there. She's looking for foods that go "pop"— the ones that grab at the senses, exuding passion and personality, demanding attention.

Taste, said Rodriguez, is the star of innovation and its goal is to "deliver flavor in a remarkable format." But purple-cow foods exhibit other potent sensory cues as well. "Auditory stimuli are essential for products to be winners . . . the crunch of a fritter, the juicy pop of citrus," she said. "Aroma is the sense of memory and has incredible emotional power, compelling salivation and craving. . . . [A] sense of seeing visualizes shapes, textures, and colors that captivate consumers."

These combinations bring bold and memorable foods to the consumer, especially when they're presented in "packaging that screams 'Hold me/Look at me'" and are marketed with language that evokes the senses. To her food-industry audience, Rodriguez declared, "The innovation of truly remarkable products is the only way to consistently create shareholder value."

The concept of purple-cow foods gave me a shorthand way to think about a fundamental trend in the food industry—finding ways to add extra levels of stimulation. Product developers and food scientists are combining ingredients and using complex flavorings, multiple textures, appealing colors, and many other innovations to add kick to their foods. As experts at McCormick said in the company's flavor forecast, "No matter where people are eating—at home or in restaurants—one thing holds true. They crave flavor: bold, comforting, unexpected, and international."

That idea was repeated in an article I read about transforming basic dishes into "sense-sational ones." The goal, according to a food industry scientist, is to create "foods that satisfy all the senses. . . . Hot and cooling, spicy and sweet, crunchy and creamy, bitter and salty work together, with enticing aromas, to create a multisensory experience and flavor utopia."

"Never say, 'This is the best' and stop there," said one company spokesperson. "There could be something else coming along, and that's exciting. So you also look for the new and focus on the future. So I want excitement, amazement, and wow, wow, wow."

Not just sugar, fat, and salt. Not just multisensory. But all of that and a lot of wow besides. Make it stand out. Take it up a notch. Make it salient. Build a purple cow that will lodge itself in the consumer's brain.

PART THREE

Conditioned Hypereating Emerges

Overeating Becomes
More Dangerous

CHAPTER 27

For most of human history we survived on unadorned animal and vegetable products. Now we eat mostly optimized and potent foods that bear little resemblance to what exists in nature.

As I learned more about the human reward system and the power of arousal, I began to think differently about food that stimulates all of our senses. The food industry is not only generating billions of dollars for itself by designing hyperpalatable combinations of sugar, fat, and salt—it's also creating products that have the capacity to rewire our brains, driving us to seek out more and more of those products.

To understand why a chocolate-chip cookie seemed capable of getting its grip on me, I turned to Mathea Falco, who heads Drug Strategies, a Washington-based nonprofit that seeks effective approaches to substance drug abuse. "What is it about an inanimate object on the plate that plays such a large role in our minds?" I asked. "Why are some of us always thinking about it? What is it about this stimulus?"

"It's a dragon, David," she said. "And the dragon is bigger than you."

Jerome Kagan, a renowned developmental psychologist at Harvard, taught me that the most effective rewards are those that can change our feelings. Eating highly palatable food falls squarely in that category, stimulating the brain in ways that provide momentary pleasure. That pleasure acts as a substitute for other emotions since it occupies working memory, and the brain can only focus on a limited amount of stimuli at any given time.

But our behavior isn't simply driven by the pleasure we derive from highly palatable foods. These foods also possess the ability to command our attention. Sometimes that attention is warranted, given the survival value of food, and sometimes it is not, given the era of plenty in which most of us live.

Living creatures survive by focusing on the most salient stimuli in their environment. If we are chased by a wild animal, caught in a house fire, or faced with an ailing child, such circumstances demand center stage in our minds, standing out from arousals of lesser power. But that response can be co-opted, and when it is, it leads us to focus on objects we would otherwise ignore. That's what happens when jelly beans gain salience.

A salient cue that—against our wishes—comes to occupy our thoughts and stimulate our emotions can provoke impulsive behavior. Whether the response is mild or intense, almost everyone has some vulnerability to the conflicts and unwanted thoughts such a cue engenders.

I was talking with a colleague about how the neural circuits of the brain had evolved to focus on the most salient stimuli and why this can drive us to overeat. As we talked, I deliberately tore open a box of chocolate-chip cookies. He sighed and asked, "Why did you have to do that?"

I had just cued him to the availability of a thick, chunky chocolate pleasure. Suddenly, his attention was diverted from our scientific discussion to an arousal he had not sought and did not want. His conditioned brain responded immediately to the sensory properties of that cookie.

Salient food drives a cycle of overeating behavior. Highly rewarding food becomes reinforcing because we've learned that it makes us feel better, motivating us to return and do the work necessary to feel better again. "Reinforcement learning is a mechanism for the organism to figure out which course of action will lead to positive outcomes," explained Wai-Tat Fu, of the University of Illinois. Learning that a certain behavior generates reward motivates us to act. And when the motivational circuitry of our brains is activated, we come back for more.

This process is enabled by the power of memory. Our memories store the experience of consuming highly palatable food and the resulting reward. This learning circuitry makes us aware of cues that predict the emotionally valued experience so that when we sense those cues again, we also retrieve the memories associated with them. And those memories, in turn, drive arousal, so that we repeat the actions that led to pleasure.

With the wide availability of potent stimuli, this process repeats itself over and over. The more multisensory the stimuli, the greater the reward and the stronger the emotional reaction. The stronger the emotional reaction, the more potent the memories. The more potent the memories, the more powerful the cues. Action builds on response, and response generates action.

Eventually, the actions that lead to pleasure become imprinted on the brain and the habit of pursuit becomes firmly established. This is rooted in evolution—it's simply more efficient to act automatically than to devote effort to deciding whether to take action. "It is quite valuable to be able to schedule things into a habit system," said UCLA researcher Bernard Balleine.

Once our behavior becomes automatic, the emotional component—the desire to feel better—is no longer required. We saw this principle at work in the experiments that demonstrated the power of habit. The animals persisted in eating food even after they had been sickened by it. They acted against their better interests because they were guided by routine rather than by new learning.

When our brain circuits have adapted to a predictable pattern of behavior, we find ourselves in a cycle of cue-urge-reward-habit. We repeat the same action over and over because that's what we've become accustomed to doing. "Reward learning takes place, but then it becomes highly automated and below the level of conscious awareness," explained Raymond Niaura of Brown University Medical School.

At that point, we are almost literally thoughtless. Wiring embedded deep within the brain's reward circuitry becomes our guide; we heed its response not only to salient food, but also to other rewards, such as sexual opportunity and psychoactive drugs. This is a region driven primarily by reflexive action, not reasoned thought.

Neuroscientists think of the habits delineated in these neural pathways as bottom-up conditioning. "Stimulus-response–type habits are established that are largely unconscious and very hard to control," said Philip David Zelazo, a professor of psychology at the University of Toronto, who studies the development of executive function in the brain. Once habits become ingrained in the lower brain, we no longer recall how or why they developed. "You just notice over time, 'Hey, when I'm in this situation, I tend to act that way.'"

Something triggers an automatic behavior, and we respond according to our conditioning, without reflective thought or even awareness. "You just get caught in these cycles where one thing leads to another, and you're just at it again and you're not even thinking about it," said James Leckman at Yale University.

And having started, it's difficult to stop. "Once you've crossed the threshold, the floodgates open," according to Raymond

Miltenberger, a professor in the Department of Child and Family Studies at the University of South Florida and an expert in repetitive behavior disorders.

In the process we may become discontented with the discrepancy between the reward we expect and the reward we actually experience. In order to revive our prior level of satisfaction, we may feel driven to seek out something more—more novelty, more stimulation, more calories. Two pieces of cake instead of one. Chocolate peanut-butter pie to follow buffalo wings. Foods higher in sugar or fat. More variety. The ephemeral nature of the sought-after reward may drive pursuit in an increasingly feverish upward spiral.

Just as a compulsive gambler can't place a single bet and feel satisfied, many people can't stop after a few bites of hyperpalatable food. We have become conditioned to seek more reward. The barricades to repetitive behavior have been toppled. We keep looking for the next big wow.

That's what the industry has engineered, with food built layer upon layer to stimulate our senses. Foods high in sugar, fat, and salt, and the cues that signal them, promote more of everything: more arousal . . . more thoughts of food . . . more urge to pursue food . . . more dopamine-stimulated approach behavior . . . more consumption . . . more opioid-driven reward . . . more overeating to feel better . . . more delay in feeling full . . . more loss of control . . . more preoccupation with food . . . more habit-driven behavior . . . and ultimately, more and more weight gain.

All of these responses are made more acute in the face of more potent stimuli and ubiquitous cues. That's what's happening in today's high-sugar, high-fat environment. Hyperpalatable foods are hyperstimulants. And when a stimulant produces reward, we want more of it.

What Weight-Loss Drugs Can Teach Us

CHAPTER 28

If overeating is the result of changes in the reward, learning, and habit circuits of the brain, then drugs that act on those circuits should alter behavior and help control this impulse. That's exactly what a combination of two drugs—phentermine and fenfluramine, more commonly known as phen-fen—seemed to do.

Phen-fen proved to be dangerous and was pulled from the market in 1997. In some cases, it produced serious and sometimes life-threatening side effects in the heart. While no one should use this drug combination today, we can learn a lot about the biology of overeating by examining the way it worked on the brain's reward circuits. Many doctors say phen-fen was the most effective drug therapy they ever had for treating obesity.

Phen-fen acted in a complex way on two brain chemicals: serotonin and dopamine. The drug combination increased the level of serotonin, which shuts down the action of dopamine and reduces activity in the reward pathways. The overall effect was to lessen the drive for reward.

Research has shown that serotonin can also tamp down the rewarding value of drugs of abuse, such as cocaine. For example, a test animal that has been conditioned to press a lever to obtain cocaine will stop doing so after being given pharmaceuticals that promote serotonin release. This may help to explain reports in psychopharmacological journals that phentermine and fenfluramine reduce drug use.

If the same pharmacologic therapy decreases the power that both food and drugs of abuse can gain over the body, then they are in all likelihood engaging the same regions of the brain. That means the reward circuits targeted by highly palatable food are also the reward circuits targeted by drugs.

The stories physicians tell of patients who used phen-fen are remarkably similar. Over and over again, these patients reported being able to stop focusing single-mindedly on food.

"Everybody who has ever treated obese people and put them on phen-fen had a patient say to them, 'I felt normal for the first time,'" said Richard Atkinson, who directs the Obetech Obesity Research Center.

Atkinson described one such patient, who had lost 100 pounds without the aid of drugs and then struggled by sheer force of discipline to keep that weight off. Driving past a doughnut shop, the man remembered the many times he would walk inside, buy a dozen doughnuts, and eat them all in one sitting. As his weight dropped, he would pass the same store and chant fervently to himself, "Don't go in, don't go in." Usually he managed to muster enough willpower to keep going, but it took an enormous effort.

All of that changed for him when he began taking phen-fen. The doughnuts stopped dominating his thoughts. He no longer felt hungry all the time. His overwhelming sense of urgency to pursue food was gone.

Obese patients treated with phen-fen at the Najarian Center, based in Los Osos, California, had similar experiences. "At the supermarket, they bought a lot less food and they were less likely to buy junk food," said founder and director Thomas Najarian. "They were not thinking about food all day long. Food did not drive them. . . . In general, phen-fen reduced its reward value."

At the Weill Cornell Medical College in Manhattan, Louis Aronne echoed his colleagues.

"What was phen-fen like clinically for patients?" I asked. "What did they tell you?"

"They felt normal," explained Aronne. "Their relationship with food was normal. They would say things like, 'I'm there, the food is there, but I don't feel like eating the food. It used to be that I would see the food and I would go completely nuts, and that doesn't happen any longer.'"

Still another confirming anecdote came from Michael Weintraub at the University of Rochester School of Medicine and Dentistry. Prior to using phen-fen, patients would tell him, "While I'm eating breakfast, I'm thinking about the doughnut I'm going to eat at ten o'clock. And while I'm eating the doughnut, I think about lunch. And I think about dessert after lunch." Phentermine and fenfluramine, said Weintraub, "wiped that all out."

The message from clinicians was consistent: Phen-fen changed not only their patients' eating behavior, but also their perception of food. They finally felt satisfied and in control. This drug combination seemed to cut the link between the cues for rewarding food and the brain circuitry that responds to those cues.

Why We Don't Just Say No

CHAPTER 29

I began to develop an overarching theory about eating for reward: Chronic exposure to highly palatable foods changes our brains, conditioning us to seek continued stimulation. Over time, a powerful drive for a combination of sugar, fat, and salt competes with our conscious capacity to say no.

I've termed the resulting behavior "conditioned hypereating." "Conditioned" because it becomes an automatic response to widely available food and its cues, "hyper" because the eating is excessive, driven by motivational forces we find difficult to control.

Conditioned hypereating works the same way as other "stimulus-response" disorders in which reward is involved, such as compulsive gambling and substance abuse. Such disorders are characterized by a high degree of sensitivity to sensory stimuli, and they typically lead to a perceived loss of control, an inability to feel satisfied, and obsessive thinking.

I believe this is what bedevils Sarah, Andrew, Samantha, and Claudia. In order to treat conditioned hypereating, it is essential to understand the patterns of behavior associated with it.

How does conditioned hypereating override the executive control functions of the healthy human brain that should allow us to say no to highly palatable food? What explains the potency of arousal? Why should a cookie be anything more than just a cookie?

Three powerful and interdependent forces engage fundamental neural mechanisms that interfere with executive control: cues, priming, and emotions. These triggers amplify the beckoning power of highly palatable food and make it difficult for many people to turn away.

The Reach of Cues

We've learned that when a cue captures our attention, it can motivate us to act. When we're aroused by the anticipation of reward, we seek the release that changes how we feel.

On my way home from the gym, I drive past In-N-Out Burger, a popular western U.S. chain. As I near the restaurant, I'm expecting to see it and thinking about how good a hamburger and fries would taste. At once excited by the thought and uneasy about the action, I start a silent debate with myself.

Yes, today I will stop. No, I shouldn't. Yes, no, yes, no. My continued ambivalence allows me to think of nothing else. Discomfort settles over me, an anxiety of my own creation. If I pull into the restaurant, I can resolve the ambivalence and subdue the arousal. For the moment, my discomfort will disappear.

But I will be putting other forces into play. If I make that stop often enough, my response will become automatic behavior, a habit. At that point, any efforts to suppress it will only intensify the power of the cue.

Expectancy is the cue that tempts me into In-N-Out Burger, but it is not the only provocateur. Cues can gain power even if we're not consciously aware of them. Seemingly out of the blue, we may begin to think about an egg-and-bacon sandwich or a favorite doughnut, not recognizing that our desire has just been triggered by an advertisement, a memory, or a location. "You are aware of the thought, but not necessarily of what drove it," said David Kavanagh, a professor of clinical psychology at the University of Queensland in Brisbane, Australia.

Whatever the initial prompt, thoughts begin to build on thoughts, creating what Kavanagh calls an "elaborated thought." I might begin to think not only about how good that doughnut will taste, but about where I can buy it, what route I can take to get there, and how much better it will make me feel. Simultaneously, I may also be thinking that I shouldn't want it and I shouldn't eat it.

"All of those things start crowding in," said Kavanagh. "There's a lot of parallel stuff that's occurring when people are trying to engage in control at the same time they're experiencing a desire."

Distinguishing the longing for a highly palatable food from conflicted thoughts of pursuing it becomes difficult. "You're thinking about it and you're approaching it in your mind, and that feeds the affective power of the craving," says Kavanagh. "The response planning and the craving start to become very similar."

"The thoughts become larger and larger?" I asked.

"You get a much more elaborate image. You're aware of taste and smell and size and sensation in your mouth. As you elaborate that and make the image more complex, it becomes affectively more powerful and more motivating."

Increasingly insistent and expansive thoughts consume more mental space as we become more preoccupied. But we try to hold ourselves back. The emotional drivers of wanting struggle with the desperate desire to resist temptation. Behavior-activating messages that urge pursuit clash with internal messages demanding control. Our brains become battlegrounds.

Ultimately our decision to reach for that food—to relax our struggle for restraint, to give in to consumption—becomes the only possible relief from the anxiety of a war within. But the satisfaction doesn't last. By responding to a salient cue with action that generates immediate reward, we only strengthen the association between the cue and its reward. "You have the wanting, you eat the food, you experience the reinforcement again," said Marcia Pelchat of Monell Chemical Senses Center. "If you eat the salient food that you want today, it's going to be more salient tomorrow because you have more positive associations with it. You increase the number of memories that you have of the food."

Soon enough, you're cued again, desire builds, and the cycle begins anew.

The Power of Priming

Sometimes just one taste of a food—a single dose—is enough to trigger conditioned hypereating. We call that effect "priming," and it's another way to kick overeating behavior into action, even when we're not hungry.

That's what the food industry knows when it tells us, "Bet you can't eat just one." It's what Alcoholics Anonymous recognizes when it warns drinkers, "One drink, one drunk." A small quantity can be enough to generate a large response.

Although the underlying biology of priming isn't fully understood, the same neural circuitry that responds to cues seems to be at work. A highly palatable food tells the brain, "This is a desirable object, get more," Harriet de Wit, in the Department of Psychiatry at the University of Chicago, explained to me. Immediately after eating that first salt-and-fat-rich potato chip, "you want more of it than you did a minute before you had one. It is as though it is stimulating the dopamine system—the motivation and reward-seeking system—a little bit, enough to get it going to make you want more."

Priming, which is lodged in the brain's fundamental motivational circuitry, has the power to make an animal seek out more of a stimulus. Adaptive in origin, it is yet another tool our species has developed in order to survive. "It makes adaptive sense for animals to get hungrier once they find a little bit of food," said de Wit.

As with our responses to cues, priming works in part by triggering memories of past pleasure and activating the reward pathways of the brain. Priming may also be something of an "abstinence violation," suspects de Wit. "If somebody has been trying to abstain from cheesecake and has gone for a very long period of time before having just a little bit of it, that can lead to eating way too much of it," she says. "In a sense, that person gives up and a spiral of eating follows."

When we're hungry, almost any food can have a priming effect—in fact, that's one of the risks of dieting. But in the absence of hunger, only highly palatable foods are likely to spark further eating. "Having a little bit makes you want more. And then you have it, and it makes you want still more," observed de Wit.

That's when it becomes hard to stop. Martin Yeomans at the University of Sussex, in England, has done experiments in which he keeps interrupting people as they eat to ask them how hungry they are. Halfway through their meals some people rate their hunger levels higher than before they started to eat.

The power of priming is made visible in a study that looked at two highly palatable foods—pizza and ice cream. The results showed that we're motivated to seek out more of a specific stimulus when we've been primed for it.

Researchers first fed lunch to twenty-eight men so they were presumably not hungry when the rest of the experiment took place. After their meal, the men were assigned to one of three groups—one primed with pizza, one primed with ice cream, and one that wasn't primed at all. The priming was done by placing a medium-sized mozzarella pizza in front of the first group and two big bowls of vanilla and chocolate ice cream in front of the second, and then inviting everyone to take a single bite. Immediately afterward, the men filled out a form on which they rated the sensory properties of the primed food, including its flavor, smell, and appearance.

A few minutes later, both primed groups were presented with all the foods—that is, the group primed with pizza also got the two bowls of ice cream, and the group primed with ice cream also got the pizza. Everyone was then told to eat freely. People ate more of the food with which they'd been primed.

Unlike cues, priming holds power for only a short time. That means the food for which you've been primed has to be readily accessible. If you eat one piece of candy and there's a bowl of them in front of you, chances are you will keep eating more. But if no more are available or you have to search for them, the priming response may be undermined because you won't be stimulated for long enough to alter your behavior.

The Influence of Emotions

Among people who experience conditioned hypereating, emotional states often heighten the power of cues, overpower executive control, and intensify the drive to eat. "It's a form of self-medication," said George Koob, at the Salk Institute. "You're modulating your arousal. People take the food to calm themselves down."

Rajita Sinha, at Yale University's School of Medicine, said that sadness and anger have the greatest potential to drive a loss of control. "If you've got that really charged emotional situation, with both of these emotions going, chances are you'll be going to the kitchen before you know it," she said.

Because a cookie makes me feel better, it's easy to develop the habit of seeking it out when I'm sad or angry. Over time, as neural pathways link the change in my mood with the experience of eating the cookie, the association grows stronger.

"These products have some kind of hedonic, calming effect," said Koob. "In other words, they relieve the itch." The problem is that the itch comes back.

Anger and anxiety can act as a "setting condition" for cues, says Charles O'Brien, a professor at the University of Pennsylvania. "A cue that has been extinguished in the basal state [when the body is calm] again becomes active in producing craving and physiological changes when it is presented after a person has been put in an angry state."

We see this with smokers. "I can remember being in a room and there was a tense discussion, and everybody would start lighting up, to either increase their alertness or to calm themselves down," Koob recalled. "I think the same thing happens with people who learn to eat that way."

The effect is visible in imaging studies in which people undergo brain scans as they respond to cues suggesting they're about to get a milkshake. In one study, researchers first induced a negative mood by playing some dark music and asking participants to recollect a particularly depressing life experience. Afterward, the regions of the brain where the reward pathways operate showed greater activity level in response to the anticipated milkshake compared with levels among participants in a neutral mood.

"We interpreted those findings as suggesting that when emotional eaters are in a negative mood, the idea that they are about to get a milkshake makes them anticipate reward," said Eric Stice, a scientist at the Oregon Research Institute. "That's not the case for nonemotional eaters, and it is not the case for a neutral mood state. It only emerged in a negative mood state."

When emotions amplify reward, the drive for reward becomes even harder to control.

Stress also lends more power to each of the mechanisms that drive overeating through its capacity to heighten our arousal. "If you're in an agitated state, a stimulus will act on you more, will generate a little more vigor," said Bernard Balleine.

Call it the paper-clip-on-the-rat's-tail phenomenon. Pinching the animal's tail with a paper clip is a mild stressor—not so strong as to interfere with the animal's behavior, but strong enough to intensify all its usual activities.

There are limits to the arousing effect of stress. Profound stress—the death of a family member, for example—can interfere with this response and shut down overeating behavior.

To capture the impact of mild stress, Balleine suggested I visualize myself in a familiar conference room. When the tone of a meeting is relaxed, Balleine said, "You're looking around, recognizing cues, but they are not having any motor effects on you." Then the dynamic of the meeting changes, and someone makes me angry. Suddenly a cue in the room that has signaled reward in the past takes on new power.

For me, that cue is likely to be the platter of cookies sitting in the middle of the table. Under normal circumstances, I probably found its attention-grabbing effect hard enough to resist. Most likely, I was consciously willing myself not to reach for a cookie. But when stress comes into play, holding myself back becomes even harder. By intensifying my arousal and approach behavior, stress steamrolls over the cognitive voice that had been trying to say no to the cue.

"When you get into this slightly aroused state, the strongest cue in the environment will tend to elicit the motor response it has been associated with in the past," he said. "It's a level of affective arousal."

Periods of transition can make us more vulnerable. Eating foods that are high in fat and sugar seems to be one way to ease the discomfort of "transition emotions." These are the emotions we encounter as we change from one activity to the next. A meeting ends and we get in the car, or a television program is over and we walk into the kitchen. As our activities change, so does our state of arousal.

"Is there any evidence that food really makes you feel better after you've eaten?" I asked Loma Flowers, a community psychiatrist in San Francisco.

"Absolutely," she said. "People feel better after eating it. They eat for anxiety. And it soothes anxiety. It really does work like a Valium." But that effect, of course, is momentary.

When we learn that a stimulus provides gratification, that knowledge drives our wanting, arousing us further. Our focus narrows to the target of our desire, capturing our full attention and directing us toward it. The anticipation of feeling better puts us in a heightened state of focus, making us want it all the more.

What we fail to realize is that the food we ate for comfort has left its mark on the brain, creating a void that will need to be filled the next time we are cued. The result is a spiral of wanting.

How We Become Trapped

CHAPTER 30

Cues, priming, and emotional triggers all drive conditioned hyper-eating in fundamentally the same way—by stimulating mental ghosts. These ghosts are representations of past sensory and emotional associations with food that we have stored in our brains. Expectations, or what Mark Goldman, associate director of the National Institute on Alcohol Abuse and Alcoholism, calls "traces retrieved from memory," give form to these ghosts.

When we expect food to give us pleasure (positive reinforcement) or relief from distress (negative reinforcement), that expectation amplifies the reward value. Expecting something to be rewarding stimulates pursuit of that reward.

"Expectancy has powerful effects on strengthening the primary reinforcer," George Koob said. "With the script of how we behave in the presence of a stimulus already written and stored in our brains, expectancy also helps to control the choice we make between actions."

The belief that food will make us feel better contributes to our desire for food. At that point it's only a short step from wanting the food to feeling that we need it. The act of eating becomes something we do to attain a desired emotional effect.

"If most often eating alleviates my negative mood state, then over time, that cognitive memory will become the salient, predominant one," said Gregory Smith, of the psychology department at the University of Kentucky. Having come to associate the behavior of eating with a desired outcome, we begin to act more automatically to achieve that outcome.

For example, I believe a Milky Way candy bar will make me feel better because it has done so before. That expectation drives my action. I'm caught in a cycle of craving, satisfaction, and more craving. Conditioned hypereating takes on a momentum of its own.

The dominating influence of rewarding food can be marked along a continuum. Many people like and want a food, but only some of us develop elaborate thoughts about it, or a preoccupation with it. We still need to dig further to understand why some people are so much more vulnerable than others, but for those unlucky ones, an increasingly intense focus on reward can spiral into obsession.

"Thinking about cream cakes is fine, as long as it doesn't become dysfunctional for you," David Kavanagh said. "What makes it an obsession is the fact that you don't want the thought."

Someone who can't stop thinking about a cream cake when she would like nothing better than to shut it out of her mind comes to wonder, "What does it mean if I have this thought? This must mean I'm a very weak person. I'm somebody who cannot succeed at a diet."

The brain is conflicted. That generates unhappiness, followed, ironically, by the notion that only the cream cake can bring relief. We begin thinking, "I feel so awful now, but if I actually had that cream cake, I'd feel better."

The clash escalates as we try to put the cream cake out of our minds. That's known as the white bear problem—if you tell yourself not to think about white bears, soon that's your dominant thought. The research literature tells us we can suppress thoughts only for short periods of time. As soon as we tell ourselves, "I'd better make sure to avoid that thought," we start to focus on it. "An attempt at suppression is going to mean that the thought becomes more salient," said Kavanagh.

Indeed, focusing single-mindedly on *not* eating eventually pushes us to eat more. Feeling deprived only increases the reward value of food, and then usually gives way to indulgence, and often to abandon. As desire evolves into need, we do exactly what we've tried so hard not to do—we eat that cream cake. And then we feel worse, which makes us even more likely to be out of control.

To find your way out of this trap, you need to understand the functions of the brain, the drivers of conditioned hypereating, and what you can eat without triggering the reward-based behavior that leads to habit.

Conditioned Hypereating Emerges

CHAPTER 31

When I first began to talk to people about the loss of control over eating, I was met with two opposite reactions. Many people understood immediately and were themselves often painfully and personally familiar with the behavior. But a smaller group, having had no direct experience with out-of-control eating, was convinced it could be halted by exercising willpower.

I realized that if I was going to bring attention to conditioned hypereating as a major behavioral issue, I was going to have to define it more rigorously and identify some of its specific characteristics. I also needed scientific evidence to support my growing conviction that conditioned hypereating was correlated with becoming overweight.

To get started, I mostly had a lot of questions. What features define conditioned hypereating? Who is affected? How is it linked to excess weight? Why do some people at a healthy weight also exhibit conditioned hypereating behavior? I asked three colleagues at the University of California, San Francisco—Elissa Epel, an expert on cognitive health psychology; Michael Acree, a biostatistician; and Tanja Adams, a psychology postdoctorate fellow—to help me answer these questions.

The scientific literature gave us a good base on which to build our research. It told us that not every overweight person demonstrates the same set of eating behaviors in the presence of highly palatable food. It also reminded us that overeating is not the exclusive province of the overweight. Many people, fat and thin alike, lose control in the face of rewarding foods.

But those who are obese do seem to be more susceptible to the disinhibited patterns of eating that often allow rewarding foods to gain the upper hand. A revealing study showed that obese women consumed significantly more throughout the day compared to women who were not obese. (This may seem self-evident, but remember, a lot of wrongheaded ideas about why people gain weight still circulate, and it is important to understand that calories count.) More revealing for my goal of understanding behavior was the finding that the obese group ate more snacks, more evening and nighttime meals, and significantly more during nontraditional mealtimes.

Another trait shared by many people who are either overweight or obese is their tendency to keep eating beyond the point of hunger. This became evident in a survey that asked "How often do you keep eating at meals even though you are not hungry anymore?" Women who reported that they "eat beyond satiation nearly every day" were dramatically more likely to be obese than those who rarely or never did so.

Obese women were also willing to work harder for food, which is the defining trait of reinforcing behavior. In one study, two groups of women were allowed to earn points that could be traded for either high-sugar, high-fat snack foods or for access to activities such as playing video games, watching a comedy video, reading popular magazines, or playing computer solitaire. (Research has shown that these forms of entertainment are highly reinforcing.) One group was obese; the other was not.

There were no significant differences in how much either group actually liked the rewards or in the hunger level of participants. But the obese women were consistently more likely than the nonobese women to earn points for food rather than activities, reminding us that liking and wanting are not the same thing.

All of this evidence gave me a basis for investigating which eating behaviors might be associated with conditioned hypereating. Working with my colleagues, I began looking for appropriate data to analyze and eventually found it in the Reno Diet Heart Study, led by Sachiko St. Jeor, a nutritionist at the University of Nevada. Launched in 1985, the Reno study had goals entirely different from what I was interested in. Its main purpose had been to assess the relationship between cardiovascular health and weight. But no one had used the data collected in that study to ask the questions that interested me.

The Reno study was one of the largest, most comprehensive studies ever conducted on how people eat. Researchers had enrolled a total of 508 men and women across age groups. Half were overweight or obese and half were not, and they had been followed for five years to assess their weight, attitudes toward eating, and eating behaviors. Three years after the first five-year phase was completed, the researchers had been able to track down most of their original subjects to gather more information.

Their data included true-or-false responses to statements such as "sometimes when I start eating, I just can't seem to stop," "my stomach often seems like a bottomless pit," and "I am always hungry so it is hard for me to stop eating before I finish the food on my plate." We also had answers to questions such as "How often are you preoccupied with thinking about food?"

Together, the information allowed us to focus on three behaviors of interest—loss of control over eating; lack of feeling satisfied by food; and preoccupation with food. Based on what I knew about the classic symptoms of other conditioned and driven behaviors, all three characteristics could reasonably be considered expressions of conditioned hypereating.

We used a sophisticated statistical process called "latent classification analysis" to determine whether one group of people exhibited more of those characteristics. It turned out that about one-third of the study population scored high on at least two of the factors (or, in a few cases, very high on one of them).

But the most significant feature for me was how the figures broke down by weight. Some 50 percent of obese participants and 30 percent of overweight participants demonstrated the features of conditioned hypereating, as did 17 percent of those who were lean. The gender breakdown was also of interest: 56 percent of obese women and 43 percent of obese men exhibited conditioned hypereating. Those with evidence of conditioned hypereating were almost twice as likely to have been overweight early in life.

The sizable minority of lean people with features of conditioned hypereating warranted a closer look. Most of them scored high on questions that measured their ability to compensate for their food drive by concerted and conscious efforts to limit their eating. As a result, they had been able to maintain a healthy body weight during the study period—but could well face challenges in maintaining such behavior over time. This population is probably at risk for weight gain.

Clearly, a broad swath of the population is struggling with conditioned hypereating. Our data indicate that those who exhibit conditioned hypereating are twice as likely to be obese as those who do not.

Dana Small, a colleague at the John B. Pierce Laboratory and Yale University, worked with me to collect concrete evidence about the biological mechanisms driving conditioned hypereating. We studied the issue from two angles: how humans behave in the face of highly rewarding food and how their brains actually respond.

First we further developed a scale that allowed us to distinguish "high" and "low" degrees of conditioned hypereating, based on the participants' responses to eleven statements about eating behavior. These included, "When it comes to foods I love, I have no willpower," and "I have days when I can't seem to think about anything else but food." The behavioral tests confirmed that people who scored higher on the conditioned hypereating scale were more willing to work for food.

So that she could study their response to cues, Small also asked the subjects to smell chocolate and then to taste a chocolate milkshake. Normally, a pleasing aroma becomes less pleasant over time as we habituate to it. Not so with conditioned hypereaters. People who scored higher on the scale of conditioned hypereating reported that the odor became *more* pleasant over time.

Then we looked at what was happening in people's brains. The differences in the reward centers were striking. High-scoring individuals exhibited an enhanced level of neural activity as they responded to the cue of a chocolate odor (this is the anticipatory phase, when reward is expected) and to the taste of a milkshake (this is the consumption phase).

Especially interesting was the response in the amygdala. This area of the brain, which normally allows us to anticipate reward, was also activated among conditioned hypereaters while they were eating. "The heightened amygdala response drives the whole circuit out of whack," said Small. This suggests that the act of eating, when we might expect cue-induced anticipation to lessen, instead stimulates this vulnerable population. It also offers physiological evidence of what is observable in the real world—eating rewarding food can enhance the drive for more rewarding food.

Remember those brain pathways that allow us to focus on our environment's most salient stimuli and avoid the wild animal, escape a burning home, or tend to a sick child? Those pathways have been captured by the highly stimulating foods that are now available everywhere.

Based on these findings, an argument can be made that conditioned hypereating is a syndrome, or a condition characterized by a cluster of symptoms. We also have reason to assert that conditioned hypereating is associated with body weight.

Framing conditioned hypereating in those terms helps us think about the common biological mechanisms at play among those who are affected and makes it easier to agree on a diagnosis. At the same time, it highlights the power of environmental exposure. In other contexts, such as infectious diseases and chemical toxins, we understand that environmental factors can be associated with a cluster of symptoms, but we have not yet recognized this quality about eating.

That said, defining conditioned hypereating as a cluster of symptoms also has limits. Although many people exhibit the defining characteristics to at least some degree, we can't say they all have the same condition, although we suspect they may all be at risk. Before we can apply the label appropriately, we need to know more about the brain responses of people who cluster somewhere in the middle of the conditioned hypereating continuum.

Meanwhile, we shouldn't consider these distinctive patterns of behavior abnormal or pathological. Rather, they are a psychological adaptation to the environment that occurs among certain susceptible individuals. As learned responses driven by the motivational circuits of our brains, these patterns almost certainly contribute significantly to the exploding obesity epidemic.

Tracing the Roots of
Conditioned Hypereating

CHAPTER 32

Clues to the puzzle of conditioned hypereating extend back many decades. In recent years, the extraordinary advances we have made in neuroscience have given us the ability to examine old information in new ways.

In the 1970s, Stanley Schachter, a Columbia University social psychologist, became convinced that overweight people did not respond appropriately to internal signals, such as hunger, satiety, or a need for fuel. Our knowledge about the brain's ability to focus on salient stimuli and the nature of the reward system was not available then, but Schachter hypothesized that overweight people ate in response to external cues, rather than internal signals. His theory came to be known as "externality."

Schachter's cracker study, which compared the eating behaviors of thin and overweight subjects, pointed to ideas we did not fully grasp at the time. He first divided his participants into two groups, offering one all the sandwiches they wanted to eat and asking the other only to fill out a questionnaire about food. Then he gave everyone the same opportunity to sample five different types of crackers.

Not surprisingly, the thin people who had already eaten the sandwiches ate fewer crackers than the thin people who had simply completed the questionnaire. But those who were overweight ate about the same number of crackers whether or not they had eaten the sandwiches first. Schachter theorized that the sight of food was exerting more pull on the overweight population than any internal messages reporting an absence of hunger.

A roast-beef sandwich experiment produced similar results. Richard Nisbett, also then at Columbia, offered his study subjects varying amounts of food, either placing one sandwich on a table or loading it up with three full sandwiches. He also told both groups they could help themselves to more sandwiches from a nearby refrigerator.

People who were overweight ate what they were given but did not seek out more food—if they could see it, they ate it. Visual cues took on preeminent importance. Those who were thin were more consistent in their eating patterns—they ate about a sandwich and a half, regardless of how much food was presented to them and whether or not they had to make trips to the refrigerator for more.

Such studies helped establish externality as the dominant theory of weight gain for more than a decade. Through the 1970s most textbooks offered it as the primary explanation for the eating behavior of the overweight. Then Judith Rodin, then at Yale University's Department of Psychology, who once worked closely with Schachter to develop the externality theory, raised questions about its validity.

Externality was too "simplistic," she wrote in a seminal article in *American Psychologist* in April 1981. Convinced the theory didn't hold up to closer scrutiny, Rodin pointed out that other researchers saw significant differences in how people in every weight category responded to external stimuli. Particularly confounding was the fact that some thin people also ate a lot more when they saw food or smelled it.

Rodin's criticism gained traction, and the emphasis of weight research shifted away from the influence of external cues and toward the concept of restraint, which attributes overeating to dieting. Restraint theory says that people restrict their eating in order to lose weight, but they are unable to maintain that discipline indefinitely. Eventually they lose control, overeat, and gain back the lost pounds.

In time, cracks also appeared in the notion that restraint theory could offer a full explanation for weight gain, and researchers have recently come to regret having prematurely cast aside the theory of externality.

Decades ago, Schachter and Rodin each set out to find a single mechanism that distinguished people who are overweight from those who are not. And they both demonstrated something important, without fully understanding the implications. The externality theory recognized the power of cues—we now understand that's because they amplify the rewarding aspects of highly palatable food. Restraint theorists saw, accurately, the risks of deprivation—which we have come to realize increases the drive for reward.

Based on what we have learned in more recent years, externality and restraint are two different manifestations of one thing: conditioned hypereating.

Nature or Nurture?

CHAPTER 33

A fundamental question about conditioned hypereating is whether it will turn out to be genetic or environmental in origin. Is it passed down from one generation to the next, inherited in much the same way that we inherit blue eyes or short stature? Or does it reflect patterns of eating acquired at home and at school, with friends and in the workplace, in response to broad trends promoted by the food industry? We don't yet have the definite answer, but we do have clues.

Myles Faith, of the Center for Weight and Eating Disorders at the University of Pennsylvania School of Medicine, is an expert on the genetic basis of childhood eating behavior and obesity. Faith measured the tendency of children to eat in the absence of hunger. In one study he allowed a group of five-year-olds to eat as much dinner as they wanted, until they reported feeling full and stopped voluntarily. Following dinner, these children were offered snack foods for a period of ten minutes. Both the main meal and the snacks were the kinds of highly palatable foods that drive overeating.

Faith also collected data about maternal weight as part of this study because fifty years of research has clearly established that a mother's weight is one of the best predictors of the weight of her child. Based on the prepregnancy weights of their mothers, Faith classified five-year-olds as at "high risk" or "low risk" for obesity. Boys at high risk were more likely to reach for the snacks, even though a few minutes earlier they had said they were full. The high-risk boys ate twice the calories the low-risk boys did. (Faith did not find this same effect in girls.)

Something about our families—either the genes we inherit or the environment we share—seems to promote overeating behavior. But Faith wasn't willing to speculate on which had the greater effect. "We know it is familial, but we cannot separate out genes from environment," he said.

Digging more deeply into the available data, I looked at two studies involving twins, a population often favored by researchers trying to determine the relative contributions of genes and the environment. In one study, Swedish researchers found "a great importance of genetic factors in the eating behavior of a large, unselected population of young adult male twins." Even so, inheritance was not the dominant influence; they estimated that genetics contributed to a bit less than half of an individual's total tendency to eat in an uncontrolled manner.

In the other twins study, researchers reached the same conclusion. Cynthia Bulik, an expert in eating disorders at the Department of Psychiatry at the University of North Carolina at Chapel Hill and one of the study's authors, called the loss of control over eating "a moderately heritable behavior trait."

Somewhat higher estimates can be found elsewhere in the research literature. "Eating in the absence of hunger . . . is under substantial genetic control," concluded the authors of still another study. They estimate the heritability of eating without hunger at 51 percent (meaning that genetics accounts for 51 percent of an individual's total proclivity for the behavior).

But other studies have cast uncertainty on all these findings. For example, one analysis of questionnaires completed by twins suggested that loss of control was not, in fact, a heritable trait, even though it was correlated with weight. Another study estimated heritability of disinhibited eating patterns at about 17 percent—but also found a significant correlation between spouses, which suggests that disinhibition may reflect what we do at home, rather than what's in our genes.

Currently available research, then, is inconclusive. Certainly there are big differences in how individuals respond to external stimuli—some of us are more impulsive, while others are better at avoidance behavior. Most studies do suggest that genes play some part in eating behavior, but also insist on the role played by environmental factors. The argument is only about which influence is predominant.

My sense is that eating behavior itself may not be genetically determined, but how we respond to stimuli probably is, at least to some degree. One thing is certain—to whatever extent genes put us at risk for conditioned hypereating, they are able to express themselves only in the presence of highly rewarding foods. "You have environmental factors that basically release the underlying genetic susceptibility," said Cynthia Bulik.

A genetic predisposition has evolved over time in humans and animals, but a conducive environment is necessary to trigger hypereating. That's exactly what we have today.

Warning Signs in Children

CHAPTER 34

To understand when conditioned hypereating takes the brain hostage, it is useful to consider the age when we first see indications of reward-driven eating. The process seems to begin in early childhood—and it now appears to be developing among younger and younger children.

We have long thought that infants and preschool children intrinsically adjust their food consumption over a period of a day to take in a consistent number of calories. This is known as compensation, and a body of research attests to it. Give a preschooler food that is more energy dense than usual—that is, one with more calories in the same volume of food—and the child will compensate by subsequently eating less of other foods. This is part of the body's innate drive for homeostasis.

But that self-regulatory system is changing.

Susan Johnson, who directs the Children's Eating Laboratory at the University of Colorado Health Sciences Center, said that research has evidenced a population-wide shift over time. She told me that in the 1980s, children ages two to four were compensating for about 90 percent of any extra calories added to their diet. By the 1990s, they were compensating for only about 45 percent of those added calories.

In her own studies, Johnson sees three- and four-year-olds who are able to pack in very large meals, sometimes consuming as much as 800 calories in one sitting. They just keep asking for more. "I did not see this kind of behavior in the past," she commented. "Fifteen years ago I would have said with great confidence that preschoolers compensate. But in the studies we have been doing of late, I see an incredible amount of dysregulatory behavior."

Johnson has also examined a slightly older population: children ages five to twelve. Her study compared the impact of drinking two different fruit-flavored beverages (that tasted similar but had different calorie content) on how much children ate at a subsequent meal. Those who ate less after drinking the high-calorie beverage, compared with what they ate after drinking the low-calorie beverage, were said to have compensated.

Johnson found that school-age children compensate to some degree, but not fully. And their capacity to compensate declined with age, year after year, especially among girls. The older they got, the less they compensated.

For example, after drinking a high-calorie beverage, five-year-old girls reduced their consumption of other foods to compensate for about 80 percent of the extra calories. That meant they were still taking in 20 percent more calories than those who drank the low-calorie beverage. By age eight, the girls were compensating only for 60 percent of the extra calories in the high-calorie beverage, and by eleven, that figure hovered at around 30 percent.

Loss of control, one of the defining characteristics of conditioned hypereating, seems to be a growing trend, even among youngsters. "I'm sensing a newer kind of disinhibition in children in some of the portion-size work we have been doing," said Johnson. "I never saw children who ate and ate and ate until you finally had to cut them off and say, 'You're done.' They are eating to excess now."

Jennifer Fisher, an expert in pediatric nutrition at the Center for Obesity Research and Education at Temple University, has observed the same thing. On different lunchtime occasions she served a group of children ages three to five either an age-appropriate portion of macaroni and cheese or a portion that was about double that size. Both meals were accompanied by milk, applesauce, carrots, and sugar cookies. Some of the children who were served the double portion of mac-and-cheese ate a lot more of it than others, but on average, this group consumed about 25 percent more mac-and-cheese calories than those given the smaller portion. The children partially compensated by eating less of the accompanying foods, but they still ate a total of 15 percent more calories during the meal.

"Large entrée portions may constitute an 'obesigenic' environmental influence for preschool-aged children by producing excessive intake at meals," concluded the authors. In other words, when they were served more, they ate more.

In a follow-up study with the same population, Fisher fed everyone an age-appropriate portion of macaroni and cheese, and then offered them a number of toys and a large tray with generous portions of ten snack foods, including popcorn, potato chips, nuts, pretzels, cookies, candy, and ice cream. Although the children had said they were no longer hungry, they were allowed to eat whatever they wanted for ten minutes before researchers measured how many calories they had consumed.

Those who ate more of the snacks turned out to be the same ones who had eaten more when they were served double portions of macaroni and cheese in the earlier study. Lacking the control to eat only when hungry, they seemed uniquely vulnerable to the food cues embedded in large portions.

Most likely there have always been people who showed early signs of conditioned hypereating as children. But as stimulating food becomes increasingly available, we're seeing more and more of this behavior. And troubling eating behaviors are becoming apparent at ever-younger ages.

The Culture of Overeating

CHAPTER 35

The question "Is food available?" once had social and economic implications. We were really asking "Are we facing famine?" "Can we afford food?" That framework has changed in Western societies. Now we usually mean "Can I buy food nearby?" "Can I eat it any-where?" In today's America, the answer to these questions is usually yes. This makes it the ideal laboratory in which to study conditioned hypereating.

Our encounters with food are intense, and they are frequent. The number of neighborhood food stores and restaurants grew markedly in the 1980s and beyond, coinciding with increasing rates of obesity. Highly palatable foods are now available anytime, day or night, wherever we may be. Rare is the community that lacks constant access to restaurants, convenience stores, and vending machines. We have drive-through fast food; cars outfitted with cup holders; and gas stations, pharmacies, and even health clubs that sell snacks and other food.

But the ready availability of food affects more than our ability to purchase it easily. It also means that we're able to *eat* it easily, whether it's in our cars or on the run, in social settings or at work. Social mores once kept us from eating on the street or walking into a colleague's office while munching on popcorn, but we no longer think of that kind of behavior as rude. "The barriers have been lowered," Unilever scientist David Mela said to me.

These days, most meetings and almost all social occasions are constructed around food. "It is always there," said Mela. "There is great frequency of coming into contact with places where food is being sold or where other people are eating."

Mela, who is based in the Netherlands, was particularly aware of differing patterns in the office. "We go to a meeting in America and somebody will inevitably bring in a huge plate of bagels and cream cheese and muffins and all of these things. For Europeans it comes off as bizarre, but it just seems to be expected here. Everybody seems to be expecting that a lot of food will suddenly show up."

The contemporary context of our lives makes it possible to eat just about all the time. And many people do. "Food availability and the opportunity to consume are ubiquitous, and that has been a huge driver of energy intake for children and adults," Susan Johnson of the University of Colorado told me.

A breakdown in meal structure, with the distinction between meals and snacks increasingly blurred, also promotes increased consumption and, ultimately, conditioned hypereating. It becomes a self-perpetuating cycle, with conditioned hypereating spurring a further breakdown in meal structure as out-of-control eaters pursue every opportunity to consume food.

Back in the 1950s, "people ate meals," said Meredith Luce, a dietitian in private practice in Orlando. "They ate them together as a family. . . . Snacks were the sole property of growing children, to provide an extra opportunity to nourish the growing body. Adults didn't eat snacks."

But snacking is now the norm, and the data show that it, too, rose in the 1980s and 1990s. Worse, snacking generally occurs without a compensating caloric reduction at mealtimes, especially when snacking patterns are erratic. People don't eat smaller breakfasts, lunches, or dinners just because they snack throughout the day.

Elsewhere in the world, cultural patterns have tended to reduce the risk of conditioned hypereating. Countless articles, some based on research, some on speculation, have tried to explain the so-called French paradox—the fact that the French generally have lower rates of both cardiovascular disease and obesity than Americans, even though the French diet is higher in fat. One theory suggests that the types of fat the French consume lessen their risk. Another says that drinking red wine with meals does the trick. Still other commentators suggest that the French are healthier because their lives are generally less stressful than those of Americans or that they have genetically based metabolic differences.

None of these theories seems well supported by the facts. A more evidenced-based hypothesis is that while the French linger longer over meals, they eat smaller portions. And portion size, we know, helps drive conditioned hypereating.

Researchers based their conclusions about portion size on several kinds of analysis. First, they compared serving sizes at restaurants in Paris and Philadelphia and found that American portions averaged 25 percent larger. That held true both in chain restaurants, such as Pizza Hut and the Hard Rock Café, and in comparable bistros, local Chinese restaurants, *crêperies*, and ice cream parlors in each country.

Second, they analyzed restaurant reviews in *Zagat* guides to the two cities and found that reviewers in Philadelphia were far more likely than those in Paris to comment about large portion sizes. Furthermore, all-you-can-eat or buffet options were highlighted in the Philadelphia guide but never once mentioned in the Parisian reviews.

Finally, they studied comparable French and American cookbooks. *Joy of Cooking* and *Je sais cuisiner* showed a consistent trend:

American recipes generally yielded larger servings of meat and soup courses and smaller servings of vegetables.

Historically, another protective factor in France has been the tradition of eating two or three structured meals a day in the company of others, with no snacks in between. For a long time French restaurants wouldn't even serve meals at times other than those they considered conventional lunch and dinner hours.

"In France we still have a very strong meal structure," France Bellisle, an obesity researcher at the Hôtel-Dieu Hospital in Paris, told me.

"There's a cultural notion that you don't eat between meals?" I asked.

"That's right. You don't do that. You learn very early on as children that you just don't do that."

When she teaches, Bellisle often says to her students, "What, you have not brought anything to eat into the classroom? If we were in America, you would have brought your coffee, your doughnuts, your chocolate bar with you to eat."

Not in France. "Nobody has given even a fraction of a second to the thought that they could have brought food into the classroom," she said. "They've never done it before, and they are not tempted to do it. There is nothing in the environment that stimulates such inappropriate eating at an inappropriate time."

But the norm of eating only at certain times of the day, with its built-in safeguard against overeating, is under siege outside America's borders, even in France, as snacks, fast-food restaurants, and other temptations are beginning to emerge. As the availability of hyperpalatable food is exported, it will become more apparent that conditioned hypereating does not respect national borders.

Jean-Pierre Poulain, who directs the Centre d'études du tourisme et des industries de l'accueil at the Université de Toulouse–le Mirail, sees signs of a gradual cultural shift away from notions about proper meals and toward what he calls "vagabond feeding." He refers to this as the "destructuration" of eating habits in France. While vagabond eaters still consume structured meals in a social context, they also eat alone on multiple occasions throughout the day.

France Bellisle has observed the same trend. "Food cues are becoming more and more numerous, more and more present in the French environment," she says. As a consequence, more people are likely to become obese, a pattern that is starting to emerge in the French population, especially among children.

As meal patterns break down and the French gain cultural flexibility in when and where they can eat, eating for reward begins to overtake eating for hunger—and satisfaction becomes elusive. "The satiety mechanism that takes place between meals cannot take place if you eat constantly," Bellisle said. "Instead of experiencing the metabolic effects of satiety, you will lose the notion of what they feel like."

Although environmental changes in France have so far been less drastic and the weight gain in the population is less extreme than in many other developed countries, the trend is unmistakable. The social framework that supports conditioned hypereating is slowly being erected.

Still, America remains in the vanguard. A segment of the population seems especially vulnerable to the stimuli that lead to conditioned hypereating, but in the end this is behavior that anyone can develop. Learning to overeat is an incremental process that grows with repeated exposure.

What came first? Did changes in how, when, where, and how much we consume food lead to conditioned hypereating? Or did conditioned hypereating alter social and commercial patterns so that stimulating food became that much easier to secure?

We don't yet know. In either case, a cycle has been set in motion. Ultimately it begins to seem more surprising that some people manage to eat normally than that many do not.

PART FOUR

The Theory
of Treatment

Invitations to the Brain

CHAPTER 36

Despite the challenges, we do have opportunities to break the cue-urge-reward-habit cycle and treat conditioned hypereating. It's important to have a framework for thinking about treatment, a framework rooted in theories of how we learn and the knowledge contained in many different scientific fields. More specific treatment strategies follow in the next section, building on the theories presented here.

To protect ourselves from stimuli that arouse us and drive us to act, we first need to recognize how vulnerable we are to those stimuli. In conditioned hypereating, food cues are the stimulus, overeating the habitual response. These cues, said James Leckman, professor of child psychiatry and pediatrics in the Child Study Center at Yale University School of Medicine, are "invitations to the brain."

"The ability to respond to urges for food is built in, but if you give in to those urges too often, the system becomes dysregulated. Then you're hypersensitive to these cues," Leckman explained. "To control our brains, we have to be mistrustful of our brains. We have to recognize they are the vehicle to invite us to do things that at some point in our evolutionary past may have been very useful, but have gotten completely out of control."

Raymond Miltenberger dramatized the extent of human vulnerability in his description of compulsive hair pulling, a stimulus-response disorder that primarily afflicts girls and women. Once a hair puller grasps a single hair on her scalp, telling herself, "I can just pull one, that will be okay," she has basically lost her struggle for restraint. To cope with her affliction, she must first recognize the automaticity of her response—and understand that if she pulls out a single hair, she'll pull out twenty more. Only then will she be ready to learn intervention techniques, and to use them.

Effective intervention draws us away from the conditioning power of a stimulus before it triggers its usual response. It reminds us that it's possible to say no. Intervention begins with the knowledge that we have a moment of choice—*but only a moment*—to recognize what is about to happen and do something else instead.

The cornerstone of treatment for conditioned hypereating is developing the capacity to refuse the cue's invitation to the brain in the first place. That refusal must come early, and it must be definitive. "It's only at the very beginning, when the invitation arises, that you have any control over it," Leckman affirmed. At that point it's still possible to turn away from the stimulus. Once we get started, a cascade of events—stimulation, response, and more stimulation—is likely to drive behavior.

If we do manage to say no, our vulnerability to the stimuli doesn't simply disappear. We never fully unlearn earlier responses. "The old habit is still there," said Mark Bouton, a professor of psychology at the University of Vermont. Bouton studies the relationships among context, conditioning, and memory, and he has helped shape current thinking about how humans can alter their behavior. "We can learn something new, but when you learn something new, you don't necessarily get rid of the old thing."

Because earlier associations linger, they can all too easily surface under the right circumstances. Animal experiments have demonstrated this reaction. Rats learn to fear a tone if they are given a shock every time they hear it. The fear eases if that tone is subsequently repeated without an accompanying shock, but they don't entirely "unlearn" the connection. With the right manipulations, their fear can readily be rekindled.

The same principle applies when we have had a positive emotional response to a stimulus. Once established, the connection between a cue and a memory is never fully severed. Many people who haven't smoked for decades still feel the urge for a cigarette at certain times. Cigarettes remain a "hot" stimulus with a promise of reward.

Despite that legacy, new learning is possible, and most of the time it can prevent us from acting on our urges. We can practice new behaviors and learn new thoughts to keep the old ones at bay. Eventually these can become as automatic as our past responses, and when they do, the stimulus begins to cool.

Avoiding risky situations is one approach, but in a world of omnipresent food cues—in All-U-Can-Eat America—that isn't enough. It's simply impossible to avoid the temptation of highly palatable food all the time. To succeed, you will need to be able to employ a variety of other cognitive and behavioral tools. And then you will need to practice using them, with determination and commitment, until you can alter the reactions that are generated by stimulation.

Reversing the Habit

CHAPTER 37

Refusing a cue's invitation to the brain means reversing long-standing habits. In the beginning, you'll need to control your actions carefully, but in the long term, you'll replace one set of automatic behaviors for another. As Raymond Miltenberger said, the new response needs to become "so well entrenched and so automatic and part of your repertoire that now when you walk past tempting food, you say, 'Boy, that smells good, but it's not in my plan.'" And you keep on walking.

To do so requires repeated practice and enough behavior change to establish a track record of success. That, in turn, will reinforce your capacity to persevere. Ultimately, there must also be a motivational component to enduring change. You'll have to learn new habits that are rewarding enough to keep you from engaging in the old ones.

"We're talking about something that's very difficult to do," said James Leckman. "And if you fail in some of your early attempts, or if you give a try and have only limited success, it's very easy to get discouraged and feel like, 'It's just beyond my power and control to manage this.'"

A sense of powerlessness is one of the biggest obstacles to success. If you feel you have no choice but to engage in a behavior, the arousal that drives it will persist. But if you develop a sense of your own capacity for control and recognize that you need not engage in habitual behavior, that sense of arousal will begin to diminish.

The ability to change entrenched habits rests with you. Four major components of habit reversal grow out of the literature of behavioral and cognitive psychology and have proven effective in dealing with repetitive behaviors: awareness, competing behavior, competing thoughts, and support. A fifth, emotional learning, has not traditionally been a part of habit reversal, but it may be the missing piece for treating the most recalcitrant habits. That category certainly includes conditioned hypereating and the driven behavior that is at its core.

Following the tenets of habit reversal can help you overcome conditioning and regain control of your behavior.

Awareness is the first step.

Being aware means that you have a conscious knowledge of the risks of a given situation. "You have to figure out the situation that leads you to eat, that leads you to start the chain of behaviors," said Miltenberger. "That is the absolute first step—to catalogue all of the stimuli, all of the situations, all of the cues that start that chain."

Leckman talked about recognizing "premonitory urges," urges that foreshadow the action you automatically take. Premonitory urges are a characteristic feature of stimulus-response disorders. "The gate that's usually there to hold back the flood of sensory information doesn't work as well in some of these disorders," Leckman noted. More sensation makes it into the conscious awareness of vulnerable people, forcing them to confront more powerful urges. They respond with familiar and repetitive behavior that relieves those urges, at least momentarily.

"This is obsessive-compulsive disease, this is Tourette's, this is life," Leckman said. By that, he meant we all respond to sensory stimuli to some degree or other, whether or not we have a diagnosable disorder. "It's not so much a question of, 'Do you have it or not?'" he explained. "The question is, 'How much of it do you have?'"

Experience tells us that sensory signals, stressful situations, and forceful memories are all invitations to out-of-control eating. To have any power over those cues requires first that we notice them and know the behavior they stimulate.

"Once you're cued, once you have the premonitory urge, is it too late?" I asked.

"No," insisted Leckman. "That's the point at which you've got a moment of control."

It is at that moment, he explained, that "you say, 'Thank you. I'm aware of the urge. And now I have a moment of decision. Am I going to walk through that door and accept that invitation? Or am I going to turn away and walk through another door?'"

Becoming aware that there's a choice to be made means bringing the setting, and your habitual response, into conscious thought. "You have to ask people to specifically pay attention so that they can begin to self-monitor," said Matthew State, professor of child psychiatry and genetics at Yale School of Medicine. "Once they pay attention, they have a capacity to extinguish the behavior."

The second component of habit reversal is engaging in competing behaviors.

To resist what Miltenberger calls "the pull of the behavior," we need to develop and learn alternative responses that are incompatible with it. Rather than coming home at night and going straight to the refrigerator, you change your routine and don't even enter the kitchen. You drive a different route to work in order to avoid the fast-food corridor that tempts you, or you make a list and ask a family member to go to the grocery store so you don't risk off-limits purchases.

To compete successfully with old habits, this competing behavior needs to be planned before you encounter a cue. You need to know exactly how to respond when your brain receives an unwanted invitation.

"You've got to be prepared with some other behavior, because the closer you get to eating, the more powerful it becomes, the more reinforcing," said Miltenberger. "If you intervene early and start a new chain that will prevent you from going down the other path, then you're more likely to be successful."

To break the pattern of stimulus and response, you must have a road map to guide you through high-risk settings. Substituting competing behaviors for habitual responses demands that you use your executive control functions, which can override the more primitive, hardwired circuitry of the brain. Doing that, said Leckman, requires a lot of new learning.

The third element of habit reversal is formulating thoughts that compete with, and serve to quiet, the old ones. "I think we take for granted how much of what we do is verbally mediated, governed by talking our way through a problem," said the Canadian psychologist Philip David Zelazo. In essence, we write a cognitive script that helps us carry out new behavior and deal effectively with the old.

Our thoughts, and the language we use to express them, can remind us of the consequences of bad habits, guide us to other actions, and heighten the reinforcement value of success. We can introduce ideas that countermand others. Instead of "That pint of chocolate ice cream looks really good to me; I'll have just a few bites," we can say to ourselves, "I know that I can't have one bite, because it will lead to twenty." We can remind ourselves of our goals: "If I don't eat that now, I'll feel better about myself tomorrow." Or we can repeat statements of self-efficacy: "I don't have to respond that way; I can respond this way," or "I can do this; I can control this."

Instead of responding habitually to the promise of immediate reward, we can make ourselves conscious of the long-term impact of eating highly palatable food. This shift of attention is a tool for gaining cognitive control that "involves changing the way you think about the meaning of the stimulus," according to Kevin Ochsner, who studies the psychological and neural processes involved in emotion, self-regulation, and perception at Columbia University.

By learning to think not only of the pleasure of a sugar cookie but also of its direct contribution to weight gain, we can begin to seize cognitive control. "Thinking about outcomes changes how you feel about the situation," Ochsner explained.

By changing the way we talk to ourselves about food, we can endorse new ways of thinking and learn how to shift the meaning we assign to something we once wanted. "You're providing a mental reimagining of the stimulus and using that to control your behavior," said Ochsner.

The fourth component of habit reversal is support. None of these changes is easy to make, and having someone around who can help you recognize and avoid cues—and acknowledge your success—makes the whole process much easier. Ultimately, the choices we make are ours alone, but supportive family, friends, colleagues, and health professionals can make a big difference.

People often engage in habitual behavior in private. "I've got a plan, I know what I'm supposed to do, but if I'm home alone I can easily short-circuit that plan," said Miltenberger. "If I have support from a person who knows my plan and who can be there, it's more likely I'll be successful. It would be embarrassing to overeat in front of my friend or spouse to whom I just made a commitment."

Support is a way of sustaining and reinforcing our motivation not to engage in conditioned hypereating, adds Miltenberger. "That's how you make it more likely that you'll be able to resist the immediate, strongly reinforcing situation. Now you've got this other contingency, this person to whom you've made a commitment. It's going to be hard to break that commitment when that person is with you."

Of course, you must find the *right* kind of support. Otherwise, your support system can work against you, endorsing the type of behavior you're trying to reverse. A study published in the *New England Journal of Medicine* showed that social networks can promote obesity—people with friends, siblings, and spouses who are obese are more likely to be obese themselves. If your support system does not reinforce your goals, you're better off going it alone.

But the right support can make a difference. For one thing, social engagement itself can serve as a "competing behavior," or substitute reward. It can also reduce the anxiety that accompanies giving up old behavior and the ambivalence you may feel about saying no. And finally, the prospect of disappointing the people you care about, or earning the disapproval of someone who is trying to help, can keep you on track.

Rules of Disengagement

CHAPTER 38

At the heart of conditioned hypereating lies the impulsive nature of the behavior. Because people with conditioned hypereating are so sensitive to food cues, they tend to make eating decisions on the spur of the moment. To compete with the chaotic nature of that behavior, we need to develop a set of rules to keep us from becoming aroused.

Setting rules helps us make the steps of habit reversal real. Rules provide structure, preparing us for encounters with tempting stimuli and redirecting our attention elsewhere. As a type of "top-down processing" executed with awareness, rules stand in contrast to the bottom-up, reflexive conditioning that typically dictates our response. Rules are conscious; they can be expressed in words. We can reflect on them and apply them to new situations.

We know that we shouldn't eat foods rich in sugar, fat, and salt when we're trying to lose weight, just as we know we shouldn't smoke or drink to excess. But it isn't easy to act on that kind of abstract knowledge. Simply knowing the right behavior isn't enough.

What we need is to develop a planned response when we encounter a stimulating food that drives conditioned hypereating. "That protects you against automatic contingencies that are going to be primed all around you in the environment, and that you can't control," explained Walter Mischel of Columbia University's Department of Psychology, who has dedicated his career to the study of personality and self-regulation. "A plan connects specific actions to specific possibilities."

Preparing for situations in which we actually encounter such foods is a lot more useful than having a good idea ("I should stop eating high-fat foods"). Concrete "if-then" rules can be useful and effective. The idea is to have a countermanding action for a risky situation: "If I encounter this cue, then I regulate my response to it in this way."

"When you have those rules in mind, they can help prepare you for what you need to do," said Kevin Ochsner. Once you're in the moment—experiencing the emotional force of the cue—this becomes a lot harder.

Rules work in part by giving us an alternative to a conditioned response, forcing us "to engage in contrary behavior that is incompatible with habitual behavior," said Matthew State of the Yale School of Medicine. When my brain receives the signal that salient foods are nearby and recalls their pleasure, I remember my rules, which tell me, "Don't stop. Pass them by. Turn your attention elsewhere." Set that rule, stick with it, and in time your desire will decrease.

We have the science to demonstrate that this works. Adults who are placed on either a low-carbohydrate, high-protein diet or a low-calorie, low-fat diet did not develop cravings for the restricted food. Once the stimuli that have been paired with the food are gone, the preference for eating the food diminishes.

Rules aren't the same thing as willpower. Willpower pits the force of reinforcing stimuli against your determination to resist, a clash of titans that can become very uncomfortable.

"What's the difference between just using willpower to resist food and having a rule?" I asked Silvia Bunge, whose research at the University of California, Berkeley, focuses on cognitive control.

"If you develop a rule, that will allow you to better inhibit the behavior, because you'll have a context that provides some kind of reason for inhibiting in the first place," she said. "A rule makes explicit the negative consequences of giving in to your impulses and the positive consequences of not giving in. Without any kind of context or motivation, there's really no reason that you would inhibit the response of wanting it."

Rules are guided by higher brain functions, said Bunge, and they need to be "kept in mind" so that they substitute for unconscious action. There's that idea of a cognitive script again—the strategy of using words and thoughts consciously to craft a new response to habit-driven cues. "The more specific the rules are, the easier it is to hold them in mind and to represent an alternative action." Categorical rules—"I don't eat french fries," "I will not have dessert"—are the easiest to follow.

With practice, new responses can eventually become as automatic as the old ones. "If I'm being cued, if I'm being stressed, and that sets off my wanting, how can rules overcome all the effects of a hot stimulus?" I asked Mischel.

"They are not going to, unless they have been practiced and also made automatic," he observed. "Unless your implementation plan goes from being a good idea to something that becomes an automatic behavior pattern, I don't think you get anywhere."

Using an analogy to alcohol, Mischel emphasized that it's not enough for someone to say, "I am dying from this addiction, so I really don't want to drink anymore." The thought alone won't make it happen. The shift from wanting to behave differently to actually doing so requires setting rules and practicing them until they become programmed behavior.

The goal, Mischel said, is "to create rules that pass control of the external stimuli to the self." Only then can we make the essential transition from a desire to change to change itself.

Every time I approach the food court at the San Francisco airport, I'm tempted to stop for fried dumplings. The representation of that behavior is etched in my brain—I can see myself doing it, and I know I'll be rewarded. But an incompatible behavior—refusing temptation and walking on by—is also represented there. Those opposing representations vie with each other for dominance. "It's a competition between these representations of actions, and whichever one is strongest is going to win," said Silvia Bunge.

The drive for sugar, fat, and salt tends to be the stronger representation, she notes. "The salient thing, based on bottom-up drives, is to stop at the food court." That's what learning and habit dictate. That's what gets the neurons firing. That's the response that satisfies my basic desire.

But to achieve other goals, like maintaining weight loss and eating healthier food, I need to behave differently. The problem is that my brain hasn't been trained to respond to the message "No, it would be better for my health and my looks if I don't do this." It is more accustomed to responding to an immediate orosensory reward. But that doesn't mean that the longer-term reward can't eventually take on more salience.

That's where the prefrontal cortex (a part of the brain responsible for executive control) plays a key role, boosting the force of goals other than obtaining the reward of highly palatable foods. "It literally sends excitatory inputs to the weaker representation, amping that up, causing stronger activation of those neurons," said Bunge. "It can lead to an increase in activity of the neurons that is going to control your ability to walk away."

In other words, the habit-driven response of stopping at the food court competes with the executive functions signaling me to walk past it. Over time, if I'm successful at turning down the salience of a cue often enough, its intensity will diminish as new learning substitutes for the old. By increasing the activation of neurons that represent one behavior ("keep going"), the prefrontal cortex succeeds at suppressing the alternative ("stop and eat"). That creates an opportunity, Bunge said, for "the action plan that's getting the top-down input from the prefrontal cortex to win the race."

The action plan offers me a tool for refusing invitations to the brain.

Experience has taught me something essential about the neuronal excitement I get as I near the food court: The urge to stop doesn't last. If I can maintain focus and repeat my rules—"Do not detour; go right to the baggage claim"—I can redirect my attention away from the stimulus. Once I'm safely beyond its enticing call, my neurons settle down and I'm not tempted to turn around and go back. I've accepted that those fried dumplings are unavailable to me.

That's my personal experience with a broader lesson: Rules that make food unavailable can modulate how we respond to cues. The sensory signals of a piece of fried chicken don't evoke the same neural activity if we know that it is not available. A photograph of fried chicken may not activate the reward pathways to the same degree if we're on a mountaintop miles away from the nearest KFC.

Alain Dagher, a neurologist at Montreal Neurological Institute at McGill University, used imaging technology in a study of smokers to learn how anticipation influences brain activity. All his participants had brain scans, but only some were told in advance that they would be able to smoke immediately after the test was completed. The others understood that they couldn't have a cigarette for another four hours and that a carbon-monoxide monitor would be used to ensure that they complied.

Dagher's MRI scans showed that areas of the brain involved in arousal and attention were essentially shut down in the population that did not expect to be able to smoke afterward. "We confirmed with our study that you could reduce the behavior response and the brain imaging response to cigarette cues by reducing expectancy of reward," said Dagher. "Somehow these people have the ability to suppress that response. If a reward is deemed unavailable, it affects what we thought was a very basic and automatic response."

Apparently, when the brain knows that a reward will not be forthcoming, it shifts its attention elsewhere. Rules are designed to take advantage of that capacity by shutting out the possibility of pursuing a food reward and forcing us to focus on something else.

Over time, it can become second nature to follow those rules. But until then, rules need to be "kept in mind" so that they are available to guide behavior in the moments we need them. That requires attention, practice, and advance planning, motivated by the expectation that you will ultimately derive emotional satisfaction in new ways. Your ability to follow your own rules will eventually carry its own reward.

Emotional Learning

CHAPTER 39

Learning to act in a new way requires either being drawn toward something you want or being pushed away from something that no longer seems desirable. Learning comes most readily when the two occur together.

More than many habits, conditioned hypereating involves stimuli we have come to depend on for comfort. Their positive emotional charge drives our behavior.

"We have cultivated very positive associations with the stimuli at a gut level," said Philip David Zelazo of the University of Toronto. We can look at a piece of cherry pie, consider only one dimension of it—its appealing taste—and evaluate it as something we want.

But Zelazo tells us we can also see something much more complex. "There are infinite ways you can look at a piece of cherry pie. Our attention, our memories, our expectation feed into the kind of cue it becomes for us." As we become more consciously aware of those dimensions, that piece of pie can begin to look very different.

To alter our behavior, we need to change our emotional appraisal of salient food. We begin that process by recognizing our capacity to assign food a value, either good or bad. If we learn to view the pursuit of sugar, fat, and salt in a negative light, and to imbue with equal emotional significance behavior that encourages us to turn away from it, we can reverse a habit.

Psychologist Arnold Washton offered a vivid description of the emotional underpinnings of old habits, and the challenge of mastering new learning, when he related the story of a medical student who struggled with addiction. The first time the young man was caught diverting drugs at work, he was encouraged to enter rehabilitation. The second time, he was again urged to seek treatment and warned that he would be expelled from medical school if he stole drugs again.

The young man, said Washton, "will tell you that he wants nothing more in life than to finish his MD/PhD program and be a physician, that this is of the greatest value to him, that his entire self-esteem, his self-worth, rides on this." And yet the student took drugs a third time. "Evidently to him the reinforcement value of the drugs is still far greater than the reinforcement of his career path."

Changing that kind of behavior requires almost heroic effort, acknowledged Washton. "What ends up being critical is the way in which you're appraising the meaning of the stimulus," he explained. "You can move from one highly charged affective appraisal to another—from 'That's going to be fantastic' to 'That's the most disgusting thing in the universe; I don't want to come near it.'"

As you begin to evaluate a familiar stimulus in a new way, you protect yourself from its compelling draw. Developing negative associations, which is sometimes called counterconditioning, has proved useful in reducing tobacco use. Over the past decade many adults have come to view cigarettes differently—not as sexy and glamorous, but as repulsive and deadly. One colleague told me that every time he felt tempted to smoke, he put his nose into a jar

packed with cigarette butts and inhaled deeply. The negative association with that act has helped him move from abstractly recognizing that he should stop smoking because it's bad for his health to
a deeply felt understanding that this product is not a friend but a
detested enemy.

"He has acquired an emotional feeling about smoking that has
him disgusted so vividly that even the thought of approaching a cigarette is aversive," explained Walter Mischel. "It activates negative
feelings and thoughts. Presumably, his brain activity is going to
steer him away from this."

"We talk to patients about playing the tape until the end," said
Arnold Washton. "The cognitive strategy is to become well practiced
in recognizing when you're having euphoric recall and selectively
remembering only the good parts. Then, in your mind, you play the
scenario out to the end and you say, 'This is what's going to happen.
I'll feel good for two minutes, and then I'll feel horrible.'"

At the same time, new behavior must come to have an emotional
value that carries its own rewards. "Unless a person makes the cognitive shift, where it's more reinforcing to have a life without the
substances than it is to have a life with them, recovery is not obtain-
able," said Washton.

Mischel agreed. "Not smoking becomes the thing the individual
feels good about. Smoking has become aversive rather than pleasurable." It may not seem that food can become as readily aversive as
cigarettes, but for my part, very large portions now strike me as gen-
uinely disgusting. And consider the burger from the Claim Jumper
Restaurant, which piles avocado, cheddar cheese, applewood-smoked
bacon, and sweet onion rings on the meat. Contemplate the real message in the attempted humor of its name, and distaste may temper
desire: It's called the Widow Maker Burger.

Cues to foods that are high in sugar, fat, and salt create emotional
tension—a psychic itch, if you will—and eating becomes a strategy

for easing the stimulus-induced tension. This becomes habit, made automatic by the repeated experience of gaining reward and the learning attached to it.

Over time, those associations automatically activate a positive memory, said Russell Fazio, a professor in the psychology department at Ohio State University and an expert on the formation and evolution of human attitudes. "That automatically activated positivity will be the starting point for perceptions and judgments," he said.

The fact that a smoker knows cigarettes are harmful or that the obese person understands that eating fried food contributes to her weight problem does not necessarily interfere with that automatic response. Motivation and opportunity are required as well. "If the individual is properly motivated, you can override the impact of the automatically activated attitude, but that's effortful, and it requires mental resources," explained Fazio. "Many times our resources are sufficiently taxed in day-to-day life that we just can't engage in that kind of motivated overriding of our impulses."

To change our associations with a stimulus, we need to make a "direct attack," Fazio says, on the way we evaluate it. In his studies, Fazio exposes subjects to a visual stream of information designed to create new pairings in our minds. That's what advertising agencies do when they link an Olympic athlete to a pair of sneakers or an attractive woman to a piece of new technology. "The consequence is that we actually produce a change in the automatically activated attitude," he said.

People who want to curb their overeating need to make a similar shift in order to maintain self-control over the long run. "The dieter who is successful eventually manages to have negativity automatically activated in response to the presence of a chocolate cake," said Fazio.

"How do you get to the point where the sugar isn't inherently reinforcing?" I asked.

It's a matter of how we construe the object, Fazio explained. "Everybody knows that chocolate cake is high in calories and should be avoided if you are on a diet. The idea is to have that construal dominate over the other possible construal as a treat." The goal is to extinguish the learned associations that encourage us to pursue reward in the form of sugar, fat, and salt, and instead to develop new associations that turn us away from them. The experts make this point in many different ways. James Leckman describes it as a way of refusing invitations to the brain. Behavioral psychologists use the term counterconditioning, and Kevin Ochsner talks about the process of changing the way we appraise a stimulus. Washton focuses on the need to make a cognitive paradigm shift, and in the annals of psychology, the concept is known as making a critical perceptual shift.

It all means essentially the same thing: looking at a stimulus in new ways. How we make that shift will vary from individual to individual. For me, it was about altering my perceptions of large portions. Once, I thought a big plate of food was what I wanted and needed to feel better. Now I see that plate for what it is—layers of fat on fat on sugar on fat that will never provide lasting satisfaction and only keep me coming back for more. With that critical perceptual shift, large portions look very different to me. I have changed the reward value of the stimulus.

To build on this information and treat conditioned hypereating, we need to understand two key principles and how they're linked.

As we have seen, cue-induced behavior is automatic behavior. Once the association between food cues and emotional reward has become embedded in the brain, highly rewarding food steals our attention.

Second, our perception of a food stimulus directly influences our behavior in response to it. If we think rewarding food is a friend, we're likely to pursue it. If we think it's an enemy, we'll turn from it with distaste.

At first blush, those principles appear somewhat contradictory. If behavior is automatic, why does our view of the stimulus matter? The answer is that managing our eating behavior depends on our ability to alter automatic responses to food cues and gain conscious control over them. We do that most effectively by engaging the higher functions of the brain to change our perceptions.

In the presence of a stimulus, conditioned hypereaters tend to engage the higher brain regions in less-than-useful ways. Sometimes we formulate rationalizations that allow us to act on our desire for reward. Thoughts like "I deserve this" or "I'll only have a small piece" are strategies for easing our discomfort about behavior we know is not in line with our goals.

And sometimes we use higher brain functions to engage in an internal debate about the pros and cons of a food choice. Telling ourselves, "This would taste good, but I know I shouldn't eat it," is an attempt to gain control (although it does carry the risk of back-firing if you become too preoccupied with the stimulus).

There's another, more productive way to use the brain's executive functions: by formulating strong opinions about the stimulus. When you perceive hyperpalatable food as negative—and place that recognition in your working memory so you can access it quickly—you're better equipped to interfere with the automatic response and make healthier food choices.

Effective treatment of conditioned hypereating is dependent upon making that perceptual shift and learning new behavior that eventually becomes as rewarding as the old.

PART FIVE

Food Rehab

The Treatment Framework

CHAPTER 40

The nation's weight problem is evidence, in part, that we have gotten a lot of bad advice. New diets are constantly being developed and marketed to help us change our behavior, our thought processes, our emotions, or the food combinations we put on our plates. Although some of these programs do help us shed pounds, none of them has allowed us to keep weight off over the long haul.

What's missing has been an understanding of how we lost control over eating in the first place and how we can use that knowledge to our advantage. The nature of the problem—our focus on food as a reward—suggests the solution. It is time to begin thinking about Food Rehab.

Readjusting your expectations about food requires gaining new perspective. My own perspective shifted as I worked on this book. I described a meal I had recently eaten at a San Francisco restaurant to a woman regarded as one of the top food coaches in the country. I thought my dinner had been about the right size, and I felt pleased that I had skipped dessert. But when I described exactly what I had eaten as an appetizer and a main course, she was blunt in her assessment. "You just ate twice as much as you needed," she said.

I was stunned. In that moment, I realized I had lost track of what I needed to feel satisfied. Since then, I've worked hard to figure it out, and I've learned to find reward in smaller amounts of foods I enjoy. Over time, doing that has gotten much easier. In fact, gaining a sense of control has become its own reward. I no longer need to derive quite so much of my satisfaction from sugar, fat, and salt.

Food Rehab is the key to viewing food stimuli in new ways. Once we decide to seek reward from avenues other than endless quantities of hyperpalatable foods, we can begin to restructure our environment and strengthen our behavior to support new learning and the pursuit of new rewards.

A few essential principles lie at the foundation of Food Rehab:

- Conditioned hypereating is a biological challenge, not a character flaw. Recovery is impossible until we stop viewing overeating as an absence of willpower.

- Treating conditioned hypereating means recognizing it as a chronic problem that needs to be managed, not one that can be completely cured.

- Every time we act on our desire for sugar, fat, and salt, and earn a reward as a result, it becomes harder for us to act differently the next time. Effective treatment breaks the cue-urge-reward-habit cycle at the core of conditioned hypereating.

- The loss of control that characterizes conditioned hypereating is magnified by diets that leave us feeling deprived.

- New learning can stick only when it generates a feeling of satisfaction. We can't sustain a change in behavior if it leaves us hungry, unhappy, angry, or resentful.

- Restoring control over eating requires us to take a comprehensive approach, one that has many interlocking steps. To gain the upper hand, we need strategies that address the multiple behavioral, cognitive, and nutritional elements of conditioned hypereating.

- Lapses are to be expected. Most of us are never fully cured of conditioned hypereating. We remain vulnerable to the pull of old habits, although with time and the rewards that accompany success, they do lose some of their power. With practice, we can find ways to use "slips" to our advantage, as tools for recognizing where we might stumble and reminders of the need to develop new learning.

- Eventually, we can begin to think differently about food, recognizing its value to sustain us and protect us from hunger, and denying it the authority to govern our lives.

The elements of the Food Rehab program outlined here have been used and tested in other contexts and still need to be rigorously evaluated for the treatment of conditioned hypereating. Nonetheless, I believe they can offer you some help.

To change the way you eat, you'll need to focus on how you approach food, craft a plan to which you can devote concentrated attention, and recognize that making progress is incremental and effortful. The suggestions presented here are very practical and very forgiving. They recognize that it won't be easy to change your habits. Situations will arise when the old reward value of food is almost impossible to resist. This isn't a sign of failure, but simply a reminder that it is difficult to unlearn old behavior.

I don't offer a one-size-fits-all technique, because I know it will not work. New learning that sticks is new learning that resonates for *you*. It takes individual experimentation to determine how you can structure your environment and strengthen your behavior. The idea is to mix and match the tools presented here and to find the ones that work best for you.

Planned Eating

CHAPTER 41

As we've discussed, treating conditioned hypereating means, in part, developing new eating behaviors to compete with the old ones. Think of this approach as "planned eating," which is rooted in clinically proven techniques of behavior modification and built on four elements: replacing chaos with structure, just-right eating, choosing foods that satisfy you, and eating foods you enjoy. Together, this package deconditions your habitual response to highly palatable food and its cues and gives you a specific alternative behavior to substitute.

In time, planned eating can recondition your behavior. The trick is to identify foods that you can learn to eat in a controlled way and that are at least as reinforcing as the foods you once overate.

Replacing Chaos with Structure

Planned eating calls upon you to replace chaos with structure. This structure is designed to keep you away from salient stimuli in the environment, protect you from cues, and curb the impulsive behavior that drives you toward reward. It tells you what is permissible and what is not, taking away the need for you to make decisions about food in vulnerable moments. It gives you competing and repeatable behaviors that guide you past temptation and toward foods that satisfy. It allows you to set up a parallel food universe while continuing to participate in normal social and work activities.

The rules that support your structure must be simple enough to fit with your busy life, but specific enough to remove uncertainty from the food equation. Instead of facing a day filled with the unplanned eating opportunities that drive out-of-control behavior, you must develop a set of meal plans and a repertoire of satisfying foods. Those meals should offer sufficient variety to keep you interested, but enough predictability that you can avoid being stimulated and don't have to make continuous decisions about what to eat.

That kind of predictability is the secret behind meal replacements—those all-in-one powders, shakes, and packaged foods that promote weight loss so effectively. The unyielding structure of meal replacements inhibits the mindless and repetitive eating that takes place in a world without boundaries. But this works only for short periods of time. You probably can't tolerate meal replacements for long and still participate in the business and social activities that fill most of our lives.

Structure offers a more lasting approach, allowing you to function in the real world so you can still enjoy restaurants and the company of the friends and family who invite you to join them for dinner.

At first, structure is imposed from the outside—with meal plans that tell you what you can eat, when, and how much. You determine in advance what you'll put on your plate at mealtimes and for snacks, you write out your menus, and you block out everything else. One overarching and rigid rule will be your guide: If it isn't part of your structure, you don't eat it. The idea is to eliminate your mental tug-of-war.

When you first begin to practice this, there's no room for deviation. You need to ease the tension of temptation, to quiet the warring voices that say, "I want that food. I shouldn't have that food. I'm going to eat that food."

But over time that can change. Once you've established new patterns and reconditioned yourself to nonchaotic eating, you'll be able to open the door to other foods. There is no real timetable, but as you learn to protect yourself from hunger and realize that small amounts of food can be satisfying, you will begin to feel more comfortable adding some flexibility to your meals. As you master the art of portion control, establish new habits, and realize that the triggers of overeating are beginning to lose some of their power, you may be able to end the total ban on foods high in sugar, fat, and salt.

If you adore hamburgers, you'll eventually be able to structure meal plans that allow you to eat hamburgers. Not monstrous burgers layered with cheese and bacon, but good-tasting hamburgers all the same. Few foods will be totally out of bounds. You'll be able to enjoy the pleasure of food without feeling the guilt of overindulgence.

Just-Right Eating

Planned eating means choosing food in appropriate quantities—figuring out how much you should put on your plate so you feel satisfied until it's time to eat again. For most people, a just-right meal is one that will keep away hunger for about four hours. A just-right snack should keep you satisfied for about two hours.

It is important to think in advance about what a meal or a snack should look like, and then to put only that much on your plate. Feedback signals from the stomach come long after you have consumed too much, and the increased activity of the brain makes it difficult for people with conditioned hypereating to stop eating if there is more food in front of them. Serving yourself just-right meals is an automatic safeguard against the habit of going back mindlessly for more.

People with conditioned hypereating tend to overestimate how much food they need to hold them comfortably until it is time to eat again. That's why I was so startled by the food coach who told me I had eaten two meals at one sitting.

When your plan is built around just-right eating, this doesn't happen. A useful way to gauge what will truly satisfy you is to eat only half of your usual meal. Then pay attention to how you feel thirty minutes later, and ninety minutes after that. If you are experiencing real hunger, try the same experiment again with three-quarters of your standard portion. Chances are good that you will find one of those servings to be enough—beyond that, you are eating for reward, not satiety. It often comes as quite a shock to realize how much less you can eat.

Some people count calories because they find it the easiest way to know how much they are eating. Others are willing to weigh their food to determine portion size. But those strategies are impractical for most of us because they take too much time and are too difficult to do. A better approach is to develop an intuitive sense of how much you need to feel satisfied. By paying close attention to how much food you eat and how long it sustains you, you learn that portions smaller than you've come to expect will hold you perfectly well.

There is a strong cognitive element to this process: What I perceive to be satisfying will help me determine whether it actually is. If you say, "I'm going to be hungry after I eat that" or "That won't be enough" when you're served a plate of food, then you'll probably want more.

But if you believe the food in front of you will fill you up, it's likely to do so. Patricia Pliner, a professor of social psychology at the University of Toronto, Mississauga, has demonstrated that if people feel they have been served a meal, they say they are less hungry afterwards than if they have considered what they ate to be an appetizer.

Once you learn that smaller portions won't leave you hungry, you can begin conditioning yourself to think "That was enough," "That filled me up," or, best of all, "That was just right."

Choosing Foods That Satisfy You

Choosing *what* to eat is as important to planned eating as deciding how much to eat. For many years we didn't fully appreciate that, which explains why standard weight-loss advice once emphasized eating a restricted diet consisting primarily of low-fat foods. Most people couldn't do that because they didn't feel satisfied—and any diet that keeps you hungry is guaranteed to fail.

Scientific studies of satiety have advanced in recent years, and we now know that most people find protein the most satiating macro-nutrient. Emptying from the stomach at the relatively slow pace of 4 calories a minute, protein reduces hunger and makes it easier for us to comply with caloric restrictions. Simple sugars offer the least satiation, because they empty from the stomach at the rate of about 10 calories a minute. That provides only a transient effect; sugary foods will typically satisfy hunger only for about an hour.

Similarly, foods high in fiber tend to be satisfying because they're assimilated by the body more slowly. These are foods that are generally intact—that is, as they were designed by nature rather than processed by industry. Examples are whole-wheat flour and brown rice, rather than their white counterparts; meat instead of products built around meat fillers; and apples instead of applesauce. High-fiber foods retain the tissue that's part of their architecture and empty more slowly from the stomach.

Fat is somewhat more complex. Because it empties from the stomach at just 2 calories per minute, fat can increase satiety. But the body processes those signals slowly, and until it does, we can keep eating high-fat foods without feeling full. This gives rise to the concept of a "fat paradox." Especially in combination with sugar, or sugar and salt, the high reward value and equally high caloric load of fat become very problematic.

Neither sugar nor refined carbohydrates that behave much like sugar in the body, such as white flours and pasta, belong in the diet in significant amounts. They break down too readily in the mouth, they're too quickly processed in the gastrointestinal tract, and they comprise too many of the calories that we could otherwise reserve for more satiating foods.

Putting all this together gives us a basic formula for satiety: foods that occur in nature, consisting primarily of high-fiber or complex carbohydrates (such as whole grains and many vegetables), combined with protein and a small amount of fat. Obviously, not every meal has to have every one of these constituents, but we're much more likely to be satisfied by meals in which these foods dominate.

Essentially, that means a diet based largely on lean protein and whole grains or legumes, supplemented with fruits and nonstarchy vegetables. On a typical day meals might include an omelet for breakfast; a grilled chicken sandwich for lunch; two snacks, such as a piece of cheese and a cup of fruit; and fish with leafy greens for dinner.

Within these parameters it's important to identify those foods that will satisfy *you*—and this is very personal. I know people who will eat a few strips of bacon or a small portion of cheese for breakfast, a plain, reasonable-size hamburger for lunch, and a medium serving of pasta and salad for dinner, and they control their eating well.

Eating Foods You Enjoy

The only eating plan that will work for you is one built around the personal likes and dislikes you have accumulated over a lifetime. This is the secret behind the many weight-loss regimens that have captured popular attention: Whether these diets have you eating mostly protein, lots of complex carbohydrates, or a grapefruit every morning, the key to their success is that you enjoy the permitted foods.

Once you are confident that you have established structure and can eat satisfying food in appropriate amounts, nothing will automatically be off-limits. But from a practical point of view, most combinations of sugar, fat, and salt will remain in the danger zone because they are so stimulating that most people can't limit themselves to suitable portions.

What you may be able to do is learn to savor the food you *can* control. Consciously paying attention to the pleasures of taste and the experience of eating food can be an effective way to deepen its reward value.

Everyone needs rewards, and eventually your eating behavior may worsen if you don't get them. You can incorporate rewards into your structure by choosing the ones you can control—biscotti, frozen yogurt, a small piece of good chocolate, or a fruit dessert. This strategy is known in some circles as "harm reduction," and it's a valuable way to avoid feeling deprived.

Mental Rehearsal

You might think of all this as a game against a powerful opponent. You can't expect to win every encounter, but with continued practice and training you can get a whole lot better. A sports analogy applies in another way as well: Whether the quest involves athletics or food, mental rehearsal improves performance.

There are two purposes to mental rehearsal—one cognitive, the other motivational. The cognitive process allows you to envision your strategies, routines, and game plans before actually executing them. The motivational value comes from enhancing your sense of competence and self-confidence, reducing your anxiety, and helping you stay focused. Rehearsal reduces the chaos in which conditioned hypereating often occurs, positioning you to succeed.

When it comes to eating behavior, mental rehearsal helps you anticipate cues and build the skills necessary to respond to them. It takes only a minute or two to rehearse your performance, preferably just before you enter a high-risk environment in which you're likely to be cued. The idea is to run through every step in advance of the event itself. Visualize yourself deciding not to reach for bread when it is passed around the table. Imagine choosing a dinner that's part of your eating plan instead of one that is layered and loaded. Peter Gollwitzer, a professor of psychology at New York University, calls these "implantation intentions"—you implant your intended response in your brain with "if-then" propositions ("If I encounter this situation, then I'll behave in this way").

Your aim is to focus on the task at hand, rather than becoming distracted by external stimuli. Elite athletes do this by anticipating their every move in advance, whether it's watching a mental home movie of a golf swing or visualizing a response to an opponent's play on the tennis court. In that moment before an athlete springs from the diving board, her attention is focused on the routine she has practiced over and over again, not on the roar of the crowd. She sees her own performance and uses verbal cues—for example, a one-word mantra repeated silently—to ward off distractions and refocus her concentration.

Mental rehearsal helps solidify your commitment to controlled eating by helping you focus on your intentions and maintain control over your thoughts.

Letting Go of the Past

CHAPTER 42

Understanding what triggers overeating, and planning accordingly, gives you a much greater chance of taking control over the process. But for a long time to come, you'll still have to fight the conditioned responses that drive overeating. You'll still have to deal with the emotions propelling you toward highly palatable foods. Like much of the information on a computer hard drive, the neural pathways that created the cue-urge-reward-habit cycle can't easily be wiped out. They can, however, be managed.

If you're exposed to a cue and consistently manage *not* to seek out a reward, new learning begins to take hold in your brain, and the cue begins to lose its powerful association. Think back to Alain Dagher's experiment with smokers. Those who were told they wouldn't be able to have a cigarette for several hours after a brain scan showed fewer signs of arousal than those who expected to smoke immediately after the test was completed. The intensity of the cigarette's pull was reduced for smokers who didn't expect a reward.

As a conditioned response becomes less automatic, the cue becomes decoupled from the reward. The drive begins to ease, and in time, the stimulus can cool.

Seizing Conscious Control

Seizing conscious control is mostly a matter of paying attention and recognizing how quickly that attention can be hijacked. It means being mindful of the stimuli that trigger automatic behavior—a hot slice of pizza, taco chips at a Mexican restaurant, or those aromatic Charlie cookies—and replacing them with foods that sustain you. Mindfulness also allows you to recognize how entertainment—bustling crowds, loud music, bright lights, or the company of good friends—and the desire to feel better can wrest away your capacity to focus on what you eat.

Staying alert to emotional stressors is part of seizing conscious control, so that instead of responding habitually, you're equipped to act defensively. Having learned that food can make us feel better, at least in the short term, we've developed the habit of turning to it when emotional tensions are running high. Past experience narrows our focus, leading to the distorted perception that food is the *only* way to deal with potent emotions. Our conditioned response to stress is to eat.

A useful tool to help you step back from the habit of reaching for food when you're under stress is to label the feelings you're experiencing. You can begin simply by saying, "I feel sad," "I feel tired," or "I feel fearful." Recognizing your emotions and describing them helps you to look more objectively at your options for coping. Indeed, many of us do feel better for a brief while after we eat foods high in sugar and fat. But the distortion in our thinking is that the new mood will last or that there is nothing else we can do to achieve the same effect. Ask yourself, "Will eating help me truly deal with this feeling?" Most of the time it won't.

That knowledge allows you to widen your focus and consider

other responses. Rajita Sinha talks about "keeping your frontal cortex active"—in other words, making conscious choices about how you'll respond to strong emotions so repetitive behavior doesn't take over.

Handling the emotional challenges that spark overeating is easier if you're prepared for them. Consider what makes you feel better in a situation when you're experiencing psychic turmoil. It might be something as simple as a telephone call to a friend, a walk around the block, or a set of stress-reduction exercises. Have a list of alternate responses ready, so that when strong emotions kick in and steer you toward food, you can quickly choose to do something different.

The goal, says Sinha, is "to build the brain to better adapt to all situations."

Getting Out of the Path of Cues

Once cues have conditioned your behavior, you'll typically experience tension when you're around them and only eating brings relief. And so whenever possible, you want to avoid being cued in the first place.

When you're bombarded with stimuli, it is impossible to find the quiet space that will allow you to focus on new learning. If the cues keep coming—if you see candy every time you open your cupboard, if you keep returning to places where you habitually overeat—you'll be relying on sheer willpower, day after day, to resist highly palatable foods.

Breaking the grip held by these foods begins with eliminating most of them altogether. But remember that total abstinence—that firewall we have urged you to build—is necessary only until you have learned to manage risk.

For now, here are some guidelines.

Figure out what leads to overeating. Make a list of the foods and the situations you can't control. Knowing what generates an urge and ultimately hijacks your behavior allows you to erect barriers against it. Be especially alert to the power of location as a cue.

Refuse everything you can't control. Cut out all the foods on that list, and don't expose yourself to situations that promote the cycle of overeating behavior. Stay away from restaurants that layer and load meals, and at the supermarket don't buy the highly processed foods that are high in sugar, fat, and salt. Avoid meals with friends whose food habits set your eating spiral in motion. If someone puts something you overeat in front of you, push it away.

One evening I checked into a hotel room and found a plate of freshly baked chocolate-chip cookies waiting for me. I knew I could easily eat them all, and I knew with equal certainty I didn't want to do that. There was only one way to gain the upper hand, and I had to act quickly. I tossed those cookies into the trash, getting them out of my sight and stopping my conditioned behavior before it even began.

Have an alternate plan. Habit dictates that I stop for those fried dumplings at the San Francisco airport, but awareness reminds me that I don't want to. Now when I land I take steps to protect myself. I've trained myself to take a different route through the airport so I don't walk by them. My alternate plan allows me to resist a cue that would otherwise draw me in.

Limit your exposure. If you can't avoid the cue altogether, then limit the amount of time you're exposed to it. The longer you're in a stimulating environment, the more you're likely to consume. That's often the problem in a social situation—you may be able to turn away from a cue initially, but its presence will be a continued temptation until you give in. As soon as you've eaten what you know will sustain you, go somewhere else. Otherwise, the activated brain that characterizes conditioned hypereating will keep fueling your desire.

Remember the stakes. Along with devising a plan, remind yourself of what unfolds if you don't move away from cues. Think through your habitual response. Recall the inevitable chain of behaviors that lead to the first bite and then keep you going until the food is gone. Remember how you feel afterward.

Direct your attention elsewhere. Keep your working memory engaged with other thoughts in order to crowd out cue-generated responses. When you're bored or distracted, give those thoughts a place to reside.

Learn active resistance. When other people are putting you at risk, you have a right to resist. Protect yourself by reframing seemingly well-meaning acts as hostile ones. It's okay to feel angry at the marketing and advertising techniques designed to get you to eat more, at the huge portion sizes served at restaurants, and at the layered and loaded food you encounter everywhere.

Dealing with Urges

Despite your most determined efforts to stay out of the path of cues, the contemporary food environment ensures that they'll find you. Techniques for dealing with the resulting urges include "thought stopping"; conditioning a cue with negative, instead of positive, associations; and talking down the urge.

Thought stopping. Thought stopping, a term coined by Richard Rawson of UCLA, who works with recovering drug addicts, is a definitive decision not to respond to the pull of a reward: Encounter a stimulus, and shut off the action it provokes. "Think of it like television," says Rawson. "Change the channel."

Turning off a thought has to be almost immediate. "You're not helpless about this; you can make a decision, but you have to make the decision quickly," said Rawson. The more seconds you spend thinking about what to do in the face of an urge, the greater the chance that you'll ultimately give in to it. Once you begin to debate "Should I or shouldn't I?" you've lost the battle.

Experience a cue, switch off the associated thought. No ambiguity, no maybes. Don't waste time in debate; don't struggle with your response. Just get it out of your working memory. Internalize a response to urges that is absolute, even rigid, leaving no room for doubt.

Until you have gained the upper hand over trigger foods, an attempt at moderation won't work. "It is almost as if there needs to be a total reversal," said Arnold Ludwig, of the University of Kentucky. "The 'yes' becomes a 'no,' not 'maybe,' or 'I'll try.'" Opposites take on equal force, so you can make a categorical shift from one end point to another, but you can't stop anywhere in between.

In order to distract yourself from a reward and keep unwanted thoughts from taking hold, you need to engage your mind with something else. Turning to other goal-directed activities—ones you care about, feel motivated to pursue, and are able to concentrate on—can occupy enough mental space to prevent cue-induced thoughts from lingering there.

For some people, discovering that there's something else they can do in the face of a stimulus is a revelation. They've become so locked into the cue-urge-reward-habit cycle that they've lost sight of the fact that other responses are possible.

"We try to get them to think about their own thinking, and for many, that's not typical," said Rawson, speaking of the drug-using population. "There's a whole teaching process that goes on around getting them to understand that this isn't just an automatic stream of consciousness that has no beginning and no end." Drug users can learn to stop a thought and direct their attention elsewhere—and so can you.

Conditioning cues with negative associations. Another strategy is conditioning cues with negative, rather than positive, associations. This is counterconditioning, and like thought stopping, it has to be done immediately and without ambivalence.

When cued by a plate of nachos, think, "That's hundreds of calories I don't want and that will stay with me."

Passing by an ice cream shop, tell yourself, "If I eat this, I'll feel awful about myself later."

The idea is to undercut the reward value of the food, and cool down the stimulus. This is often a new idea for people struggling with compulsive behavior, who tend to act without considering consequences. Gamblers don't consider their dwindling bank accounts; compulsive shoplifters aren't focused on the humiliating phone calls they'll have to make to their spouses after they're arrested.

If they did put those kinds of outcomes at the forefront of their thinking, they might be better able to control their behavior. At the University of Minnesota, Jon Grant asks patients with a history of shoplifting to write out a shopping list before heading into a store, and to put just two items on that list: handcuffs, to remind them of a previous arrest, and a bologna sandwich, to jog their memory of what they probably ate during the night they spent in jail. "You're making people acutely aware of the consequences of behavior," he said. "I also remind them of their self-hatred afterwards."

In addition, Grant asks his patients to imagine a familiar scenario—walking into a store, confronting the desire to take something, and doing it. Then he has them record their feelings about the aftermath. "Okay, you take something. What does it feel like as the steel handcuffs go on your arms? What does it feel like when you notice somebody is looking at you? Okay, now you're calling your spouse, what do you feel like? Are you worried that you're losing your children? What does that feel like?" Listening repeatedly to the tapes of their humiliation reminds shoplifters of the repercussions of this act. For the same reason, Grant suggests they make a list of these consequences and post it in a prominent place as a daily reminder.

Similar techniques help some people control their overeating. It may be an unflattering photograph on the refrigerator or a list of all the things you don't like about being overweight taped to the kitchen table. These not-so-subtle memory tools promote awareness and demonize the things you once associated with reward. Over time, this can change the impact of a cue.

Talking down the urge. If you can't get an involuntary thought out of your mind, you may be able to learn responses that will quiet the stimulus. Think of this as talking down the urge. Here are possible responses to thoughts of food:

- Eating that food will satisfy me only temporarily.

- Eating this is going to keep me stuck in the cue-urge-reward-habit cycle.

- Eating this will keep me trapped. The next time I'm cued, I'm going to want this again.

- Eating this will make me feel bad.

- If I eat this, I'm demonstrating that I can't break free.

- I'll be happier if I don't eat this.

- I'll weigh less tomorrow if I don't eat this.

You might also try looking for an empowering word or phrase to keep in mind, one you can call on when you need to resist a stimulus. Repeating to yourself "I am in control" or "I am a healthy person who makes healthy choices" can be surprisingly useful.

Exercise: An Alternative Reward

Exercise is one of the best substitutes for the kind of reward we get from highly palatable foods. Its value is not so much that it burns calories as that it helps you achieve a long-term sense of well-being.

Although you would have to walk ten miles a day to lose the same weight as reducing your food intake by 1,000 calories, exercise is essential over the long term. Indeed, it may be the most important predictor of sustained weight loss, because it is a substitute reward. A substantial body of science tells us that exercise engages the same neural regions as other mood-enhancing rewards and produces similar chemical responses. Just as a smoker thinks he needs a cigarette, someone who exercises regularly comes to depend on the positive effects it produces.

Exercise can also reinforce an altered self-image. You begin to identify yourself as a healthy, athletic person, someone capable of making positive choices, and that in turn gives you an incentive to maintain control. New habits begin to substitute for old ones, making it easier to stay faithful to your eating plan.

You don't need vigorous exercise to achieve these benefits. If you've been sedentary all your life, a short daily walk is enough to make a difference. As you gradually change your routines to incorporate more physical activity, you'll be able to steadily increase intensity over time.

Eating Is Personal

CHAPTER 43

To eat with control, we need to eat in ways that match the realities and preferences of our own lives. The magic comes when we rearrange our actions, alter our environment, and construct the rewarding behavioral repertoires that allow us to do that.

A woman I'll call Penny showcases some of the strategies that can help. Ironically, she is married to Andrew, the journalist I profiled earlier in this book, the man who found M&M's harder to cope with than pursuing jihadists.

Penny eats what her body needs for fuel and avoids food that won't sustain her. That was apparent one afternoon on a long road trip up the New Jersey Turnpike. Penny and Andrew were driving north from Washington, and they were in a hurry. When Penny said she was hungry, Andrew suggested a fast stop at a gas station so she could pick up a candy bar. Penny told him not to bother.

It was a moment that revealed a lot about how she approaches food: "Even though I'm really hungry, I can't eat that," she explained. "It's not going to make me feel better. It's not going to satisfy me."

What she wants, instead, is food that will fill her stomach in a lasting way. Put a plate of cookies before her, and she'll say, "No, thanks." She finds that protein suits her better, and for lunch will often eat a chicken salad or a turkey sandwich, with one slice of bread removed. Steak and salad is one of her favorite dinners.

Penny doesn't bother to measure the volume of food she eats, but she has developed an instinctive sense of the quantity that's right for her. She isn't waiting for a signal from her body to stop or a message from her stomach that says, "You're full." She has simply figured out what to eat to feel satisfied, but not overstuffed. "I eat what my body needs to run," she says. "I know how food is going to make me feel."

I asked Penny how her approach contrasts with Andrew's. One big difference, she said, is that she pays attention when food arrives, and he doesn't. "Without even noticing, his brain seems to say, 'Oh, there's something good here.' He puts the food in his hand and he eats it." By contrast, she consciously registers the presence of food and then decides what to do next. "I look at it and say, 'Oh, there's food. Am I hungry? Is it good? Let me focus on it.'"

She always asks herself how eating something will make her feel. "Am I going to feel better off after I eat this? Am I going to be satisfied?"

Such questions never seem to cross Andrew's mind.

Penny does something most of us do not. She makes her own set of rules, and then she follows them. Those rules have not been imposed by any diet-of-the-moment, and they are not universal, but they work for her. Each of us can do something similar, crafting rules rooted in our own needs and wants. That puts us on the path to eating for nourishment, not stimulation, and helps us feel satisfied, not deprived.

Before you are ready to identify the kinds of strategies that will work for you, you have to be ready to change—and deciding to do that is also highly personal.

A man I'll call Frank had struggled with weight since childhood.

He was always a "fat kid," the one who would eat frosting right out of the can and thwart his mother's efforts to keep Little Debbie cakes out of his reach. He would eat dinner at home and then go off to visit friends who ate later so that he could eat again.

By the time he reached his late twenties, Frank was seventy pounds overweight. But it was not just the weight that bothered him. The evening he sat alone consuming a large pepperoni, mushroom, and green pepper pizza from Papa John's was the evening he knew he had to change. He felt physically ill, but what really scared him was the recognition that he could not control his behavior.

Convinced of the need for action, Frank took a series of steps to structure his eating throughout the day. For him, the best strategy proved to be identifying three or four options that would satisfy him at every meal and cutting out all high-fat, high-sugar foods. Without counting calories, he became much more cognizant of portion sizes. To protect himself from overeating, he made it a point not to go longer than three hours without a meal or an appropriate snack, and he began turning down dinner invitations that were likely to distract him from his plan. "Put yourself into a routine, and you take away the temptation by not making it available," said Frank, explaining the core principles of his approach.

What also proved essential to him was viewing control of overeating as a personal challenge. Frank, like Penny, built a strong emotional foundation for his approach to food. By writing eating scripts for themselves, they have both learned to enjoy what they eat and to feel good about it—not just for the moment, which is the effect of hyperpalatable foods, but over the long term.

Jordon Carroll, a weight-loss consultant in New York City, tries to instill the same kind of conditioning and drive in her clients. She is their guide to eating in the real world, where food can be enjoyed and controlled despite food cues, business demands, stress, and social expectations. Carroll tells her clients never to say, "I'm on a diet," because she thinks that implies temporary deprivation, and she is training them in lifelong behavior change.

Although Carroll has never studied the biological basis of conditioned hypereating, she understood the concept when I described it. "If we allow an object to be more powerful, it will always have power over you," she said.

Her techniques are designed to diminish that power through a personalized eating plan. To develop that plan, she learns firsthand what a client's business day looks like, often by spending hours at a corporate office or watching a trader run around the floor of the New York Stock Exchange. She also spends a lot of one-on-one time in conversation with clients to identify their stresses and figure out where they're likely to go astray. Building on that information, Carroll then works with her clients to create meal plans that are simple and structured enough to become automatic. "With structure there is no chaos," she says.

Her golden rule is to "eat small and follow the meal plans." She trains her clients to recognize and then be able to eat about 2 ounces of protein for breakfast, 2.5 to 4 ounces for lunch, and 4 to 6 ounces of protein for dinner (4 ounces for a woman, 6 for a man), plus four ½-cup servings of fruit and vegetables a day. In essence, Carroll helps them structure just-right meals.

"What if a waiter brings out a 10-ounce portion at dinner?" I asked.

"You're going to cut off one-third of it and give it back. Don't put it on a nearby plate. Get it away from you."

Her approach is generally flexible. For example, a client is welcome to eat more for lunch and less for dinner, as long as that person has learned to eyeball food and estimate proper portions. And the occasional pizza, or even a piece of Kentucky Fried Chicken? Not at first, Carroll says, but eventually that will be fine too, as long as the client is capable of keeping the portion size reasonable.

Once again, the key is that meal plans have to be personal. "It's about the individual," she explains, emphasizing that people shouldn't have to eat anything they don't like or avoid all foods they love forever. But everyone needs to understand his or her own vulnerabilities—one person might be able to snack on crackers with control, but someone who is likely to eat the whole box should not get started with even a single bite.

In essence, people with conditioned hypereating need to become their own food coaches.

Avoiding Traps:
On Obsession and Relapse

CHAPTER 44

One characteristic that defines long-term success is the ability to eat normally without becoming obsessive about food. Most people with conditioned hypereating take a long time, and struggle hard, to reach that place. Until they do, they can easily fall into a trap that painfully reminds me of those childhood finger cuffs that hold you tighter as you pull harder.

That's because, as we have seen, awareness is essential to control—it's necessary to prevent yourself from automatically reaching for the cake nearby. Many people can protect themselves only with a focus that initially does border on obsession. George Ainslie, a behavioral economist, talks about an internal policing process that involves a very high degree of regimentation.

And yet when you focus hard on avoiding a food reward, you risk increasing its reward value instead. Your heightened awareness of those cookies means you must repeatedly deal with the urges they provoke.

The danger is in becoming overly focused on food and your

eating plan. Obsession typically develops in the face of conflicting desires. When you use all of your emotional energy to avoid a behavior, you can become anxious and tense. You begin to feel deprived, which fuels further struggle as you try to resist the call to ease that deprivation by giving in. The process of being cued, and the conflict it engenders, becomes mentally exhausting.

John Foreyt, a leading obesity researcher, described a patient who has maintained her weight for almost two decades, but only by working at it every minute of every day. She has designed highly restrictive rules for herself, eating almost exactly the same food year in and year out—the same breakfast, the same lunch, the same dinner, with only the smallest variations in the kind of grilled fish or meat she might choose.

Foreyt asked whether this woman was a success story. That is something only his patient can decide. An outsider might consider her rules obsessive, but they do allow her to maintain her weight, and she has made the choice to live with them.

Nonetheless, I think you can do better. The eventual goal is to gain enough control to move past full-blown obsession.

With its power to take us hostage, a stimulus-response disorder like overeating can be deeply demoralizing. When something as seemingly inconsequential as a chocolate-chip cookie assumes so much power in our lives, it can make us feel that we're somehow less than fully capable adults. That leads to distressing thoughts: Why am I unable to stop this behavior? How can I be so inadequate?

But when you gain the upper hand, the opposite effect can also occur. The satisfaction of breaking the cycle that leads to the pursuit of unhealthy food can be reinforcing in its own right.

With the ability to control your response to cues comes the reward of self-mastery. When cued, you are aware that you could easily act on the resulting urge—but you choose not to. That assertion gradually strips the cue of its power. In time, you cease to be someone caught in the clutches of conflicting desires, and with this transformation comes a new sense of competence and pride.

Along the way, setbacks are inevitable. When your commitment to staying in control clashes with your desire for reward, you move closer to a situation in which relapse can occur. If your guard is down at the first sign of an urge, it can be tempting to respond to an especially appealing cue. That lapse opens the door to an internal dialogue in which you begin to justify giving in to temptation. A bad day at work, a child's misbehaving, even a disappointing step on the scale can become your justification.

Soon you're inventing excuses for pursuing reward. "I'm entitled to this. . . . It will cheer me up. . . . I've been good this week. . . . I can eat just a little." In a series of small steps, you put yourself into a position where it becomes easier to access a reward, an internal battle begins ("Should I eat this or not?"), and your determination to say no eventually buckles.

Some people find it especially hard to stay in control when they are at the highest end of their weight spectrum—at that point, the goal of weight loss may just seem too remote to be achieved. For others, the greatest challenge comes after reaching their sought-after weight, when they recognize that their struggle will never be completely over and that the battle with conditioned hypereating is lifelong. Accepting those realities helps to keep you vigilant. Keeping relapse at bay is not about being strong enough to beat the temptation of eating stimulating food, but about being smart enough to deal with it.

Making the Critical Perceptual Shift

CHAPTER 45

Ultimately, the goal of Food Rehab is not only to change your eating behavior, but also to fundamentally alter your perceptions of hyperpalatable foods. The enduring ability to eat differently depends on coming to view these foods as enemies, not friends.

It is not enough to be told that you shouldn't overeat, or that foods high in sugar, fat, and salt will only get you to eat more foods high in sugar, fat, and salt. No one can persuade you with intellectual arguments that such foods will not relieve stress but will only make it worse. The moment you're thinking, "I deserve this," or "I'll only eat a little," no one can remind you that you'll feel differently after the meal.

But as you learn new approaches to eating and recognize the powerful influence of hyperpalatable foods, you will internalize these ideas more fully. Only then can you see that food has kept you trapped in a cue-urge-reward-habit cycle. Only then can you accept that food rewards are short-lived and that their more enduring effect is to sustain your desire to keep eating. That's when you realize that if you stay trapped, you'll never eat enough to feel satisfied, and that's when you'll stop expecting food to make you feel better. That's when awareness of the long-term consequences of conditioned hypereating hits with full force.

When this happens, you begin to assign different value to foods. Your attitude shifts and you begin to see foods in a new light. You have made that critical perceptual shift.

PART SIX

The End of Overeating

"Our Success Is the Problem"

CHAPTER 46

Just as conditioned hypereaters need to make a critical perceptual shift, so too does the food industry. A candid assessment of its manufacturing and marketing processes is a reasonable place to begin, and in fact, this is already starting to happen. Europe, where criticism of industry practices has been growing, is ahead of the curve here.

Not long ago I flew to London to talk with top executives of one of the world's largest global food companies. They were taking a beating from the British press about the industry's role in the obesity epidemic. Some members of Parliament were exploring their regulatory options, such as revising food labeling requirements. The company invited me, along with European colleagues who had government experience with food regulation, to help them think about their responsibilities.

I was asked to make a ten-minute presentation. I opened my set of PowerPoint slides to the one that showed a circle with the names of deadly diseases listed around its perimeter. At the center of the circle I'd written "obesity." After outlining obesity's role in stroke, hypertension, high cholesterol, and diabetes, I provided some numbers documenting the tremendous rise in the incidence of obesity and explained the flaws in the commonly held notion that our weight is set at a predetermined point.

I continued my presentation with an overview of the information contained in this book. When I said that people tend to eat excessively if food is readily accessible, I could see the executives' facial expressions begin to change. They understood that I was going to the heart of their business model. I described the stimulating qualities of sugar, fat, and salt, especially in combination, and told them that the brain is wired to focus on the most salient stimuli. "The more potent and multisensory you make your products, the greater the reward and the greater the consumption," I said bluntly.

By way of analogy, I described the way nicotine gains the power to provoke desire. By itself nicotine is only moderately reinforcing, but that begins to change with the building of layer upon layer of sensory stimulation: The sight of the packaging, the crinkling sound of the wrapper, the tactile sensation as you light a cigarette and hold it between your fingers, and the sensory characteristics of the first puff all bolster the reinforcement. Factor in the times of day and the location where you often smoke, and smoking becomes conditioned behavior. Cues, coupled with the emotional salience that the tobacco industry has embedded in cigarettes through decades of strategic advertising, intensify the drive for nicotine, which then becomes highly reinforcing.

Shifting back to food, I told my audience that industry tactics and social norms bolster the reinforcing properties of sugar, fat, and salt in much the same way—through their appeal to the senses, the power of advertising, ready availability, and cultural patterns that allow us to eat all the time.

Put it all together, I said, and "You end up with a highly reinforcing product that provokes conditioned and driven behavior."

For a moment there was complete silence in the room. Then one executive spoke up.

"Everything that has made us successful as a company is the problem," he said.

And then, to their credit, they began to rethink their strategies about labeling and portion size.

Industry Cracks the Code

CHAPTER 47

In Santa Monica, California, I introduced myself to Wolfgang Puck, award-winning chef-owner of Chinois on Main, known as a "temple of Asian-French fusion" cuisine. I asked him why he thought consumers were overeating. Without any prompting from me, he answered, "It's sugar, fat, and salt. People can't get enough."

And portion size? I asked, pointing to the large plate of food I had just been served. "I tell people to slow down and share," he said ruefully.

Puck observed that consumers have adapted over time to eating what's on their plates. "The first time, people didn't eat it. The second time, they didn't eat it. The third time, they ate it. We did it together."

Later, I spoke about the food industry with Joseph Stiglitz, a Columbia University professor and a Nobel laureate in economics.

"Does the industry know that what they feed us gets us to eat more?" I asked.

"The industry has jacked up what works for it," he said. "The learning is evolutionary." Practical experience, not scientific experimentation, has been its guide. The industry does not need laboratory rats when it can try out its ideas on humans. Its decision makers do not have to analyze human brain circuitry to discover what sells.

A research chef at Chili's was certainly aware of consumers' response to the products he creates. "We come up with craveable flavors and the consumers come back, even days later," he said. "There is a psychological craving. It's all part of habit."

The superstimulating nature of food is only part of the equation. The power of wanting is stoked with equal force by marketing, with its appeal to the emotions and its capacity to amplify the reinforcing properties of sugar, fat, and salt. The combination is irresistible.

Food marketing gains its influence over us in three ways. First, it creates positive perceptions about a product, encouraging us to seek it out. Our behavior is directly affected by the way we view an object—we seek out things framed in a positive light and avoid those with a negative cast.

Second, the message of marketing is that we'll gain a pleasurable emotional experience from our purchase. Food commercials don't generally tout food quality or nutritional value; they promise to make us feel good. "They're marketers of good times. Fun. Feeling connected, feeling involved, feeling loved," said an industry expert in Australia. "It's always about being happy—just do a favor for yourself, come to this fun place. Eat happy." Marketing caters to the emotions.

Third, marketing is designed to present us with cues associated with rewards. "We do the learning for you," explained this expert, reminding me of the connection between frequent exposure to cues and the learning that propels us toward food. The goal is to have a type of food or the name of a restaurant or product pop into our minds frequently and seemingly unexpectedly. We may not know why we're suddenly thinking about Burger King, but we can be sure marketing is at work.

Effective marketing is itself a reinforcer, driving us to pursue reinforcing food. The industry has created a tool that reinforces the reinforcer—and it's doing everything possible to rev it up even further.

With its ability to create superstimuli, coupled with its marketing prowess, the industry has cracked the code of conditioned hypereating and learned exactly how to manipulate our eating behavior. It has figured out the programming that gets us to pursue the food it wants to sell.

Our challenge is to figure out how to respond.

Fighting Back

CHAPTER 48

If they could, many food companies would likely be satisfied with making conditioned hypereaters out of all of us so they could sell more product. Yet the power to resist ultimately rests with us. While a combination of human biology, personal experience, and a determined industry may explain why we overeat, we still have the ability to make choices about whether we allow this triumvirate to dominate our behavior. The fact that the industry helps create this problem, and takes advantage of it, doesn't render us helpless.

When hyperpalatable food is offered to us, we're not obliged to consume it. When it's on the menu, we don't have to order it. But this takes more than willpower. We need to cultivate skills that will cool down the stimulus, and we need to practice them. Alcoholics Anonymous tells alcoholics that they're not to blame for their disease—but that they must take responsibility for their behavior. It acknowledges their vulnerability to the power of alcohol, yet refuses to accept that as an excuse for drinking.

Reconciling automatic drives with cognitive processes is one of the great struggles of the human species. Whether it's the allure of alcohol, drugs, sex, or food, many of us are driven by automatic responses that lead us to act in ways that are at odds with how we would like to act. This sets up a conflict that gives the stimulus even more power. Ultimately, bringing our conflicting desires into synch is the most effective way to act the way we would like.

It *is* possible to learn to eat the food you want in a planned and controlled way. As individuals, we can practice this, and we can get better at it.

And, as a society, we can identify the forces that drive overeating and find ways to diminish their power with comprehensive labeling, public education campaigns, regulation of marketing, and new perspectives on what kinds of behavior are acceptable and appropriate. We need to start rethinking our ideas about the right time and place to eat in business and social settings.

We can lead long and healthy lives without consuming alcohol, tobacco, or other drugs of abuse, so treatments for those addictions can be built around the principle of abstinence. But since we can't survive without eating, we need other strategies for changing our perception of foods that are superstimulants and for keeping them at bay. The highest goal—not only for those of us who are conditioned hypereaters, but also for a responsible industry—is to find food that provides emotional reward without driving overeating.

Effective strategies for weaning people from hot stimuli are often built around substitute rewards. Programs such as Alcoholics Anonymous, Al-Anon, and Narcotics Anonymous offer the fellowship of others with similar problems. Exercise can soothe certain desires, because it generates the same kinds of chemical rewards in the brain that food does.

The substitute for rewarding food is often other rewarding food—not the kind that drives conditioned hypereating, but the kind we can nonetheless enjoy. The choice is individual, depending on what relieves our negative feelings and makes us feel good without the baggage and calories of superstimuli. To avoid harm, we have to be able to purchase those foods in reasonable quantities and eat them in appropriate settings.

Shining a light on our automatic behavior can also help. Treatment for many stimulus-response disorders involves recasting the provocateur. Some approaches pull the desire from its internal hiding place and make it external to the body so we can see it as a foreign object that we have the power to reject. In obsessive-compulsive disorder, for example, patients learn to talk back to a stimulus. People with anorexia are taught to see their disease as an outside force. The idea is to learn to say, "Anorexia is doing this to me. It is not 'me' who doesn't want the food, it is anorexia telling me I don't want the food."

The "truth campaign," the largest antitobacco education campaign ever focused on young people, takes a related approach, promoting the idea that the desire for cigarettes comes not from the self but from a manipulative and profit-driven industry. Cigarettes have been successfully redefined in this framework as products deliberately peddled to appear as objects of desire.

These techniques, which have proven to be effective in battling other stimulus-driven conditions, suggest the possibility of successful clinical and strategic interventions for conditioned hypereating. They also prove that public policies can make a difference. Four possible strategies deserve special attention.

First, restaurants should list the calorie counts of all foods they serve on the menu—by mandate, if they're not willing to do so voluntarily. Along with giving consumers key information on which to base eating decisions, this provides an incentive for restaurants to offer more meals for people who are seeking to follow the guidelines of just-right eating (300 calories for breakfast; 400 to 500 calories for lunch; 500 to 700 calories for dinner). These meals should be flavorful and salient, and restaurants should promote them at least as aggressively as their more indulgent offerings.

Second, all food products should convey prominently on their labels the percentage of added sugars, refined carbohydrates, and fats they contain.

Third, well-funded public education campaigns should address the issue of "big food." People need to hear repeatedly, from many sources, that selling, serving, and eating food layered and loaded with sugar, fat, and salt has negative, unhealthy consequences.

And fourth, food marketing should be monitored and exposed. When the industry promotes superstimulants that lead to conditioned and driven behavior, it's not presenting neutral information; it's promoting harmful behavior.

We need to develop strategies and solutions to this public health problem, because we need to protect our children. I am a pediatrician, and this is one of my most profound concerns. Our greatest gift to future generations of young people would be to find a way to prevent the cue-urge-reward-habit cycle from ever taking hold.

Few of us are immune from the eating behavior motivated by cue-stimulated wanting. The ubiquitous presence of food, large portion sizes, incessant marketing, and the cultural assumption that it's acceptable to eat anywhere, at any time, have combined to put more and more people at risk. We see the results as increasing numbers of people become conditioned hypereaters.

We have allowed this epidemic to unfold, and we can find ways to reverse it. Social norms dictate what kinds of behavior are appropriate and what is deviant. They provide guidelines for how we live our lives, encouraging certain kinds of behaviors and inhibiting others. While there will always be those who trespass beyond what's considered socially acceptable, the vast majority of people feel most comfortable living within the standards set by their peers.

This is why redefining norms is such a powerful tool. We've learned from the major public health battles of the past that while legislation and regulation play a major role, the greatest power rests in our ability to change the definition of reasonable behavior. That's what happened with tobacco—the attitudes that created the social acceptability of smoking shifted, and many of us began to see smoking as deviant, and even repulsive, behavior. A consensus emerged that the cigarette, and the industry that manufactured it, was abhorrent. We moved from glorification to demonization.

A change in perspective cannot be imposed with mandates, but must evolve as a social consensus. The goal is not to vilify all food and those who serve it, but to change our thinking about *big* food, those huge portions of layered and loaded food with little nutritional value. We need to look differently at the people and the places that serve it. When their power to manipulate our behavior becomes fully transparent, cues will lose their capacity to entice. Instead of expecting food to materialize at every social and business occasion, we'll realize that many offers of food outside mealtimes do not serve anyone's interest.

In the future, new social norms and values will emerge, and food choices, offered in smaller portion sizes, will seem "right" to us. That will be what we come to expect, and that will be what we want.

Until then, you'll have to set your own rules for eating in a controlled manner and maintaining a healthy weight. To live within a framework of planned eating, you'll have to understand your own behavior around food and pay attention to everything you eat. You'll need to seek out alternative rewards that satisfy you and find support from people who care about you. You'll need to bear in mind how the brain processes stimuli and how that drives your behavior in the presence of food and food cues. And you'll always need to remember what the food industry is trying to sell you and why.

Only then will you be able to see clearly what's on your plate.

A FINAL WORD

As I've acknowledged in the preceding pages, I'm firmly in the camp of the overeaters. For much of my life, sugar, fat, and salt held remarkable sway over my behavior. I have lost weight, gained it back, and lost it again—over and over and over. I have owned suits in every size.

There is almost nothing else in my life that I do on impulse, without first giving it a great deal of thought. But stimulating food, and the cues that surround it, have the power to make me act without conscious awareness and against my own will. At times the quest for reward has trumped my cognitive capacities.

And so I admittedly had something of a personal agenda as I began researching and writing this book. I expected my journey to lead me deeper into the worlds of nutrition and human physiology, and it did. But it also pushed me into an exploration of how our behavior is governed by the workings of the mind.

We have known for a long time that certain stimuli, such as alcohol, sex, drugs, gambling, and food, can exert powerful effects on our actions. Much more recently we have begun to learn that these stimuli have a common, underlying mechanism, and the same general effect: They command our attention, occupy working memory, change how we feel, and become the focus of our single-minded thoughts.

Their power to control the way we think and behave lies at the core of many of our most impulsive and obsessive behaviors. But the influence of salient stimuli is felt not only in the realm of pathology, but also in the emotional responses of our daily lives. Whether we are pulled toward a reward because of its positive appeal or pushed there as a way to avoid a negative emotion, such as anxiety, we often react without awareness to a force we do not recognize.

For centuries, philosophers, theologians, and scientists have tried to discern the reasons we lose control over our behavior. Paul and Augustine saw it as weakness of the flesh. Siddhartha's crises of desires are at the core of Buddhism. Freud suggested that many of our instinctual behaviors are driven by the desire for pleasure. Jung used the term "Shadow" for multiple complexes or fragmentary personalities within us that cause discomfort. Contemporary psychiatrists and psychologists such as Roberto Assagioli write about "multiplicity of mind"; F. Michler Bishop refers to the "mind as a committee"; and Richard Schwartz discusses the parts that make up the self.

Although they represent many different disciplines, they all have sought to explain the same thing: why we sometimes act independently of our conscious intentions. Neurobiologists have also helped to advance our understanding as they pinpoint the mechanisms that are involved in our responses. Nonetheless, much mystery remains. We still do not understand why the same biological principles do not affect all of us equally. True, millions of people exhibit conditioned hypereating, but millions of others do not. Some of us have the instinct to turn away from salient stimuli; some of us are drawn impulsively toward them. And among those who do approach salient stimuli, only some respond most vigorously to food, while others are more aroused by something else.

As we gain insight into the fundamental mechanisms that drive our behavior, the consequences of the food culture and the environment we have created become more apparent. Understanding the nuances of our own biology casts the food industry's business plans in a very different light. What did we expect to happen when this industry embarked on a highly profitable business model that made foods high in sugar, fat, and salt widely available; conditioned us to associate their products with positive emotions; and created environments that foster these positive associations?

As we gain more insight into the problem, we also become better equipped to understand what works—and what does not—to control weight. We now must face the reality that until we fundamentally alter our eating behavior, we will continue to squander billions of dollars on ineffective weight-loss schemes. The sooner we create and implement a framework that promotes prevention and treatment strategies that work, the sooner we will regain control over our minds and bodies.

And then things can begin to change.

ENDNOTES

p. xii. Dr. Phil: *The Oprah Winfrey Show*, June 26, 2001.

p. xiv. Andrew: Andrew is a pseudonym, as are the names of others who shared their personal stories with me and appear later in this book, including Claudia, Frank, Jacob, Maria, Penny, Rosalita, and Samantha.

p. xvii. People who lack control: In her book *Fat Girl*, the late author Judith Moore described her single-mindedness with food: *"I daydream crab legs dipped in hot butter or crab cakes dribbled with garlic aioli. I consider toasted cheese sandwiches or homemade lemonade pinkened with macerated strawberries or carrot cake with brown sugar frosting that I ate once, 20 years ago, or those cheeseburgers. Foods I ate once and liked I think about the way people think about old lovers. I entertain memories of clam strips and tartar sauce and coleslaw from an outdoor food stand in Maine or an ice cream flavor—Honey Vanilla—that Häagen-Dazs used to make. For thirty minutes I think about Honey Vanilla."* (p. 10)

The author also recognized her own vulnerability: *"My mouth is dangerous. My lips and my teeth and my tongue are always ready. My mouth wants to bite down on rough bread and hot rare pepper steak and steamed broccoli sprayed with lemon juice."* (p. 12)

Moore understands her torment. *"I am frightened of food. I flinch when I consider ice cream, especially flavors beyond strawberry, vanilla, and chocolate. Caramel macadamia crunch might as well be the A-bomb. I am so scared of salty nuts and unctuously sweet caramel. I am scared of the frozen cream that melts along my tongue and walls of my cheeks."* (pp. 12–13)

Yet the author did not display signs that would lead doctors to diagnose her with an eating disorder. *"I have never lugged home sacks of food and binged. I have never taken diet pills or made an appointment with a quack diet doctor. Nor have I done the vomit or laxative route."* (p. 9)

Still, food is never far from her mind, and once she begins eating, she is unable to stop. Her own behavior is a mystery to her. *"Down the street an old-time bakery makes plain, unfashionable and not all that tasty pies. The filling for these pies come from commercial-sized cans and the crusts are premade. These pies, from three blocks away, call 'Judith, Judith.' An unopened bag of potato chips or an unopened box of vanilla wafers can sit in my pantry for months. I need exercise no self-control not to open these bags and boxes. However, once I open the containers, I can't quit eating. I want every chip, all the wafers. I do not know why this is."* (p. 10)

Reprinted by permission from Penguin Group (USA) Inc., Judith Moore, *Fat Girl: A True Story*. New York: Hudson Street Press, © Judith Moore, 2005.

p. xix. My goal in this book: This book is an effort to dissect the relationships between the stimulus of palatable food and the response of eating. A synthesis of the science available as of this writing, it is neither the end of work in this field nor a full explanation of the obesity epidemic. I have focused on the opioid and dopamine circuitry of the brain, that complex and mysterious two-pound intermediary between the stimulus and the response, but there is much more to be learned. We are far from a full understanding of how a variety of other neurotransmitters, neuromodulators, and chemical messengers modify eating behavior, and I look forward to the continued investigation by many scientists into the role that ghrelin, leptin, neuropeptide y, orexins, melanocortins, agouti proteins, CRH, cholecystokinin, and other molecules play in this process.

Vast scientific territory remains unexplored here. In particular, we will benefit from further research into the pathology of eating disorders. Understanding bulimia and binge eating will help shed light on the basic mechanisms of eating behavior, as will more knowledge of rare disorders that cause people to eat huge amounts of food, such as Prader-Willi syndrome, bilateral temporal lobe disease, and posterior hypothalamic tumors. As well, there is much to be learned from studying diseases like anorexia nervosa and cancer cachexia, and from examining the effects of exogenous substances, including the cannabinoids and antipsychotics, on eating behavior.

Also helpful will be a deeper understanding of eating disturbances that are remarkable for their specificity. These include desires for specific foods—such as pica among people who are iron-deficient, salt cravings in the face of dehydration, and licorice craving where there is adrenal insufficiency—and aversion to others, such as cabbage among people with gallbladder disease and meat among people with gastric cancer. These experiments of nature, which are not discussed in this book, hint at how tightly regulated the processes dictating appetite must be. Nor have I considered the endocrine system, and its many influences on eating behavior. For example, when blood sugar drops, we experience a desire for carbohydrates, and when we don't eat, we receive physiological cues that elicit a craving for food. More knowledge there, as well as about systemic endocrine disorders associated with abnormal eating behavior, such as hyper- and hypothyroidism and Cushing's syndrome, will also help in our understanding of obesity.

p. 3. Weight stayed remarkably stable: "Existing prospective studies suggest relative consistency in body weight patterns over time. . . . Two-thirds of the participants maintained their weight within 5 kg of their original weight classification." The referenced studies were published in 1977 and 1979. J. Grinker, D. Rush, and P. Vokonas, "Changing Body Habitus among Healthy Older Men: The NAS Boston VA Study of Weight Stability in Healthy Male Volunteers Aged 40–80 Years," *Diabetes Research and Clinical Practice* 10 Suppl 1 (1990): S89–94.

In the past, men and women usually gained weight during the first twenty years of adulthood before reaching a plateau, followed by weight loss in the older decades. One study showed that a population of white women ages 25 to 35 at baseline gained a total of 7.7 kg over a twenty-year period (white men, 7.3 kg); white women and men ages 36 to 47 at baseline gained 4.5 kg over the next twenty years; white women ages 48 to 60 at baseline gained 0.9 kg over twenty years (white men, 0.5 kg). T. J. Sheehan, S. DuBrava, L. M. DeChello, and Z. Fang, "Rates of Weight Change for Black and White Americans over a Twenty Year Period," *International Journal of Obesity and Related Metabolic Disorders* 27, no. 4 (2003): 498–504.

For longitudinal weight patterns over adult years, see I. Lee, S. N. Blair, D. B. Allison, A. R. Folsom, T. B. Harris, J. E. Manson, and R. R. Wing, "Epidemiologic Data on the Relationships of Caloric Intake, Energy Balance, and Weight Gain over the Life Span with Longevity and Morbidity," *Journals of Gerontology. Series A, Biological Sciences and Medical Sciences* 56 (2001): 7–19.

p. 3. In the 1980s, something changed: "The average annual growth rate of median BMI was lowest between 1900 and 1976 and has been rising to 0.5% per annum between 1988 and 2000." L. A. Helmchen and R. M. Henderson, "Changes in the Distribution of Body Mass Index of White US Men, 1890–2000," *Annals of Human Biology* 31, no. 2 (2004): 174–81. According to the authors, "In 1890–1894, median BMI declined with age, but by 2000 the age pattern had been reversed." See Table 1: From 1890 to 1894, men ages 40 to 49 had a mean BMI of 23.3; ages 50 to 59, a mean BMI of 23.0; ages 60 to 69, a mean BMI of 22.9. By contrast, from 1999 to 2000, men ages 40 to 49 had a mean BMI of 27.8; ages 50 to 59, a mean BMI of 29.1; and ages 60 to 69, a mean BMI of 29.2.

p. 3. Overweight had spiked dramatically: Flegal reviewed the National Health and Nutrition Examination Survey (NHANES), conducted by the National Center for Health Statistics, part of the Centers for Disease Control and Prevention, which takes a snapshot of the US civilian population. Among the thousands of participants are children and adults, men and women, and people of all races and ethnicities who are interviewed in their homes about their health status, disease history, and diet, and then given a thorough physical exam. The first such survey was conducted in 1960; questions about nutrition were added in 1971. NHANES-I was conducted from 1971 to 1974; NHANES-II, from 1976 to 1980; NHANES-III was conducted in two phases—phase 1, from 1988 to 1991, and phase 2, from 1991 to 1994. Beginning in 1999, NHANES became a continuous annual survey, with survey data released every two years.

p. 4. Fare-thee-well: Interview with Katherine M. Flegal, PhD, senior research scientist, National Center for Health Statistics, Centers for Disease Control and Prevention, January 9, 2005.

p. 4. Flegal's team wrote up its data: R. J. Kuczmarski, K. M. Flegal, S. M. Campbell, and C. L. Johnson, "Increasing Prevalence of Overweight among US Adults. The National Health and Nutrition Examination Surveys, 1960 to 1991," *JAMA* 272, no. 3 (1994): 205–11. This analysis was based on a sample population of 8,260 adults over age 20 who participated in NHANES-III, phase 1. Across all race/sex population groups, ages 20 to 74, the prevalence of overweight increased from 25.4 percent in NHANES-II (conducted from 1976 to 1980) to 33.3 percent in NHANES-III, phase 1 (conducted from 1988 to 1991). Median BMI increased from 25.3 in NHANES-II to 26.3 in NHANES-III, phase 1.

p. 5. Bigger over the decades: C. L. Ogden, C. D. Fryar, M. D. Carroll, and K. M. Flegal, "Mean Body Weight, Height, and Body Mass Index, United States 1960–2002," *Advance Data from Vital and Health Statistics* 347 (2004).

p. 5. During childhood and adolescence: The prevalence of overweight children increased between 1980 and 2004, with the heaviest children getting heavier (there was no further prevalence increase between 2004 and 2006). C. L. Ogden, M. D. Carroll, and K. M. Flegal, "High Body Mass Index for Age among US Children and Adolescents, 2003–2006," *JAMA* 299, no. 20 (2008): 2401–5; C. L. Ogden, K. M. Flegal, M. D. Carroll, and C. L. Johnson, "Prevalence and Trends in Overweight among US Children and Adolescents, 1999–2000," *JAMA* 288, no. 14 (2002): 1728–32; C. L. Ogden, M. D. Carroll, L. R. Curtin, M. A. McDowell, C. J. Tabak, and K. M. Flegal, "Prevalence of Overweight and Obesity in the United States, 1999–2004," *JAMA* 295, no. 13 (2006): 1549–55.

p. 5. Heaviest people: K. M. Flegal and R. P. Troiano, "Changes in the Distribution of Body Mass Index of Adults and Children in the US Population," *International Journal of Obesity and Related Metabolic Disorders* 24, no. 7 (2000): 807–18.

Mean-distribution plots were used to compare the distribution of BMI in NHANES-II and III and show "some upward shift in the distribution of BMI for every sex-age group. All age-sex groups also show greater differences in the upper portion of the distribution . . . there is also increased skewness in the distribution of BMI for every sex-age group. . . . In most groups, the largest differences are approximately 3–4 BMI units and are seen at the highest percentiles of the distribution."

p. 6. Doctors and health care professionals: E. L. Harvey and A. J. Hill, "Health Professionals' Views of Overweight People and Smokers," *International Journal of Obesity and Related Metabolic Disorders* 25, no. 8 (2001): 1253–61; L. L. Brandsma, "Physician and Patient Attitudes toward Obesity," *Eat Disord* 13, no. 2 (2005): 201–11.

p. 7. Compared food intake: S. M. Pearcey and J. M. de Castro, "Food Intake and Meal Patterns of Weight-Stable and Weight-Gaining Persons," *American Journal of Clinical Nutrition* 76, no. 1 (2002): 107–12.

p. 8. Group of children: A. J. Stunkard, R. I. Berkowitz, D. Schoeller, G. Maislin, and V. A. Stallings, "Predictors of Body Size in the First 2 Y of Life: A High-Risk Study of Human Obesity," *International Journal of Obesity and Related Metabolic Disorders* 28, no. 4 (2004): 503–13. Whether their parents were obese or lean, differences in what the children ate, rather than what they burned, predicted the degree of their weight gain. "Total energy expenditure doesn't differ much between the two groups, but food intake is strikingly different." Author interview with Albert J. "Mickey" Stunkard, MD, Professor Emeritus of Psychiatry, University of Pennsylvania, April 20, 2005.

p. 8. Vigorous exercise: K. E. Ebersole, L. R. Dugas, R. A. Durazo-Arvizu, A. A. Adeyemo, B. O. Tayo, O. O. Omotade, W. R. Brieger, D. A. Schoeller, R. S. Cooper, and A. H. Luke, "Energy Expenditure and Adiposity in Nigerian and African-American Women," *Obesity (Silver Spring)* (2008). The study, comparing a group of women in Nigeria to a group in Chicago, suggested that food intake, rather than energy expenditure, was the main factor responsible for weight gain.

p. 8. Burn more energy: Author interview with Dale A. Schoeller, PhD, professor, Department of Nutritional Sciences, University of Wisconsin–Madison, Institute on Aging, November 6, 2007.

p. 9. Feedback system known as homeostasis: A. E. Macias, "Experimental Demonstration of Human Weight Homeostasis: Implications for Understanding Obesity," *British Journal of Nutrition* 91, no. 3 (2004): 479–84; L. M. Kaplan, "Body Weight Regulation and Obesity," *Journal of Gastrointestinal Surgery* 7, no. 4 (2003): 443–51.

p. 9. Brain is the command center: M. W. Schwartz and D. Porte Jr., "Diabetes, Obesity, and the Brain," *Science* 307, no. 5708 (2005): 375–79; M. K. Badman and J. S. Flier, "The Gut and Energy Balance: Visceral Allies in the Obesity Wars," *Science* 307, no. 5717 (2005): 1909–14; J. G. Mercer and J. R. Speakman, "Hypothalamic Neuropeptide Mechanisms for Regulating Energy Balance: From Rodent Models to Human Obesity," *Neuroscience and Biobehavioral Reviews* 25, no. 2 (2001): 101–16.

p. 9. Maintain energy balance: Lee Kaplan, MD, PhD, director of the Weight Center, Massachusetts General Hospital (presentation at "Practical Approaches to the Treatment of Obesity," an annual Harvard Medical School Department of Continuing Education conference). "There is a central regulatory system . . . ," said Kaplan. "The body is very good at matching energy intake and energy expenditure to a very close tolerance. The tolerance is about 0.15 percent, averaged on a daily basis. . . . The mechanism by which this process of balancing food intake and energy expenditure occurs is a simple biological feedback controlled by parts of the brain. . . . If you decrease your energy intake so that you lose weight arbitrarily, you will become hungrier so that you return the energy intake to a higher level. If you arbitrarily try to gain weight, the opposite will occur. . . . The epidemic of obesity is not divorced from the system; the epidemic of obesity is a disruption of this system. It's not McDonald's only; it's McDonald's as it disrupts this system. It's not your genes only; it's your genes as they affect the balance of this system."

In a conversation with me on November 19, 2003, James O. Hill, PhD, Professor of Pediatrics, director, Center for Human Nutrition, University of Colorado–Denver, one of the nation's leading experts on weight, emphasized the changed environment: "For most of mankind's history our challenge was getting enough food to meet our energy needs. . . . If you look at how our physiology really developed, it developed in a situation where we had to be very physically active in daily living. We had to go out and kill the wild beast. Weight was controlled simply because we had to be very physically active and our challenge was to get enough food to meet our needs."

See also M. W. Schwartz and K. D. Niswender, "Adiposity Signaling and Biological Defense against Weight Gain: Absence of Protection or Central Hormone Resistance?" *Journal of Clinical Endocrinology and Metabolism* 89, no. 12 (2004): 5889–97.

Those who maintain eating and exercise behaviors that led to weight loss for a year are significantly more likely not to gain that weight back. M. T. McGuire, R. R. Wing, M. L. Klem, W. Lang, and J. O. Hill, "What Predicts Weight Regain in a Group of Successful Weight Losers?" *Journal of Consulting and Clinical Psychology* 67, no. 2 (1999): 177–85.

p. 9. Robert De Niro: Author conversation with actor Robert De Niro, July 27, 2005. Lee Kaplan, MD, PhD, director of the Weight Center at Massachusetts General Hospital, first told the De Niro story at "Practical Approaches to the Treatment of Obesity," an annual Harvard Medical School Department of Continuing Education conference.

p. 10. Motivational pathways: Jutta Heckhausen and Heinz Heckhausen, *Motivation and Action* (New York: Cambridge University Press, 2008); Johnmarshall Reeve, *Understanding Motivation and Emotion*, 4th ed. (Hoboken, NJ: Wiley, 2005); Rick A. Bevins and Michael T. Bardo, *Motivational Factors in the Etiology of Drug Abuse* (Lincoln: University of Nebraska Press, 2004); Eva Dreikurs Ferguson and Beth Eva Ferguson Wee, *Motivation: A Biosocial and Cognitive Integration of Motivation and Emotion* (New York: Oxford University Press, 2000).

p. 11. Artificially stimulating: Almost a half century ago, P. J. Morgane, a faculty member in the Department of Physiology at the University of Tennessee Medical School, implanted electrodes in various regions of rats' brains, and then sent a stimulating pulse through those electrodes for four, three-hour periods spread out over 20 days. When the far-lateral hypothalamus was stimulated, rats already fed to satiation showed a dramatic tendency to keep on eating. P. J. Morgane, "Distinct 'Feeding' and 'Hunger Motivating' Systems in the Lateral

Hypothalamus of the Rat," *Science* 133 (1961): 887–8; P. J. Morgane, "Electrophysiological Studies of Feeding and Satiety Centers in the Rat," *American Journal of Physiology* 201 (1961): 838–44; P. J. Morgane, "Evidence of a 'Hunger Motivational' System in the Lateral Hypothalamus of the Rat," *Nature* 191 (1961): 672–4; P. J. Morgane, "Medial Forebrain Bundle and 'Feeding Centers' of the Hypothalamus," *Journal of Comparative Neurology* 117 (1961): 1–25.

p. 13. Palatable foods: Author interview with Peter Rogers, PhD, head of department, professor of experimental psychology, University of Bristol, England, August 10, 2005. For more on the influence of palatability, see M. R. Yeomans, "Taste, Palatability and the Control of Appetite," *Proceedings of the Nutrition Society* 57, no. 4 (1998): 609–15; M. R. Yeomans, J. E. Blundell, and M. Leshem, "Palatability: Response to Nutritional Need or Need-Free Stimulation of Appetite?" *British Journal of Nutrition* 92 Suppl 1 (2004): S3–14; E. M. Bobroff and H. R. Kissileff, "Effects of Changes in Palatability on Food Intake and the Cumulative Food Intake Curve in Man," *Appetite* 7, no. 1 (1986): 85–96; David J. Mela and Peter J. Rogers, *Food, Eating, and Obesity: The Psychobiological Basis of Appetite and Weight Control* (London; New York: Chapman & Hall, 1998); S. M. Green and J. E. Blundell, "Effect of Fat- and Sucrose-Containing Foods on the Size of Eating Episodes and Energy Intake in Lean Dietary Restrained and Unrestrained Females: Potential for Causing Overconsumption," *European Journal of Clinical Nutrition* 50, no. 9 (1996): 625–35.

p. 13. Adam Drewnowski: Author interview with Adam Drewnowski, PhD, director, Nutritional Sciences Program, University of Washington, June 30, 2005; A. Drewnowski, "Energy Intake and Sensory Properties of Food," *American Journal of Clinical Nutrition* 62, no. 5 Suppl (1995): 1081S–85S; A. Drewnowski and M. R. Greenwood, "Cream and Sugar: Human Preferences for High-Fat Foods," *Physiology and Behavior* 30, no. 4 (1983): 629–33.

Consumption of high-fat, high-sugar foods correlates most significantly with increased BMI. J. I. Macdiarmid, A. Vail, J. E. Cade, and J. E. Blundell, "The Sugar-Fat Relationship Revisited: Differences in Consumption between Men and Women of Varying BMI," *International Journal of Obesity and Related Metabolic Disorders* 22, no. 11 (1998): 1053–61.

p. 14. Cheesecake Factory: Author interview with Stephen Kalil, executive chef at the Culinary Innovations Center at Frito-Lay and president of the Research Chefs Association, October 6, 2008. In an earlier capacity, Kalil was *chef de cuisine* for Culinary Research and Development at The Cheesecake Factory.

p. 14. Bliss point: Howard R. Moskowitz, Sebastiano Porretta, and Matthias Silcher, *Concept Research in Food Product Design and Development* (Ames, Iowa: Blackwell, 2005).

p. 14. Salt curve: Author interviews with Dwight Riskey, PhD, former Frito-Lay executive, November 4, 2004, and September 26, 2005.

p. 14. When the mix is right: Author interview with Barry Levin, MD, clinical professor, Pharmacology and Physiology, Department of Neurology and Neurosciences, New Jersey Medical School, August 12, 2005; B. E. Levin, A. A. Dunn-Meynell, B. Balkan, and R. E. Keesey, "Selective Breeding for Diet-Induced Obesity and Resistance in Sprague-Dawley Rats," *American Journal of Physiology* 273, no. 2, pt. 2 (1997): R725–30.

p. 15. Variety and ready availability: Author interviews with Anthony Sclafani, PhD, Distinguished Professor, Department of Psychology, Brooklyn College,

City University of New York, June 11, 2004, and August 29, 2005; A. Sclafani and D. Springer, "Dietary Obesity in Adult Rats: Similarities to Hypothalamic and Human Obesity Syndromes," *Physiology and Behavior* 17, no. 3 (1976): 461–71.

p. 16. Experiments with humans: J. M. de Castro, F. Bellisle, A. M. Dalix, and S. M. Pearcey, "Palatability and Intake Relationships in Free-Living Humans: Characterization and Independence of Influence in North Americans," *Physiology and Behavior* 70, no. 3–4 (2000): 343–50.

p. 16. Researchers at the National Institutes of Health: D. E. Larson, R. Rising, R. T. Ferraro, and E. Ravussin, "Spontaneous Overeating with a 'Cafeteria Diet' in Men: Effects on 24-Hour Energy Expenditure and Substrate Oxidation," *International Journal of Obesity and Related Metabolic Disorders* 19, no. 5 (1995): 331–7.

p. 18. Leading food consultant: Author interview with anonymous food consultant, August 12, 2004.

p. 22. Set point theory: R. E. Keesey and M. D. Hirvonen, "Body Weight Set-Points: Determination and Adjustment," *Journal of Nutrition* 127, no. 9 (1997): 1875S–83S.

p. 22. If the set point worked: A number of scientists have raised doubts about the set point theory. A body of research by David A. Levitsky, PhD, professor of psychology/nutritional sciences, Cornell University, shows that what we eat does not depend solely on signals sent by the brain to maintain a stable weight. For example, when study subjects were overfed—consuming 135 percent of what they had eaten during the baseline portion of the study and gaining weight in the process—they did not subsequently restrict their food intake enough to return to their baseline weight. D. A. Levitsky, E. Obarzanek, G. Mrdjenovic, and B. J. Strupp, "Imprecise Control of Energy Intake: Absence of a Reduction in Food Intake Following Overfeeding in Young Adults," *Physiology and Behavior* 84, no. 5 (2005): 669–75.

In another study, Levitsky found that preschool children "did not adjust the amount consumed in response to the energy density of the meal" and concluded that "the eating behavior of children is similar to adults in that they display very poor regulation of energy intake and are responsive to environmental stimuli." G. Mrdjenovic and D. A. Levitsky, "Children Eat What They Are Served: The Imprecise Regulation of Energy Intake," *Appetite* 44, no. 3 (2005): 273–82.

Other research suggesting limits to set point theory includes D. A. Levitsky, "Putting Behavior Back into Feeding Behavior: A Tribute to George Collier," *Appetite* 38, no. 2 (2002): 143–8; D. A. Levitsky, "The Non-Regulation of Food Intake in Humans: Hope for Reversing the Epidemic of Obesity," *Physiology and Behavior* 86, no. 5 (2005): 623–32. David Wirtshafter, PhD, professor, Departments of Psychology and Neuroscience, and John D. Davis, MD, at the Department of Psychiatry, both at the University of Illinois–Chicago, pointed out that the ability of rodents to gain weight prior to hibernation and of birds to store fat before they begin their migratory journeys raises doubts about the set point theory. D. Wirtshafter and J. D. Davis, "Set Points, Settling Points, and the Control of Body Weight," *Physiology and Behavior* 19, no. 1 (1977): 75–8.

Some biologists have proposed adjustments to make set point theory more persuasive. The "absence of protection" model suggests that obesity results from a system that was never designed to work in a world of limitless food—that we are more adept at defending body weight when too little food is available than at dealing with too much efficiently. One partial explanation may be that when leptin levels fall below a certain threshold, the body recognizes it as a signal to build up its storehouse of energy—but the opposite effect does not occur when leptin levels rise above that threshold. The "central resistance" model suggests that some people have biological imperfections that impede their ability to respond to the insulin and leptin signals designed to help them alter their food intake or energy expenditure. M. W. Schwartz and K. D. Niswender, "Adiposity Signaling and Biological Defense against Weight Gain: Absence of Protection or Central Hormone Resistance?" *Journal of Clinical Endocrinology and Metabolism* 89, no. 12 (2004): 5889–97.

p. 23. Settling point theory: John P. J. Pinel, *Biopsychology*, 6th ed. (Boston: Pearson Allyn and Bacon, 2007); D. Wirtshafter and J. D. Davis, "Set Points, Settling Points, and the Control of Body Weight," *Physiology and Behavior* 19, no. 1 (1977): 75–8.

p. 29. A substance reinforcing: For a discussion of reinforcement and self-administration, see Bankole A. Johnson and John D. Roache, *Drug Addiction and Its Treatment: Nexus of Neuroscience and Behavior* (Philadelphia: Lippincott-Raven, 1997).

p. 29. Choc and Crisp: M. F. Barbano and M. Cador, "Differential Regulation of the Consummatory, Motivational and Anticipatory Aspects of Feeding Behavior by Dopaminergic and Opioidergic Drugs," *Neuropsychopharmacology* 31, no. 7 (2006): 1371–81; M. F. Barbano and M. Cador, "Various Aspects of Feeding Behavior Can Be Partially Dissociated in the Rat by the Incentive Properties of Food and the Physiological State," *Behavioral Neuroscience* 119, no. 5 (2005): 1244–53. See also H. P. Weingarten, "Conditioned Cues Elicit Feeding in Sated Rats: A Role for Learning in Meal Initiation," *Science* 220, no. 4595 (1983): 431–3.

p. 30. Carleton University: K. Brennan, D. C. Roberts, H. Anisman, and Z. Merali, "Individual Differences in Sucrose Consumption in the Rat: Motivational and Neurochemical Correlates of Hedonia," *Psychopharmacology* 157, no. 3 (2001): 269–76.

p. 31. Sara Ward: Author interview with Sara Jane Ward, PhD, Department of Pharmaceutical Sciences, Temple University, May 19, 2006. S. J. Ward and L. A. Dykstra, "The Role of CB1 Receptors in Sweet Versus Fat Reinforcement: Effect of CB1 Receptor Deletion, CB1 Receptor Antagonism (Sr141716a) and CB1 Receptor Agonism (Cp-55940)," *Behavioural Pharmacology* 16, no. 5–6 (2005): 381–8.

p. 31. Vanilla milkshake: A. M. Naleid, J. W. Grimm, D. A. Kessler, A. J. Sipols, S. Aliakbari, J. L. Bennett, J. Wells, and D. P. Figlewicz, "Deconstructing the Vanilla Milkshake: The Dominant Effect of Sucrose on Self-Administration of Nutrient-Flavor Mixtures," *Appetite* 50, no. 1 (2008): 128–38. "In this study, we hypothesized that the complex mixture of corn oil, sucrose, and flavor is more reinforcing than any of these components alone. We observed a concentration-dependent increase in reinforcers of sucrose solutions received (0%, 3%, 6.25%, and 12.5%) in both fixed ratio and progressive ratio procedures, but with equicaloric corn oil solutions (0%, 1.4%, 2.8%, and 5.6%) this finding was replicated only in the fixed ratio procedure. Likewise, addition of 1.4% oil to 3% or 12.5% sucrose increased fixed ratio, but not progressive ratio, reinforcers received relative to those of sucrose alone. Finally, addition of 3% vanilla flavoring did not change self-administration of 3% sucrose or 3% sucrose plus 1.4% oil solutions."

For a study that suggests added sugar or salt in the diet increases fat intake, see P. M. Emmett and K. W. Heaton, "Is Extrinsic Sugar a Vehicle for Dietary Fat?" *Lancet* 345, no. 8964 (1995): 1537–40; and K. Kudo, T. Saito, Y. Sano, and T. Okuda, "Extrinsic Sugar as Vehicle for Dietary Fat," *Lancet* 346, no. 8976 (1995): 698.

p. 32. Visual cue gains power: For an early demonstration that conditioned cues can produce feeding in sated animals, see H. P. Weingarten, "Conditioned Cues Elicit Feeding in Sated Rats: A Role for Learning in Meal Initiation," *Science* 220, no. 4595 (1983): 431–3. Researchers Gorica Petrovich, Peter Holland, and Michela Gallagher showed that "cue-potentiated feeding depends on the integrity of neural fibers connecting the basolateral amygdala and lateral hypothalamus." G. D. Petrovich, P. C. Holland, and M. Gallagher, "Amygdala and Prefrontal Pathways to the Lateral Hypothalamus Are Activated by a Learned Cue That Stimulates Eating," *Journal of Neuroscience* 25, no. 36 (2005): 8295–302.

p. 32. Cycle of cue-urge-reward: R. A. Wise, "Brain Reward Circuitry: Insights from Unsensed Incentives," *Neuron* 36, no. 2 (2002): 229–40; R. A. Wise, "Dopamine and Food Reward: Back to the Elements," *American Journal of Physiology—Regulatory, Integrative and Comparative Physiology* 286, no. 1 (2004): R13; R. A. Wise, "Drug-Activation of Brain Reward Pathways," *Drug and Alcohol Dependence* 51, nos. 1–2 (1998): 13–22; R. A. Wise, "Forebrain Substrates of Reward and Motivation," *Journal of Comparative Neurology* 493, no. 1 (2005): 115–21; R. A. Wise, "The Parsing of Food Reward," *American Journal of Physiology—Regulatory, Integrative and Comparative Physiology* 291, no. 5 (2006): R1234–5; R. A. Wise, "Role of Brain Dopamine in Food Reward and Reinforcement," *Philosophical Transactions of the Royal Society of London. Series B: Biological Sciences* 361, no. 1471 (2006): 1149–58; N. D. Volkow and R. A. Wise, "How Can Drug Addiction Help Us Understand Obesity?" *Nature Neuroscience* 8, no. 5 (2005): 555–60.

p. 32. Conditioned place paradigm: Derek van der Kooy, "Place Conditioning: A Simple and Effective Method for Assessing the Motivational Properties of Drugs," in *Methods of Assessing the Reinforcing Properties of Abused Drugs*, ed. Michael A. Bozarth (New York: Springer-Verlag, 1987).

p. 32. Associate snack foods with location: P. A. Jarosz, P. Sekhon, and D. V. Coscina, "Effect of Opioid Antagonism on Conditioned Place Preferences to Snack Foods," *Pharmacology, Biochemistry and Behavior* 83, no. 2 (2006): 257–64.

p. 33. Three other features of food: Author interview with Frances K. McSweeney, PhD, Regents professor, Department of Psychology, Washington State University, June 2006; E. S. Murphy, F. K. McSweeney, R. G. Smith, and J. J. McComas, "Dynamic Changes in Reinforcer Effectiveness: Theoretical, Methodological, and Practical Implications for Applied Research," *Journal of Applied Behavior Analysis* 36, no. 4 (2003): 421–38.

p. 35. Encoded for palatability: Author interviews with Howard L. Fields, MD, PhD, director, Wheeler Center for the Neurobiology of Addiction, University of California, San Francisco, August 27, 2004, and May 12, 2006; S. A. Taha and H. L. Fields, "Inhibitions of Nucleus Accumbens Neurons Encode a Gating Signal for Reward-Directed Behavior," *Journal of Neuroscience* 26, no. 1

(2006): 217–22; S. A. Taha, S. M. Nicola, and H. L. Fields, "Cue-Evoked Encoding of Movement Planning and Execution in the Rat Nucleus Accumbens," *Journal of Physiology* 584, pt. 3 (2007): 801–18; S. A. Taha, E. Norsted, L. S. Lee, P. D. Lang, B. S. Lee, J. D. Wooley, and H. L. Fields, "Endogenous Opioids Encode Relative Taste Preference," *European Journal of Neuroscience* 24, no. 4 (2006): 1220–6.

p. 36. Single cell: Author interview with Edmund T. Rolls, professor, Experimental Psychology, University of Oxford, England, September 26, 2005; E. T. Rolls, "Brain Mechanisms Underlying Flavour and Appetite," *Philosophical Transactions of the Royal Society of London. Series B: Biological Sciences* 361, no. 1471 (2006): 1123–36; Edmund T. Rolls, *The Brain and Emotion* (Oxford: Oxford University Press, 1999); Edmund T. Rolls, *Emotion Explained*, Series in Affective Science (New York: Oxford University Press, 2005); E. T. Rolls, "Taste, Olfactory, and Food Texture Processing in the Brain, and the Control of Food Intake," *Physiology and Behavior* 85, no. 1 (2005): 45–56; I. E. de Araujo, E. T. Rolls, M. L. Kringelbach, F. McGlone, and N. Phillips, "Taste-Olfactory Convergence, and the Representation of the Pleasantness of Flavour, in the Human Brain," *European Journal of Neuroscience* 18, no. 7 (2003): 2059–68.

p. 36. Just one of the senses: taste: Taste has "acute emotional primacy. . . . Reward value appears to be a fundamental dimension of gustatory sensation." A. K. Anderson and N. Sobel, "Dissociating Intensity from Valence as Sensory Inputs to Emotion," *Neuron* 39, no. 4 (2003): 581–3.

p. 37. Orosensory self-stimulation: Author interview with Gerard P. Smith, MD, Professor Emeritus of Psychiatry, Department of Psychiatry, Joan and Sanford I. Weill Medical College of Cornell University, July 20, 2006; Gerard P. Smith, "Accumbens Dopamine Is a Physiological Correlate of the Rewarding and Motivating Effects of Food," in *Neurobiology of Food and Fluid Intake*, 2nd ed., Handbook of Behavioral Neurobiology, ed. E. Stricker and Stephen C. Woods (New York: Kluwer Academic/Plenum, 2004); G. P. Smith, "Accumbens Dopamine Mediates the Rewarding Effect of Orosensory Stimulation by Sucrose," *Appetite* 43, no. 1 (2004): 11–3.

p. 37. Relieve pain or stress: P. S. Grigson, "Like Drugs for Chocolate: Separate Rewards Modulated by Common Mechanisms?" *Physiology and Behavior* 76, no. 3 (2002): 389–95; E. Blass, E. Fitzgerald, and P. Kehoe, "Interactions between Sucrose, Pain and Isolation Distress," *Pharmacology, Biochemistry and Behavior* 26, no. 3 (1987): 483–9; E. M. Blass and L. B. Hoffmeyer, "Sucrose as an Analgesic for Newborn Infants," *Pediatrics* 87, no. 2 (1991): 215–8; E. M. Blass and A. Shah, "Pain-Reducing Properties of Sucrose in Human Newborns," *Chemical Senses* 20, no. 1 (1995): 29–35; E. M. Blass and D. J. Shide, "Some Comparisons among the Calming and Pain-Relieving Effects of Sucrose, Glucose, Fructose and Lactose in Infant Rats," *Chemical Senses* 19, no. 3 (1994): 239–49; E. M. Blass and L. B. Watt, "Suckling- and Sucrose-Induced Analgesia in Human Newborns," *Pain* 83, no. 3 (1999): 611–23; M. Fernandez, E. M. Blass, M. Hernandez-Reif, T. Field, M. Diego, and C. Sanders, "Sucrose Attenuates a Negative Electroencephalographic Response to an Aversive Stimulus for Newborns," *Journal of Developmental and Behavioral Pediatrics* 24, no. 4 (2003): 261–6; G. E. Kaufman, S. Cimo, L. W. Miller, and E. M. Blass, "An Evaluation of the Effects of Sucrose on Neonatal Pain with 2 Commonly Used Circumcision Methods," *American Journal of Obstetrics and Gynecology* 186, no. 3 (2002): 564–8.

p. 38. Activates the opioid circuits: L. A. Parker, S. Maier, M. Rennie, and J. Crebolder, "Morphine- and Naltrexone-Induced Modification of Palatability: Analysis by the Taste Reactivity Test," *Behavioral Neuroscience* 106, no. 6 (1992): 999–1010; T. G. Doyle, K. C. Berridge, and B. A. Gosnell, "Morphine Enhances Hedonic Taste Palatability in Rats," *Pharmacology, Biochemistry and Behavior* 46, no. 3 (1993): 745–9; S. Pecina and K. C. Berridge, "Opioid Site in Nucleus Accumbens Shell Mediates Eating and Hedonic 'Liking' for Food: Map Based on Microinjection Fos Plumes," *Brain Research* 863, nos. 1–2 (2000): 71–86; A. E. Kelley, V. P. Bakshi, S. N. Haber, T. L. Steininger, M. J. Will, and M. Zhang, "Opioid Modulation of Taste Hedonics within the Ventral Striatum," *Physiology and Behavior* 76, no. 3 (2002): 365–77; M. Fantino, J. Hosotte, and M. Apfelbaum, "An Opioid Antagonist, Naltrexone, Reduces Preference for Sucrose in Humans," *American Journal of Physiology* 251, no. 1, pt. 2 (1986): R91–6; A. Drewnowski, D. D. Krahn, M. A. Demitrack, K. Nairn, and B. A. Gosnell, "Naloxone, an Opiate Blocker, Reduces the Consumption of Sweet High-Fat Foods in Obese and Lean Female Binge Eaters," *American Journal of Clinical Nutrition* 61, no. 6 (1995): 1206–12.

p. 38. Keep on eating: "The opioids are acting against the normal satiety mechanism," said Howard Fields. Author interview with Howard L. Fields, MD, PhD, director, Wheeler Center for the Neurobiology of Addiction, University of California, San Francisco, August 27, 2004.

p. 38. Supreme Mini-Treats: Author interview with Josh Wooley, MD, PhD, Center for Obesity Assessment, Study and Treatment, University of California, San Francisco, September 29, 2006; J. D. Wooley, B. S. Lee, S. A. Taha, and H. L. Fields, "Nucleus Accumbens Opioid Signaling Conditions Short-Term Flavor Preferences," *Neuroscience* 146, no. 1 (2007): 19–30.

p. 39. Opioid antagonists: M. J. Glass, E. O'Hare, J. P. Cleary, C. J. Billington, and A. S. Levine, "The Effect of Naloxone on Food-Motivated Behavior in the Obese Zucker Rat," *Psychopharmacology* 141, no. 4 (1999): 378–84.

p. 40. Hedonic hot spot: The signals of liking in response to sucrose are typically visible and audible. A rat licks its paws and moves its tongue in a distinctive fashion, an infant communicates pleasure with facial expressions, and an adult can use words. Using "Fos plumes," Kent Berridge and his colleagues at the University of Michigan were the first to map the area of the brain that appears to be the wellspring of that pleasure. Acting much as food coloring does immediately after it is dropped into a glass of water, Fos plumes can identify receptors in the brain that have been activated by an opioid injection. The Fos plumes showed that while nearly all regions of the medial shell recorded an increase in food intake following opioid stimulation, increased liking was limited to a much more restricted site of just one cubic millimeter. Author interview with Kent C. Berridge, PhD, professor, Biopsychology Program, University of Michigan, July 6, 2006. S. Pecina and K. C. Berridge, "Hedonic Hot Spot in Nucleus Accumbens Shell: Where Do Mu-Opioids Cause Increased Hedonic Impact of Sweetness?" *Journal of Neuroscience* 25, no. 50 (2005): 11777–86.

p. 41. Pursuit-and-acquisition behaviors: Dopamine plays a role not only in our pursuit of food, but in our pursuit of love, promoting and sustaining bonding in many species of animals. For example, among prairie voles, rodents that form monogamous attachments, dopamine levels increase by about 50 percent in the first 15 minutes after sexual activity. Research also shows that fully pair-bonded male voles have substantially more dopamine receptors in the nucleus accumbens, an important tool for enduring attachment. And scientists can show that blocking dopamine prevents initial partner preference from forming and ends the animal's aggressive behavior toward females who might be competing for the role of mate. B. Gingrich et al., "Dopamine D2 Receptors in the Nucleus Accumbens Are Important for Social Attachment in Female Prairie Voles," *Behavioral Neuroscience* 114, no. 1 (2000): 173–83; B. J. Aragona et al., "Nucleus Accumbens Dopamine Differentially Mediates the Formation and Maintenance of Monogamous Pair Bonds," *Nature Neuroscience* 9 (2005): 133–9.

Human beings in the throes of an early and euphoric romance are also affected by the stimulating effect of dopamine. With an angled mirror placed just outside a magnetic resonance imaging (MRI) machine, participants were able to see photographs of people they loved as they underwent MRI scans. The study subjects then looked at photographs of emotionally neutral acquaintances of the same age and gender. The comparative findings were clear: The regions of the brain known to be rich in dopamine were significantly more active when the participants looked at photos of those they loved. A. Aron, "Reward, Motivation and Emotion Systems Associated with Early-Stage Intense Romantic Love," *Journal of Neurophysiology* 94 (2005): 327–37; I. H. Franken, "The Role of Dopamine in Human Addiction: From Reward to Motivated Attention," *European Journal of Pharmacology* 526, nos. 1–3 (2005): 199–206.

p. 41. Attentional bias: Marcus Munafò and I. Albery, *Cognition and Addiction* (New York: Oxford University Press, 2006); Reinout Willem Henry Jon Wiers and Alan W. Stacy, *Handbook of Implicit Cognition and Addiction* (Thousand Oaks, CA: Sage, 2006); James A. Coan and John J. B. Allen, *Handbook of Emotion Elicitation and Assessment*, Series in Affective Science (Oxford: Oxford University Press, 2007); Adrian Wells and Gerald Matthews, *Attention and Emotion: A Clinical Perspective* (Hove, UK: L. Erlbaum, 1994).

p. 41. John Salamone: Author interview with John D. Salamone, PhD, professor, Division of Behavioral Neuroscience, Department of Psychology, University of Connecticut, June 29, 2006; M. S. Cousins, A. Atherton, L. Turner, and J. D. Salamone, "Nucleus Accumbens Dopamine Depletions Alter Relative Response Allocation in a T-Maze Cost/Benefit Task," *Behavioural Brain Research* 74, no. 1–2 (1996): 189–97; J. D. Salamone, "Functions of Mesolimbic Dopamine: Changing Concepts and Shifting Paradigms," *Psychopharmacology* 191, no. 3 (2007): 389; J. D. Salamone, M. Correa, S. Mingote, and S. M. Weber, "Nucleus Accumbens Dopamine and the Regulation of Effort in Food-Seeking Behavior: Implications for Studies of Natural Motivation, Psychiatry, and Drug Abuse," *Journal of Pharmacology and Experimental Therapeutics* 305, no. 1 (2003): 1–8; J. D. Salamone, "Will the Last Person Who Uses the Term 'Reward' Please Turn out the Lights? Comments on Processes Related to Reinforcement, Learning, Motivation and Effort," *Addiction Biology* 11, no. 1 (2006): 43–4. For additional research on the relationship between dopamine and highly palatable food, see P. Martel and M. Fantino, "Mesolimbic Dopaminergic System Activity as a Function of Food Reward: A Microdialysis Study," *Pharmacology, Biochemistry and Behavior* 53, no. 1 (1996): 221–6. On the role of dopamine in reward, see I. H. Franken, J. Booij, and W. van den Brink, "The Role of Dopamine in Human Addiction: From Reward to Motivated Attention," *European Journal of Pharmacology* 526, no. 1–3 (2005): 199–206.

p. 41. Two chambers: Author interview with Howard L. Fields, MD, PhD, director, Wheeler Center for the Neurobiology of Addiction, University of California, San Francisco, August 27, 2004; S. A. Taha and H. L. Fields, "Encoding of Palatability and Appetitive Behaviors by Distinct Neuronal Populations in the Nucleus Accumbens," *Journal of Neuroscience* 25, no. 5 (2005): 1193–202.

p. 41. Oystercatcher: N. Tinbergen, "Social Releasers and the Experimental Methods Required for Their Study," *Wilson Bulletin* 60 (1948): 6–51; Nikolaas Tinbergen, *The Study of Instinct* (Oxford, UK: Clarendon Press, 1951).

p. 41. Uncovered much the same thing: N. Tinbergen and A. C. Perdeck, "On the Stimulus Situation Releasing the Begging Response in the Newly Hatched Herring Gull Chick (*Larus a. argentatus*)," *Behaviour* 3 (1951): 1–38. Tinbergen also conducted research with the greylag goose. The research on butterflies is described in D. Magnus, "Experimentelle Untersuchungen zur Bionomie und Ethologie des Kaisermantels *Argynnis paphin L.* (Lep. Nymph)," *Zeitschrift für Tierpsychologie* 15 (1958): 397–426. This study is described and cited in J. E. R. Staddon, "Note on Evolutionary Significance of Supernormal Stimuli," *American Naturalist* 109, no. 969 (1975): 541–5.

p. 44. Supernormal stimuli: Author interview with John E. R. Staddon, PhD, James B. Duke Professor of Psychological and Brain Sciences and Professor of Biology and Neurobioogy, Duke University, August 7, 2006; J. E. R. Staddon, "Note on Evolutionary Significance of Supernormal Stimuli," *American Naturalist* 109, no. 969 (1975): 541–5.

p. 44. Contemporary writers and scientists: Deirdre Barrett, *Waistland: The (R)Evolutionary Science Behind Our Weight and Fitness Crisis* (New York: W.W. Norton & Co., 2007); Steven Witherly, "Food Pleasure: Principles & Practices, Technical Products," naffs.mytradeassociation.org/prn_witherly.pdf. I first became aware of the concept of supernormal stimuli when viewing Witherly's presentation.

p. 47. Panera's cinnamon crunch bagel: According to the company's Web site, here are the ingredients in this bagel: unbleached enriched flour (wheat flour, malted barley flour, niacin, reduced iron, thiamine mononitrate, riboflavin, folic acid), water, white flavored drops (sugar, partially hydrogenated palm kernel oil, whey powder, nonfat dry milk solids, natural flavor, soy lecithin [emulsifier]), cinnamon drops (sugar, palm oil, cinnamon, nonfat dry milk, soy lecithin as an emulsifier), bagel base (sugar, salt, malt barley flour, contains 2 percent or less of: molasses, mono and diglycerides, ascorbic acid, L-cysteine, azodicarbonamide [ADA], enzyme, ammonium chloride), honey, vanilla drops (vanilla, water, propylene glycol, alcohol, artificial flavors and caramel color), brown sugar, yeast, shortening (palm oil), topping (sugar, cinnamon, modified food starch, soybean oil). The bagel has 420 calories and 30 percent of the saturated fat daily value.

p. 48. Ultimate food carnival: T.G.I. Friday's television commercial and Web site (www.tgifridays.com), accessed January 2008.

p. 49. Complexity of the stimulus: "We are built to appreciate complex stimuli," said Andy Taylor, professor of flavour technology at the University of Nottingham, England. "I think our brains like to be stimulated. They like to have complex things to decode." Taylor uses functional MRI to analyze the individual signals sent by particular tastes and odors, and to show how these are amplified by simultaneous sensory exposure. He calls these "maps"—areas in the brain where stimuli are registered. These patterns are typically formed in childhood, with our early exposure to food. Different flavors create different maps, or neural signatures. For example, there is one map for strawberry flavor, another for cherry flavor, and still another for the combination of strawberry plus sugar. These maps become imprinted in memory.

p. 49. Gaetano Di Chiara: Author interview with Gaetano Di Chiara, MD, Department of Toxicology and Centre for Neuropharmacology, University of Cagliari, Italy, August 13, 2006; V. Bassareo, M. A. De Luca, M. Aresu, A. Aste, T. Ariu, and G. Di Chiara, "Differential Adaptive Properties of Accumbens Shell Dopamine Responses to Ethanol as a Drug and as a Motivational Stimulus," *European Journal of Neuroscience* 17, no. 7 (2003): 1465–72; V. Bassareo, M. A. De Luca, and G. Di Chiara, "Differential Impact of Pavlovian Drug Conditioned Stimuli on In Vivo Dopamine Transmission in the Rat Accumbens Shell and Core and in the Prefrontal Cortex," *Psychopharmacology* 191, no. 3 (2007): 689–703; V. Bassareo and G. Di Chiara, "Differential Influence of Associative and Nonassociative Learning Mechanisms on the Responsiveness of Prefrontal and Accumbal Dopamine Transmission to Food Stimuli in Rats Fed Ad Libitum," *Journal of Neuroscience* 17, no. 2 (1997): 851–61; G. Di Chiara and V. Bassareo, "Reward System and Addiction: What Dopamine Does and Doesn't Do," *Current Opinion in Pharmacology* 7, no. 1 (2007): 69–76; G. Di Chiara, V. Bassareo, S. Fenu, M. A. De Luca, L. Spina, C. Cadoni, E. Acquas, E. Carboni, V. Valentini, and D. Lecca, "Dopamine and Drug Addiction: The Nucleus Accumbens Shell Connection," *Neuropharmacology* 47 Suppl 1 (2004): 227–41; G. Di Chiara, G. Tanda, V. Bassareo, F. Pontieri, E. Acquas, S. Fenu, C. Cadoni, and E. Carboni, "Drug Addiction as a Disorder of Associative Learning: Role of Nucleus Accumbens Shell/Extended Amygdala Dopamine," *Annals of the New York Academy of Sciences* 877 (1999): 461–85; G. Di Chiara, G. Tanda, C. Cadoni, E. Acquas, V. Bassareo, and E. Carboni, "Homologies and Differences in the Action of Drugs of Abuse and a Conventional Reinforcer (Food) on Dopamine Transmission: An Interpretative Framework of the Mechanism of Drug Dependence," *Advances in Pharmacology* 42 (1998): 983–7.

p. 49. Excitement in the brain: Author interview with Edmund T. Rolls, professor, Experimental Psychology, University of Oxford, England, September 26, 2005; author interview with Frances K. McSweeney, Regents professor, Department of Psychology, Washington State University, June 2006; M. L. Kringelbach, "Food for Thought: Hedonic Experience Beyond Homeostasis in the Human Brain," *Neuroscience* 126, no. 4 (2004): 807–19; E. T. Rolls, "Taste, Olfactory, and Food Texture Processing in the Brain, and the Control of Food Intake," *Physiology and Behavior* 85, no. 1 (2005): 45–56; I. E. de Araujo, E. T. Rolls, M. L. Kringelbach, F. McGlone, and N. Phillips, "Taste-Olfactory Convergence, and the Representation of the Pleasantness of Flavour, in the Human Brain," *European Journal of Neuroscience* 18, no. 7 (2003): 2059–68.

p. 49. Multimodal stimuli: Dana M. Small, PhD, Associate Fellow at the John B. Pierce Laboratory, a Yale University affiliate, has devoted her career to understanding how we encode sensory information in the brain. She explained what happens when we eat a banana split. After journeys along separate pathways, the taste signals that originate in the taste buds and the odor signals originating in the olfactory bulb converge on the insula, where their sensory signals are integrated by newly created neural circuits.

As a result, when we are next exposed to a banana split, it will not be necessary both to smell and taste it in order to stimulate both senses. "If you have two
cells that fire together in time and space, the connections between those can be
strengthened," explained Small. "One cell can gain the ability to cause the other
cell to fire." Once we have experience with a banana split, we can perceive its
sweetness just by smelling it. The olfactory system activates the taste system,
"giving rise to a taste sensation in the absence of the gustatory stimulus."

The response is superadditive—that is, the effect of two sensory stimulants
is greater than the total of each one independently. "This is neural integration
occurring, and this is a hallmark of multisensory integration," said Small. "One
system is helping out another system and benefiting performance."

Author interviews with Dana Small, December 14, 2005, December 21, 2006,
and November 13, 2006; Dana Small presentation at the Fifth International Conference on Neuroesthetics (University of California, Berkeley, January 21, 2006).
See also D. M. Small and J. Prescott, "Odor/Taste Integration and the Perception
of Flavor," *Experimental Brain Research* 166, nos. 3–4 (2005): 345–57; D. M. Small,
R. J. Zatorre, A. Dagher, A. C. Evans, and M. Jones-Gotman, "Changes in Brain
Activity Related to Eating Chocolate: From Pleasure to Aversion," *Brain* 124, no.
9 (2001): 1720–33; D. M. Small, G. Bender, M. G. Veldhuizen, K. Rudenga, D.
Nachtigal, and J. Felsted, "The Role of the Human Orbitofrontal Cortex in Taste
and Flavor Processing," *Annals of the New York Academy of Sciences* 1121 (2007):
136–51; R. J. Hyde and S. A. Witherly, "Dynamic Contrast: A Sensory Contribution to Palatability," *Appetite* 21, no. 1 (1993): 1–16.

p. 51. Conditioning can happen quickly: L. C. Haverkort and A. Prakken, "Het
aanleren en afleren van 'trek in iets zoetigs' door middel van klassieke condi-
tionering" [Learning and extinction of 'appetite for something sweet' by means
of classical conditioning], MSc thesis, Department of Human Nutrition,
Wageningen University, Wageningen, Netherlands, 1992. This study is
described and cited in Cees de Graaf, "Research Review: Effects of Snacks on
Energy Intake: An Evolutionary Perspective," *Appetite* 47 (2006): 18–23.

p. 51. Spikes in dopamine activity: W. Schultz, P. Apicella, E. Scarnati, and T.
Ljungberg, "Neuronal Activity in Monkey Ventral Striatum Related to the
Expectation of Reward," *Journal of Neuroscience* 12, no. 12 (1992): 4595–610; W.
Schultz, P. Dayan, and P. R. Montague, "A Neural Substrate of Prediction and
Reward," *Science* 275, no. 5306 (1997): 1593–9; W. Schultz, "Reward Signals,"
Scholarpedia, scholarpedia.org/article/Reward_signals, modified May 20, 2008;
W. Schultz, "Behavioral Theories and the Neurophysiology of Reward," *Annual
Review of Psychology* 57 (2006): 87–115; S. E. Hyman, "Addiction: A Disease of
Learning and Memory," *American Journal of Psychiatry* 162, no. 8 (2005):
1414–22.

p. 51. Regina Carelli: Author interview with Regina M. Carelli, PhD, director of
the Behavioral Neuroscience Program, University of North Carolina–Chapel
Hill, July 10, 2006; M. F. Roitman, G. D. Stuber, P. E. Phillips, R. M. Wightman, and R. M. Carelli, "Dopamine Operates as a Subsecond Modulator of
Food Seeking," *Journal of Neuroscience* 24, no. 6 (2004): 1265–71; R. A. Wheeler
and R. M. Carelli, "Dissecting Motivational Circuitry to Understand Substance
Abuse," *Neuropharmacology* (2008); R. M. Wightman, M. L. Heien, K. M. Was-
sum, L. A. Sombers, B. J. Aragona, A. S. Khan, J. L. Ariansen, J. F. Cheer, P. E.
Phillips, and R. M. Carelli, "Dopamine Release Is Heterogeneous within

Microenvironments of the Rat Nucleus Accumbens," *European Journal of Neuroscience* 26, no. 7 (2007): 2046–54.

p. 52. Incentive salience: Author interview with Kent C. Berridge, PhD, professor, Biopsychology Program, University of Michigan, September 21, 2005; K. C. Berridge, "The Debate over Dopamine's Role in Reward: The Case for Incentive Salience," *Psychopharmacology* 191, no. 3 (2007): 391–431; K. C. Berridge, "Espresso Reward Learning, Hold the Dopamine: Theoretical Comment on Robinson et al. (2005)," *Behavioral Neuroscience* 119, no. 1 (2005): 336-41; K. C. Berridge, "Food Reward: Brain Substrates of Wanting and Liking," *Neuroscience and Biobehavioral Reviews* 20, no. 1 (1996): 1–25; K. C. Berridge, "Measuring Hedonic Impact in Animals and Infants: Microstructure of Affective Taste Reactivity Patterns," *Neuroscience and Biobehavioral Reviews* 24, no. 2 (2000): 173–98; K. C. Berridge, "Motivation Concepts in Behavioral Neuroscience," *Physiology and Behavior* 81, no. 2 (2004): 179–209; K. C. Berridge and M. L. Kringelbach, "Affective Neuroscience of Pleasure: Reward in Humans and Animals," *Psychopharmacology* 199, no. 3 (2008): 457–80; K. C. Berridge and T. E. Robinson, "Parsing Reward," *Trends in Neurosciences* 26, no. 9 (2003): 507–13; K. C. Berridge, "What Is the Role of Dopamine in Reward: Hedonic Impact, Reward Learning, or Incentive Salience?" *Brain Research Reviews* 28, no. 3 (1998): 309–69; T. E. Robinson and K. C. Berridge, "The Psychology and Neurobiology of Addiction: An Incentive-Sensitization View," *Addiction* 95 Suppl 2 (2000): S91–117; K. C. Berridge, "The Incentive Sensitization Theory of Addiction: Some Current Issues," *Philosophical Transactions of the Royal Society of London. Series B: Biological Sciences* 363, no. 1507 (2008): 3137–46.

p. 53. Proceed to completion: Steven E. Hyman, MD, "Neuroscience and the Challenge of Undoing Addiction" (presentation at "On Addiction," Picower Institute for Learning and Memory symposium, Boston, Massachusetts, May 2006).

p. 55. Lodged in our memory: Literature's most vivid example of the capacity of highly palatable foods to evoke powerful memories may be Marcel Proust's description of a taste of a tea-soaked madeleine: "No sooner had the warm liquid, and the crumbs with it, touched my palate, than a shudder ran through my whole body, and I stopped, intent upon the extraordinary changes that were taking place. . . . And once I had recognized the taste of the crumb of madeleine soaked in her decoction of lime-flowers which my aunt used to give me . . . immediately the old grey house upon the street, where her room was, rose up like the scenery of a theater." Marcel Proust, *Swann's Way*, 2 vols., trans. C. K. Scott-Moncrieff (New York: Holt, 1922).

p. 56. Hot stimulus: Author interview with Walter Mischel, PhD, Robert Johnston Niven Professor of Humane Letters in Psychology, Columbia University, April 4, 2007; J. Metcalfe and W. Mischel, "A Hot/Cool-System Analysis of Delay of Gratification: Dynamics of Willpower," *Psychological Review* 106, no. 1 (1999): 3–19.

p. 56. Potency of memory: B. C. Wittmann, B. H. Schott, S. Guderian, J. U. Frey, H. J. Heinze, and E. Duzel, "Reward-Related fMRI Activation of Dopaminergic Midbrain Is Associated with Enhanced Hippocampus-Dependent Long-Term Memory Formation," *Neuron* 45, no. 3 (2005): 459–67.

p. 56. Reward circuits can whisper: B. Knutson and R. A. Adcock, "Remembrance of Rewards Past," *Neuron* 45, no. 3 (2005): 331–2.

p. 57. Conjure up a memory: Author interview with Marcia Pelchat, PhD, associate member, Monell Chemical Senses Center, January 31, 2007.

p. 58. Homeostasis does not tolerate excesses: Author interview with Andras Hajnal, MD, PhD, associate professor, Neural and Behavioral Sciences, Penn State Milton S. Hershey Medical Center, August 25, 2006.

p. 59. Continued and intermittent exposure: Our studies on dopamine release revealed several findings: Highly palatable meals may retain their stimulating effects on the reward system for an extended period; dopamine release during intermittent and restricted consumption of these highly palatable meals was significantly higher than in response to less-palatable chow, suggesting habituation is inhibited with rewarding foods; and less palatable meals are less stimulating to the reward system when more-palatable meals are available. A. Hajnal, J. E. Nyland, E. Amderzhanova, N. K. Acharya, D. A. Kessler, "Chronic Intermittent Access to Highly Palatable Diets Results in Sustained and Augmented Accumbens Dopamine Release and Abolished Response to Regular Chow Compared to Continuous Availability," abstract, *Society for Neuroscience*, Washington, DC, 2008.

p. 59. Overcoming habituation. Author interview with Andras Hajnal, MD, PhD, associate professor, Neural and Behavioral Sciences, Penn State Milton S. Hershey Medical Center, August 25, 2006; A. Hajnal and R. Norgren, "Accumbens Dopamine Mechanisms in Sucrose Intake," *Brain Research* 904, no. 1 (2001): 76–84; A. Hajnal, "Repeated Access to Sucrose Augments Dopamine Turnover in the Nucleus Accumbens," *Neuroreport* 13, no. 17 (2002): 2213–6; A. Hajnal, G. P. Smith, and R. Norgren, "Oral Sucrose Stimulation Increases Accumbens Dopamine in the Rat," *American Journal of Physiology—Regulatory, Integrative and Comparative Physiology* 286, no. 1 (2004): R31–7; R. Norgren, A. Hajnal, and S. S. Mungarndee, "Gustatory Reward and the Nucleus Accumbens," *Physiology and Behavior* 89, no. 4 (2006): 531–5.

p. 60. Functional connectivity: Author interview with Craig A. Schiltz, PhD, Department of the Neuroscience Training Program, University of Wisconsin–Madison, August 28, 2006. Working in the neuroscience laboratory of the late Ann E. Kelley, PhD, Craig Schiltz moved two groups of rats from their home cages into two different environments (Context A and Context B), distinguished by their unique sensory cues—they smelled, looked, and felt different. One group of rats was given chocolate Ensure in Context A and water in Context B; the second group was fed on the opposite schedule (water in Context A, Ensure in Context B). After 15 days, the animals were returned to their home cages for three days, and then returned to Context A, but, this time, neither Ensure nor water was available there.

The animals that had previously been exposed to Ensure in Context A moved around significantly more than those that had been exposed to water, presumably because they were expecting to get Ensure again. They also had higher levels of corticosterone, a hormone associated with stress, most likely because they were frustrated at not gaining access to the food they had learned to associate with Context A. Researchers also measured elevated activity in certain genes linked to context, learning, and memory and detected significantly reorganized patterns of interconnected activity among Ensure-exposed rats. "If the changes in gene expression are correlated between regions, it is more likely that the activity in those regions is correlated also," said Schiltz.

The bottom line was that animals exposed to Ensure in Context A were more responsive to that environment even when the food was gone. The cues alone had taken on the power to activate the brain. C. A. Schiltz, Q. Z. Bremer, C. F. Landry, and A. E. Kelley, "Food-Associated Cues Alter Forebrain Functional Connectivity as Assessed with Immediate Early Gene and Proenkephalin Expression," *BMC Biology* 5 (2007): 16.

p. 60. Rewiring our brains: Over the past few years, researchers have identified a number of other significant changes in the brain that occur with long-term intake of highly palatable foods. The late Ann E. Kelley, PhD, Distinguished Neuroscience Professor, Department of Psychiatry, University of Wisconsin, noted that "chronic exposure seems to change certain elements of at least the opioid system and probably other systems as well . . . enkephalin MRNA is lowered . . . proenkephalin gene expression is reduced . . . " Author interview with Ann Kelley, August 15, 2006; A. E. Kelley, M. J. Will, T. L. Steininger, M. Zhang, and S. N. Haber, "Restricted Daily Consumption of a Highly Palatable Food (Chocolate Ensure®) Alters Striatal Enkephalin Gene Expression," *European Journal of Neuroscience* 18, no. 9 (2003): 2592–8.

The most pronounced effects of highly palatable foods seem to occur when the food is given to experimental animals at the same time every day. For example, rats given a 25 percent sucrose solution showed significant increase in dopamine D-1 receptor binding in the core and shell of the nucleus accumbens, compared to chow-fed animals. The study also revealed decreased D-2 binding in the dorsal striatum, as well as effects in the midbrain, cortex, hippocampus, and elsewhere. C. Colantuoni, J. Schwenker, J. McCarthy, P. Rada, B. Ladenheim, J. L. Cadet, G. J. Schwartz, T. H. Moran, and B. G. Hoebel, "Excessive Sugar Intake Alters Binding to Dopamine and Mu-Opioid Receptors in the Brain," *Neuroreport* 12, no. 16 (2001): 3549–52.

The effects of intermittency are also notable. After administering a 10 percent sucrose solution on a 12-hours-on, 12-hours-off schedule for three weeks, researchers detected significant changes in the gene expression of study animals. Specifically, opioid "mRNA levels for the D2 dopamine receptor and the preproenkephalin and preprotachykinin genes were decreased in dopamine receptive regions of the forebrain, while D3 dopamine receptor mRNA was increased." R. Spangler, K. M. Wittkowski, N. L. Goddard, N. M. Avena, B. G. Hoebel, and S. F. Leibowitz, "Opiate-Like Effects of Sugar on Gene Expression in Reward Areas of the Rat Brain," *Molecular Brain Research* 124, no. 2 (2004): 134–42. Also, "intermittent access to a sucrose solution leads to higher dopamine membrane transporter binding in the nucleus accumbens and ventral tegmental areas." N. T. Bello, K. L. Sweigart, J. M. Lakoski, R. Norgren, and A. Hajnal, "Restricted Feeding with Scheduled Sucrose Access Results in an Upregulation of the Rat Dopamine Transporter," *American Journal of Physiology—Regulatory, Integrative and Comparative Physiology* 284, no. 5 (2003): R1260–8.

Highly palatable foods also delay the release of acetylcholine (ACh), a neurotransmitter that reaches peak levels at the end of a meal, especially when animals are fed intermittently, which may allow animals to binge. P. Rada, N. M. Avena, and B. G. Hoebel, "Daily Bingeing on Sugar Repeatedly Releases Dopamine in the Accumbens Shell," *Neuroscience* 134, no. 3 (2005): 737–44.

One unanswered question is whether chronic exposure to highly palatable food results in "sensitization" or simply conditioning and learning in the brain.

Sensitization—defined as an "augmentation of a behavior in response to the repeated administration of a substance"—is a well-known drug effect. Rats given ten equal doses of amphetamines, at the rate of one per day, became more active on the tenth day than they had been on the first, said Kent Berridge. Author interview with Kent C. Berridge, PhD, professor, Biopsychology Program, University of Michigan, September 21, 2005.

Exposure, followed by deprivation, seems to have the strongest sensitization effects. One team of scientists concluded that repeatedly subjecting rats to the intoxicating effects of alcohol, and then withdrawing access, ultimately induced "marked and long-lasting voluntary ethanol consumption." R. Rimondini, C. Arlinde, W. Sommer, and M. Heilig, "Long-Lasting Increase in Voluntary Ethanol Consumption and Transcriptional Regulation in the Rat Brain after Intermittent Exposure to Alcohol," *FASEB Journal* 16, no. 1 (2002): 27–35. Intermittent exposure to amphetamines seems to have a comparable effect, according to an author interview with Bart Hoebel, PhD, professor, Department of Psychology, Princeton University, August 13, 2004.

The theory that the same thing might hold true for sugar is much more recent. In one study, Hoebel's research team gave two groups of rats access to a 25 percent glucose solution for 30 minutes a day, for 28 days. Half of those animals also had ready access to glucose in their cages for an additional 11½ hours. After the initial four-week trial period, both groups spent two more weeks without any glucose at all and then the 30-minute daily dose of glucose was reinstated. The results: The rats initially given access to sucrose 12 hours a day consumed significantly more after the abstinence period than those that had initially consumed it for only 30 minutes. N. M. Avena, K. A. Long, and B. G. Hoebel, "Sugar-Dependent Rats Show Enhanced Responding for Sugar after Abstinence: Evidence of a Sugar Deprivation Effect," *Physiology and Behavior* 84, no. 3 (2005): 359–62.

Other research shows that once an animal has been sensitized to one drug, it is likely to be sensitized to others—for example, the effects of amphetamines will be greater on an animal that has become more responsive to cocaine. And animals cycling between periods of food deprivation and unrestricted access to a sucrose-and-chow combination were strikingly more active in response to a low dose of amphetamines than a variety of comparison groups. "Sugar and amphetamine may be working via the same neural systems." N. M. Avena and B. G. Hoebel, "Amphetamine-Sensitized Rats Show Sugar-Induced Hyperactivity (Cross-Sensitization) and Sugar Hyperphagia," *Pharmacology, Biochemistry and Behavior* 74, no. 3 (2003): 635–9.

See also N. M. Avena and B. G. Hoebel, "A Diet Promoting Sugar Dependency Causes Behavioral Cross-Sensitization to a Low Dose of Amphetamine," *Neuroscience* 122, no. 1 (2003): 17–20; N. M. Avena, P. Rada, and B. G. Hoebel, "Evidence for Sugar Addiction: Behavioral and Neurochemical Effects of Intermittent, Excessive Sugar Intake," *Neuroscience and Biobehavioral Reviews* 32, no. 1 (2008): 20–39; C. Colantuoni, P. Rada, J. McCarthy, C. Patten, N. M. Avena, A. Chadeayne, and B. G. Hoebel, "Evidence That Intermittent, Excessive Sugar Intake Causes Endogenous Opioid Dependence," *Obesity Research* 10, no. 6 (2002): 478–88; C. Colantuoni, J. Schwenker, J. McCarthy, P. Rada, B. Ladenheim, J. L. Cadet, G. J. Schwartz, T. H. Moran, and B. G. Hoebel, "Excessive Sugar Intake Alters Binding to Dopamine and Mu-Opioid Receptors in the

Brain," *Neuroreport* 12, no. 16 (2001): 3549–52; P. Rada, N. M. Avena, and B. G. Hoebel, "Daily Bingeing on Sugar Repeatedly Releases Dopamine in the Accumbens Shell," *Neuroscience* 134, no. 3 (2005): 737–44; R. Spangler, K. M. Wittkowski, N. L. Goddard, N. M. Avena, B. G. Hoebel, and S. F. Leibowitz, "Opiate-Like Effects of Sugar on Gene Expression in Reward Areas of the Rat Brain," *Molecular Brain Research* 124, no. 2 (2004): 134–42; P. Cottone, V. Sabino, L. Steardo, and E. P. Zorrilla, "Opioid-Dependent Anticipatory Negative Contrast and Binge-Like Eating in Rats with Limited Access to Highly Preferred Food," *Neuropsychopharmacology* 33, no. 3 (2008): 524–35.

p. 61. Action schemata: D. S. Leland, "Effects of Motivationally Salient Stimuli in Visual Spatial Attention: Behavior and Electrophysiology" (doctoral dissertation submitted to the University of California, San Diego, 2004); S. T. Tiffany, "A Cognitive Model of Drug Urges and Drug-Use Behavior: Role of Automatic and Nonautomatic Processes," *Psychological Review* 97, no. 2 (1990): 147–68.

p. 62. Roughly parallel loops: Author interviews with Joshua Berke, PhD, assistant professor and neuroscience scholar, Department of Psychology, University of Michigan–Ann Arbor, August 20, 2006, and September 1, 2006. The ventral striatum of the brain, which includes the shell of the nucleus accumbens, is the processing center for motivational information, while the dorsal striatum is more involved in the motor activity associated with habits. In a University of Cambridge research study, the pursuit of drugs by cocaine-seeking rats initially engaged the ventral striatum, but as their cocaine use became a habit, activity also increased in the dorsal striatum. L. J. Vanderschuren, P. Di Ciano, and B. J. Everitt, "Involvement of the Dorsal Striatum in Cue-Controlled Cocaine Seeking," *Journal of Neuroscience* 25, no. 38 (2005): 8665–70.

p. 62. Control food intake: The power of habit is dramatized in a study of twenty-three people with frontotemporal dementia, a degenerative brain disease whose many behavioral characteristics sometimes include fairly dramatic changes in eating patterns. During the experiment, study subjects were allowed to eat as many sandwiches as they wished. After telling the experimenter that she was full, one woman ate five more sandwiches. At one point, she turned her back to the sandwiches, but then reached behind her to take several more. Others commented, "I really am finished," and "Don't bring any more please," yet they continued to eat.

The four study subjects who overate most had evidence of atrophy in a very specific region of the brain. Their damaged brains received signals of fullness, but apparently could not translate those signals into appropriate behavior and so instead demonstrated "inflexible, stimulus-driven feeding behavior." J. D. Woolley, M. L. Gorno-Tempini, W. W. Seeley, K. Rankin, S. S. Lee, B. R. Matthews, and B. L. Miller, "Binge Eating Is Associated with Right Orbito-frontal-Insular-Striatal Atrophy in Frontotemporal Dementia," *Neurology* 69, no. 14 (2007): 1424–33.

p. 62. Code whole sequences of behavior: M. S. Jog, Y. Kubota, C. I. Connolly, V. Hillegaart, and A. M. Graybiel, "Building Neural Representations of Habits," *Science* 286, no. 5445 (1999): 1745–9.

p. 63. Study of high-sugar food: J. R. Sage and B. J. Knowlton, "Effects of US Devaluation on Win-Stay and Win-Shift Radial Maze Performance in Rats," *Behavioral Neuroscience* 114, no. 2 (2000): 295–306. The rats could not see the food but learned to run toward a light. "That simple cue was enough to elicit an automatic, fast running response toward the baited arm," said study author Jen Sage in the Department of Psychology, University of California, Los Angeles. "I've often thought about how this relates to the role of contextual cues and automatic, inflexible responses to them, which may help maintain maladaptive behaviors."

p. 67. Hyperpalatable foods and drugs: Nora D. Volkow, MD, director of the National Institute of Drug Abuse, has elucidated the common underlying mechanisms of food and drug reward. N. D. Volkow and R. A. Wise, "How Can Drug Addiction Help Us Understand Obesity?" *Nature Neuroscience* 8, no. 5 (2005): 555–60; A. Spiegel, E. Nabel, N. D. Volkow, S. Landis, and T. K. Li, "Obesity on the Brain," *Nature Neuroscience* 8, no. 5 (2005): 552–3; P. K. Thanos, M. Michaelides, J. D. Gispert, J. Pascau, M. L. Soto-Montenegro, M. Desco, R. Wang, G. J. Wang, and N. D. Volkow, "Differences in Response to Food Stimuli in a Rat Model of Obesity: In-Vivo Assessment of Brain Glucose Metabolism," *International Journal of Obesity* 32, no. 7 (2008): 1171–9; P. K. Thanos, M. Michaelides, C. W. Ho, G. J. Wang, A. H. Newman, C. A. Heidbreder, C. R. Ashby Jr., E. L. Gardner, and N. D. Volkow, "The Effects of Two Highly Selective Dopamine D3 Receptor Antagonists (Sb-277011a and Ngb-2904) on Food Self-Administration in a Rodent Model of Obesity," *Pharmacology, Biochemistry and Behavior* 89, no. 4 (2008): 499–507; P. K. Thanos, M. Michaelides, Y. K. Piyis, G. J. Wang, and N. D. Volkow, "Food Restriction Markedly Increases Dopamine D2 Receptor (D2r) in a Rat Model of Obesity as Assessed with in-Vivo Mupet Imaging ([11c] Raclopride) and in-Vitro ([3h] Spiperone) Autoradiography," *Synapse* 62, no. 1 (2008): 50–61; N. D. Volkow and C. P. O'Brien, "Issues for *DSM-V*: Should Obesity Be Included as a Brain Disorder?" *American Journal of Psychiatry* 164, no. 5 (2007): 708–10; N. D. Volkow, G. J. Wang, J. S. Fowler, and F. Telang, "Overlapping Neuronal Circuits in Addiction and Obesity: Evidence of Systems Pathology," *Philosophical Transactions of the Royal Society of London. Series B: Biological Sciences* 363, no. 1507 (2008): 3191–200; N. D. Volkow and R. A. Wise, "How Can Drug Addiction Help Us Understand Obesity?" *Nature Neuroscience* 8, no. 5 (2005): 555–60; G. J. Wang, N. D. Volkow, and J. S. Fowler, "The Role of Dopamine in Motivation for Food in Humans: Implications for Obesity," *Expert Opinion on Therapeutic Targets* 6, no. 5 (2002): 601–9; G. J. Wang, N. D. Volkow, J. Logan, N. R. Pappas, C. T. Wong, W. Zhu, N. Netusil, and J. S. Fowler, "Brain Dopamine and Obesity," *Lancet* 357, no. 9253 (2001): 354–7; G. J. Wang, N. D. Volkow, P. K. Thanos, and J. S. Fowler, "Similarity between Obesity and Drug Addiction as Assessed by Neurofunctional Imaging: A Concept Review," *Journal of Addictive Diseases* 23, no. 3 (2004): 39–53.

The late Ann E. Kelley, PhD, Distinguished Neuroscience Professor, Department of Psychiatry, University of Wisconsin, conducted pioneering work on "natural" rewards. A. E. Kelley, "Ventral Striatal Control of Appetitive Motivation: Role in Ingestive Behavior and Reward-Related Learning," *Neuroscience and Biobehavioral Reviews* 27, no. 8 (2004): 765–76; A. E. Kelley, B. A. Baldo, and W. E. Pratt, "A Proposed Hypothalamic-Thalamic-Striatal Axis for the Integration of Energy Balance, Arousal, and Food Reward," *Journal of Comparative Neurology* 493, no. 1 (2005): 72–85; A. E. Kelley, B. A. Baldo, W. E. Pratt, and M. J. Will, "Corticostriatal-Hypothalamic Circuitry and Food Motivation: Integration of Energy, Action and Reward," *Physiology and Behavior* 86, no. 5 (2005): 773–95; A. E. Kelley and K. C. Berridge, "The Neuroscience of

Natural Rewards: Relevance to Addictive Drugs," *Journal of Neuroscience* 22, no. 9 (2002): 3306–11.

p. 68. Southwestern Eggrolls: The label on the cardboard box in which these were shipped lists the following ingredients: Filling: cooked white meat chicken, binders added, smoke flavor added (breast meat, water, maltodextrin, salt, autolyzed yeast extract, sodium phosphate, spices, soy protein concentrate, modified food starch, natural flavor, natural smoke flavor, garlic, onion, oleoresin paprika), spinach, black beans, shredded Monterey Jack cheese with hot peppers (cultured pasteurized milk, salt, red and green jalapeno peppers, enzymes), corn, red bell peppers, water, seasoning [chili powder (chili pepper, cumin, salt, oregano, dry garlic), corn syrup solids, salt, hydrolyzed soy and corn protein, spices, honey powder (honey, wheat starch), dry chicken stock, brown sugar, flavor (flavorings, salt, autolyzed yeast, chicken stock), flavor (maltodextrin, salt, flavor), dry molasses (molasses, wheat starch, soy flour), natural smoke flavor], actobind (corn starch, methyl cellulose, egg white powder, xanthan gum, guar gum), cilantro, cottonseed oil, jalapeno peppers (jalapenos, water, vinegar, salt, trace of calcium chloride and sodium benzoate [as a preservative]), garlic. Tortilla: enriched bleached wheat flour (wheat flour, niacin, iron, thiamine mononitrate, riboflavin, folic acid), water, vegetable shortening (partially hydrogenated soybean and/or cottonseed oils), sugar. Contains 2% or less of: salt, leavening (baking soda, sodium aluminum sulfate, corn starch, monocalcium phosphate and/or sodium acid pyrophosphate, calcium sulfate), calcium propionate (to preserve freshness), dough conditioners (fumaric acid, sodium metabisulfite and/or L-cysteine). Sorbic acid (to preserve freshness).

p. 68. Food consultant: Author interview with anonymous food consultant, February 15, 2006.

p. 70. Boneless Shanghai Chicken Wings: The label on the cardboard box in which these were shipped lists the following ingredients: Chicken breast nuggets with rib meat containing up to 25% of a solution of water, hydrolyzed soy protein, salt, and sodium phosphates. Battered with: water, bleached enriched wheat flour and enriched wheat flour (both enriched with niacin, reduced iron, thiamine mononitrate, riboflavin, folic acid), yellow corn flour, salt, leavening (sodium bicarbonate, sodium aluminum phosphate, monocalcium phosphate), wheat gluten, soy flour, spices, dried garlic, dried onion, spice extractives. Breaded with: bleached enriched wheat flour (enriched with niacin, reduced iron, thiamine mononitrate, riboflavin, folic acid), salt, spices, dried garlic, leavening (sodium aluminum phosphate, sodium bicarbonate), dried egg whites, dried onion. Pre-dusted with: bleached enriched wheat flour (niacin, reduced iron, thiamine mononitrate, riboflavin, folic acid) bread crumbs (enriched bleached wheat flour [wheat flour, niacin, reduced iron, thiamine mononitrate, riboflavin, folic acid], corn syrup solids, dry yeast, soybean oil, salt, mono- and diglycerides, malted barley flour, ammonium sulfate, leavening (monocalcium phosphate), calcium propionate, sorbitan monostearate). Breading set in vegetable oil.

p. 70. Margarita Grilled Chicken: The label on the cardboard box in which this was shipped lists the following ingredients: Margarita-flavored butterfly breast, boneless skinless chicken breast with rib meat containing up to a 15% solution of marinade (ultra-pasteurized orange juice, sweet & sour mix [sugar, citric acid, egg white solids, sodium citrate, partially hydrogenated soybean oil, flavoring, BHA (a preservative), artificial color (yellow #5, and tricalcium phosphate)], triple sec, canola oil, tequila, salt, dehydrated garlic, spice, dehydrated onion, potassium sorbate, sodium benzoate and gum arabic), water, whey protein concentrate product (modified tapioca starch, whey protein concentrate, sodium phosphate, carrageenan and sodium citrate), sodium phosphates, salt, black pepper.

p. 70. Nick Nickelson: Author interview with Ranzell "Nick" Nickelson, chief scientist, Standard Meat, October 2008.

p. 71. Billy Rosenthal: Author interview with Billy Rosenthal, former president, Standard Meat, October 2008.

p. 72. Ginger-citrus sauce: The label on the cardboard box in which this was shipped lists the following ingredients: medium brown sugar, water, Hoisin sauce (soybean, wheat flour, sugar, water, tomato paste, salt, lemon, caramel, garlic, vinegar, chili), rice vinegar, soy sauce (water, wheat, soybeans, salt, sodium benzoate [less than $\frac{1}{10}$ of 1% as a preservative]), minced ginger (fresh minced ginger, water, phosphoric acid, and potassium sorbate), modified food starch, chili paste (chili, distilled vinegar, salt, potassium sorbate and sodium bisulfite as preservatives), orange juice concentrate. Contains wheat and soy ingredients.

p. 74. Cinnabon story: Author interview with Jerilyn Brusseau, founder of Cinnabon, January 2006.

p. 78. Pink's is a hot-dog stand: Author communication with Gloria Pink, co-owner of Pink's.

p. 79. Eatertainment: George Ritzer, *Enchanting a Disenchanted World: Revolutionizing the Means of Consumption*, 2nd ed. (Thousand Oaks, CA: Pine Forge Press, 2005).

p. 80. Warm milk and a bottle: Author interview with anonymous venture capitalist, September 17, 2006.

p. 80. Self-indulgent treating: "Soaring Stress Levels Drive British Consumers to Splash Out on Premium Treats," *Datamonitor*, October 2004, datamonitor.com/industries/news/article/?pid=E1DD6B6E-9176-4F3D-8AB0-2929BC3B122D&type=ExpertView. Datamonitor publishes a "new consumer insight" series of reports "on consumer segments that are either ill-defined, currently untargeted or represent a high growth opportunity." Among them: "Everyday Self Indulgences 2004: Understanding the Needs and Motivations Influencing Food and Drink Treating Occasions," November 2004, and "Profiting from Consumers' Desires for Healthy Indulgences," December 2005.

p. 81. Sells for about $6,000: "Premium Indulgence: Capitalizing on the Growing Trend for Premium Indulgence," produced by Datamonitor, October 2004, "examines how often consumers opt for premium indulgence and how manufacturers should adjust their products and marketing to exploit this behavior." This is another report in the company's "new consumer insight" series.

p. 81. Conference on restaurant trends: Technomic Information Services, Restaurants 2006: Trends and Directions conference, Chicago, Illinois, June 22, 2005. Survey results by Technomic Consumer Research were included in a "data digest" provided to conference participants. "Share of stomach" data compared the number of breakfasts, lunches, and dinners eaten in restaurants, compared to the home. Insight about consumer habits, expectations, and decision making were provided, as were tips on "serving both masters (health, indulgence)," "takeout best practices," and focusing on the children's market.

p. 81. One satisfied Outback customer: Bruce Horovitz, "Takeout Takes Off: Time-Pressed Americans' Push for More Food to Go Is Reshaping the Way Restaurants Do Business," *USA Today*, June 13, 2007.

p. 83. Department of Agriculture data: United States Department of Agriculture Economic Research Service, The ERS Food Consumption (Per Capita) Data System, ers.usda.gov/AmberWaves/November05/Findings/USFoodConsumption.htm. See also USDA, Dietary Assessment of Major Trends in US Food Consumption, 1970–2005, ers.usda.gov/Publications/EIB33/EIB33.pdf.

p. 84. Evolutionary perspective: W. P. James, "Energy and Macronutrient Needs in Relation to Substrate Handling in Obesity," in *Clinical Obesity in Adults and Children*, 2nd ed., ed. Peter G. Kopelman, Ian D. Caterson, and William H. Dietz (Hoboken, NJ: Wiley-Blackwell, 2005).

p. 86. Monster Thickburger: Nutrition information for the three-pound Monster Thickburger is provided on the Hardee's Web site, www.hardees.com/menu.

p. 87. Strawberries & Crème Frappuccino: With whipped cream, the Strawberries & Crème Frappuccino (venti size) contains 750 calories, 15 grams of fat and 120 grams of sugar. Nutrition information is provided on the Starbucks Web site. See also *Nutrition Action Health Letter*, July/August 2004, 16.

p. 87. Kick-it-up-a-notch effect: Ellison Bakery described itself as "an innovative solutions company. Whether it is a completely new and cutting edge product, or just an improvement on a tried and true item, Ellison Bakery has the know-how to help customers succeed. Ellison Bakery has a line of stock products to add that special 'Kick it up a Notch' to ice cream or confection creations . . . " *Stagnito's New Products Magazine*, May 1, 2005.

p. 88. What consumers like to eat: Author interview with Gail Vance Civille, president, Sensory Spectrum, November 23, 2005.

p. 92. Positive reinforcement or reward: Richard Foltin, PhD, professor of neurobiology (in Psychiatry), New York State Psychiatric Institute, Columbia University Medical Center, gave his presentation at the Society for the Study of Ingestive Behavior, Naples, Florida, July 2006. Jennifer Nasser, PhD, RD, a researcher at the New York Obesity Research Center at St. Luke's Hospital, followed Foltin's presentation with a talk titled "Are Fat/Carbohydrate Combinations the Dietary Equivalent of a 'Speedball'?" Speedball is a combination of heroin and cocaine—the drug combination interacts with the dopamine and opioid systems, heightens perceptions of the drugs' attributes, and has reinforcing properties that are greater together than either component alone.

Nasser reviewed evidence from other researchers that suggests a "dietary speedball" has some similar characteristics: Bart Hoebel, PhD, professor, Department of Psychology, Princeton University, demonstrated that sucrose consumption releases dopamine in the nucleus accumbens, while the late Ann E. Kelley, PhD, Distinguished Neuroscience Professor, Department of Psychiatry, University of Wisconsin, showed the effects of Ensure on the brain. Studies among Pima Indians, who perceived greater creaminess in a mixture that contained sugar as well as fat, rather than fat alone, showed that the presence of sugar heightens the perception of fat. Anthony Sclafani, PhD, Distinguished Professor, Department of Psychology, Brooklyn College, City University of New York, demonstrated that rats will eat most when they are given a combination of sucrose and corn oil, showing that mixtures of fat and carbohydrates are more reinforcing than each component alone.

p. **94. Japanese food:** Author interview with Yoshiyuki Fujishima, DPhil, chemist and executive, Ajinomoto USA, January 26, 2006.

p. **95. Adult baby food:** Author interview with John Haywood, restaurant industry consultant, February 20, 2006.

p. **95. Metamorphosis:** Author interviews with anonymous food consultant, August 12, 2004, and February 15, 2006.

p. **96. Shoveling process:** Author interview with Nancy Rodriguez, president, Food Marketing Support Services, February 21, 2006.

p. **97. Deconstruct the key drivers:** Author interview with Gail Vance Civille, president, Sensory Spectrum, November 23, 2005. Gordon Shepherd, MD, PhD, professor of neuroscience and neurobiology, Yale School of Medicine, was blunt in an author interview, December 27, 2005: "The industry is geared to overstimulating the senses of the consumer so that they eat more," he said. "It is activating parts of the brain that are susceptible to being conditioned to find the product desirable and to wanting more of it."

p. **98. Oreos and Chips Ahoy:** Author interview with Robert Smith, former vice president, Research and Development, Nabisco, December 2005.

p. **99. Salting of potato chips:** Author interview with Dwight Riskey, PhD, former Frito-Lay executive, September 26, 2005.

p. **101. Consumers don't really know:** Author interview with Gail Vance Civille, president, Sensory Spectrum, December 19, 2005.

p. **104. Irresistible products:** Michelle Foley, research manager, Frito-Lay and PepsiCo, "Simply Irresistible: Understanding High Levels of Satisfaction and What It Means" (presentation at Sixth Pangborn Sensory Science Symposium at Harrogate, England, August 2005); author interview with Michelle Foley, December 13, 2005.

p. **108. Expert on consumer behavior:** Howard Moskowitz, PhD, president of Moskowitz Jacobs, "How We Understand Sensory Issues Better with Psychophysics" (presentation at Sixth Pangborn Sensory Science Symposium at Harrogate, England, August 2005).

p. **109. Make a food highly desired:** W. den Hoed and E. H. Zandstra, "What Makes a Food Desirable? Results from a Qualitative and Quantitative Consumer Study" (poster, Sixth Pangborn Sensory Science Symposium at Harrogate, England, August 2005).

p. **111. Asian cuisine:** Jennifer Lee, *The Fortune Cookie Chronicles: Adventures in the World of Chinese Food* (New York: Twelve, 2008).

p. **112. Panda Express:** 2007 sales figures from Michael W. Nuckolls, "The Billion Dollar Club," *QSRMagazine.com*, 2008, http://www.qsrmagazine.com/reports/qsr50/2008/billion.phtml. Preparation of the meat used in orange-flavor chicken is described on the Panda Express cardboard box label titled "Battered chicken dark meat chunks," which indicates the product is "prebrowned in shortening (partially hydrogenated soybean oil, TBHQ, and citric acid added to preserve freshness)." The label instructions also say "keep frozen" and provide these cooking instructions: "Deep fry in oil at 350°F for 5–6 minutes . . . "

p. **115. Arsenal the food industry uses:** Marketing materials and conversations with company representatives at the Institute of Food Technologists annual convention, New Orleans, July 2005. Additional information was posted on corporate Web sites.

p. **117. Flavor chemists can develop:** Paula Frank, "Applications—Tasty Solutions for Marinades," *Food Product Design*, March 2001, foodproductdesign. com/articles/0301ap.html.

p. 120. Tools to deliver the product: Author interview with John Haywood, restaurant industry consultant, December 6, 2005.

p. 121. Make food much more hedonic: Author interview with anonymous food consultant, December 20, 2005.

p. 125. Get you hooked: Author interview with anonymous venture capitalist, September 17, 2006.

p. 126. Crave-It! study: Author interview with Jacqueline Beckley, president, The Understanding and Insights Group, February 21, 2006.

p. 127. Context in which food is presented: B. Wansink, "Environmental Factors That Increase the Food Intake and Consumption Volume of Unknowing Consumers," *Annual Review of Nutrition* 24 (2004): 455–79.

p. 127. Affect sensory perception: B. Wansink, K. van Iterrsum, and J. E. Painter, "How Descriptive Food Names Bias Sensory Perceptions in Restaurants," *Food Quality and Preference* 16 (2005): 393–400.

p. 127. Come back for more: B. Wansink, "Environmental Factors That Increase the Food Intake and Consumption Volume of Unknowing Consumers," *Annual Review of Nutrition* (2004): 455–79.

p. 128. Barriers to consumption: Author interview with David J. Mela, PhD, senior scientist, Weight Control and Behavioural Nutrition, Unilever Food and Health Research Institute, December 5, 2005.

p. 128. One more penny: Author interview with Mike McCloud, January 19, 2006.

p. 130. Consumer-trends report: "Profiting from Consumers' Desires for Healthy Indulgences," Datamonitor, December 2005.

p. 132. Purple cows: Seth Godin, *Purple Cow: Transform Your Business by Being Remarkable* (New York: Portfolio, 2003); Seth Godin, "In Praise of the Purple Cow," *Fast Company*, February 2003.

p. 132. Foods that go pop: Nancy Rodriguez, president, Food Marketing Support Services, presentation at Institute of Food Technologists, New Orleans, August 2005; author interview with Nancy Rodriguez, February 1, 2006.

p. 133. They crave flavor: McCormick 2005 Flavor Forecast (news release).

p. 138. It's a dragon: Personal communication with Mathea Falco, president, Drug Strategies (a Washington, DC, nonprofit organization that seeks effective approaches to the problem of substance abuse), August 2005.

p. 138: Change our feelings: Author communication with Jerome Kagan, PhD, Daniel and Amy Starch Research Professor of Psychology, Emeritus, Harvard University, March 28, 2008; Jerome Kagan, *What Is Emotion? History, Measures, and Meanings* (New Haven, CT: Yale University Press, 2007).

p. 139. Reinforcement learning: Author interview with Wai-Tat Fu, PhD, assistant professor, Applied Cognitive Science Lab, University of Illinois–Urbana-Champaign, December 12, 2006.

p. 139. Schedule things into a habit: Author interview with Bernard Balleine, PhD, associate director for research, Brain Research Institute, University of California, Los Angeles, December 13, 2006.

p. 140. Reward learning takes place: Author interview with Raymond Niaura, PhD, professor of psychiatry and human behavior, Brown University Medical School, May 10, 2007.

p. 140. Stimulus-response-type habits: Author interview with Philip D. Zelazo, PhD, professor and Canada research chair in developmental neuroscience, Department of Psychology, University of Toronto, April 6, 2007.

p. 140. Triggers an automatic behavior: Author interview with James Leckman, MD, director of research, Neison Harris Professor of Child Psychiatry and Pediatrics, Child Study Center, Yale University School of Medicine, April 29, 2007.

Once the script for a behavior becomes imprinted in the brain, that behavior becomes so routine that we can respond to a stimulus without knowing we are doing so. Researchers can detect movement before subjects know they are going to move. And I can reach for a cookie before I realize I am doing so. "It is absolutely clear that there is brain activity before conscious awareness arises," said Susan Pockett, PhD, Physics Department, University of Auckland, New Zealand. Author interview with Susan Pockett, September 14, 2006.

See also G. Rees, G. Kreiman, and C. Koch, "Neural Correlates of Consciousness in Humans," *Nature Reviews. Neuroscience* 3, no. 4 (2002): 261–70; M. Wilenius-Emet, A. Revonsuo, and V. Ojanen, "An Electrophysiological Correlate of Human Visual Awareness," *Neuroscience Letters* 354, no. 1 (2004): 38–41; E. Fehrer and I. Biederman, "A Comparison of Reaction Time and Verbal Report in the Detection of Masked Stimuli," *Journal of Experimental Psychology* 64 (1962): 126–30; N. J. MacIntyre and A. J. McComas, "Non-Conscious Choice in Cutaneous Backward Masking," *Neuroreport* 7, no. 9 (1996): 1513–6; L. Weiskrantz, "Blindsight Revisited," *Current Opinion in Neurobiology* 6, no. 2 (1996): 215–20; A. Moors and J. De Houwer, "Automaticity: A Theoretical and Conceptual Analysis," *Psychological Bulletin* 132, no. 2 (2006): 297–326.

p. 140. Floodgates open: Author interview with Raymond Miltenberger, PhD, BCBA, director, Applied Behavior Analysis Masters Program, Department of Child and Family Studies, University of South Florida, May 10, 2007.

p. 142. Pulled from the market: H. M. Connolly, J. L. Crary, M. D. McGoon, D. D. Hensrud, B. S. Edwards, W. D. Edwards, and H. V. Schaff, "Valvular Heart Disease Associated with Fenfluramine-Phentermine," *New England Journal of Medicine* 337, no. 9 (1997): 581–8; M. M. Lumpkin, US Food and Drug Administration Public Health Advisory, July 8, 1997; "Cardiac Valvulopathy Associated with Exposure to Fenfluramine or Dexfenfluramine: U.S. Department of Health and Human Services Interim Public Health Recommendations, November 1997," *Morbidity and Mortality Weekly Report*, November 14, 1997.

p. 142. Acted in a complex way: Phentermine is an amphetamine-like compound. There is evidence that amphetamines may reduce appetite by dysregulating the dopamine circuitry. C. M. Cannon, L. Abdallah, L. H. Tecott, M. J. During, and R. D. Palmiter, "Dysregulation of Striatal Dopamine Signaling by Amphetamine Inhibits Feeding by Hungry Mice," *Neuron* 44, no. 3 (2004): 509–20.

There are other possible mechanisms by which amphetamines may reduce appetite: (1) through an effect as sympathomimetic agents; (2) via increased stimulation of gluconeogenesis with significant glycogen breaking down to glucose, resulting in an infusion of glucose into the circulating blood supply; and (3) via increased serotonergic tone in many parts of the brain. Author interview with Kenneth Carr, PhD, associate professor of psychiatry and pharmacology, Departments of Psychiatry (Millhauser Labs) and Pharmacology, New York University, October 12, 2006.

p. 142. Increased the level of serotonin: Eric J. Nestler, Steven E. Hyman, and Robert C. Malenka, *Molecular Neuropharmacology: A Foundation for Clinical Neuroscience*, 2nd ed. (New York: McGraw-Hill Companies, Medical Pub. Division, 2008), 161.

p. 143. Reduce drug use: J. J. Burmeister et al., "Differential Roles of 5-HT Receptor Subtypes in Cue and Cocaine Reinstatement of Cocaine-Seeking Behavior in Rats," *Neuropsychopharmacology* 29 (2004): 660–8; J. J. Burmeister, E. M. Lungren, and J. L. Neisewander, "Effects of Fluoxetine and D-Fenfluramine on Cocaine-Seeking Behavior in Rats," *Psychopharmacology* 168, nos. 1–2 (2003): 146–54; F. H. Wojnicki, R. B. Rothman, K. C. Rice, and J. R. Glowa, "Effects of Phentermine on Responding Maintained under Multiple Fixed-Ratio Schedules of Food and Cocaine Presentation in the Rhesus Monkey," *Journal of Pharmacology and Experimental Therapeutics* 288, no. 2 (1999): 550–60; R. B. Rothman, B. E. Blough, and M. H. Baumann, "Dual Dopamine/Serotonin Releasers as Potential Medications for Stimulant and Alcohol Addictions," *AAPS Journal* 9, no. 1 (2007): E1–10; author interview with Michael H. Baumann, PhD, IRP, NIADA, NIH, DHHS, November 27, 2006.

p. 143. Normal for the first time: Author interview with Richard Atkinson, MD, clinical professor of pathology, Virginia Commonwealth University, and director, Obetech Obesity Research Center, December 5, 2006.

p. 144. Not thinking about food: Author interview with Thomas Najarian, MD, director, the Najarian Center, Los Osos, California, December 8, 2006.

p. 144. Felt normal: Author interview with Louis Aronne, MD, clinical professor of medicine, Sanford I. Weill Medical College, Cornell University, December 8, 2006.

p. 144. Confirming anecdote: Author interview with Michael Weintraub, MD, president, Weintraub Pharmaceutical Consulting, November 28, 2006. Weintraub has also been head of the Clinical Pharmacology Unit at the University of Rochester School of Medicine and director of the Office of Drug Evaluation 5 at the US Food and Drug Administration.

p. 145. Overarching theory: The theory advanced in this book—that overeating is the result of changes in the reward, learning, and habit circuits of the brain in the face of an environment filled with highly palatable food—challenges the thrifty gene hypothesis, one of the major theories in the obesity field. The thrifty gene hypothesis suggests that obesity and diabetes stem from a natural selection that favored the capacity to store fat efficiently in periods of food abundance, providing protection when food shortages occur. J. V. Neel, "Diabetes Mellitus: A 'Thrifty' Genotype Rendered Detrimental by 'Progress'? 1962, repr. *Bulletin of the World Health Organization* 77, no. 8 (1999): 694–703; discussion 692–3; J. V. Neel, "The 'Thrifty Genotype' in 1998," *Nutrition Reviews* 57, no. 5, pt. 2 (1999): S2–9; J. V. Neel, A. B. Weder, and S. Julius, "Type II Diabetes, Essential Hypertension, and Obesity as Syndromes of 'Impaired Genetic Homeostasis': The 'Thrifty Genotype' Hypothesis Enters the 21st Century," *Perspectives in Biology and Medicine* 42, no. 1 (1998): 44–74.

Limits to the thrifty gene hypothesis include the fact that hunter-gatherers in equatorial regions, where famine was not a selection force, are not protected from obesity when they move to an obesigenic environment. J. R. Speakman, "Thrifty Genes for Obesity, an Attractive but Flawed Idea, and an Alternative Perspective: The 'Drifty Gene' Hypothesis," *International Journal of Obesity* 32, no. 11 (2008): 1611–7. An alternate explanation could be that there is an evolutionary survival advantage to attending to, and seeking out, salient stimuli in the environment and that there is variability in that trait.

p. 147. Elaborated thought: Author interview with David Kavanagh, PhD, professor, Clinical Psychology, Department of Psychiatry, University of Queensland, Brisbane, Australia, February 28, 2007; D. J. Kavanagh, J. Andrade, and J. May, "Imaginary Relish and Exquisite Torture: The Elaborated Intrusion Theory of Desire," *Psychological Review* 112, no. 2 (2005): 446–67.

p. 148. Have the wanting: Author interview with Marcia Pelchat, PhD, associate member, Monell Chemical Senses Center, January 31, 2007.

p. 148. Desire builds: Jeffrey M. Brunstrom, PhD, in the Department of Experimental Psychology at the University of Bristol, England, has demonstrated that cues both increase "desire" and the amount that we end up eating. D. Ferriday and J. M. Brunstrom, "How Does Food-Cue Exposure Lead to Larger Meal Sizes?" *British Journal of Nutrition* (2008): 1–8.

p. 148. Desirable object, get more: Author interview with Harriet de Wit, PhD, director, Human Behavioral Pharmacology Laboratory, Department of Psychiatry, University of Chicago, January 8, 2007; J. M. Kirk and H. de Wit, "Individual Differences in the Priming Effect of Ethanol in Social Drinkers," *Journal of Studies on Alcohol* 61, no. 1 (2000): 64–71.

p. 149. Hard to stop: Author interview with Martin Yeomans, PhD, CPsychol, Reader in Experimental Psychology Department of Psychology, School of Life Sciences, University of Sussex, Brighton, England, November 27, 2007; M. R. Yeomans, H. M. Tovey, E. M. Tinley, and C. J. Haynes, "Effects of Manipulated Palatability on Appetite Depend on Restraint and Disinhibition Scores from the Three-Factor Eating Questionnaire," *International Journal of Obesity and Related Metabolic Disorders* 28, no. 1 (2003): 144–51.

p. 149. Power of priming: C. E. Cornell, J. Rodin, and H. Weingarten, "Stimulus-Induced Eating When Satiated," *Physiology and Behavior* 45, no. 4 (1989): 695–704.

p. 150. Self-medication: Author interview with George F. Koob, PhD, chair of the Committee on the Neurobiology of Addictive Disorders, Scripps Research Institute, March 6, 2007.

p. 150. Charged emotional situation: Author interview with Rajita Sinha, PhD, director, Research Program on Stress, Addiction and Psychopathology, Yale University School of Medicine, September 5, 2007; H. C. Fox, K. L. Bergquist, K. I. Hong, and R. Sinha, "Stress-Induced and Alcohol Cue-Induced Craving in Recently Abstinent Alcohol-Dependent Individuals," *Alcoholism, Clinical and Experimental Research* 31, no. 3 (2007): 395–403; C. S. Li and R. Sinha, "Inhibitory Control and Emotional Stress Regulation: Neuroimaging Evidence for Frontal-Limbic Dysfunction in Psycho-Stimulant Addiction," *Neuroscience and Biobehavioral Reviews* 32, no. 3 (2008): 581–97; R. Sinha, "Modeling Stress and Drug Craving in the Laboratory: Implications for Addiction Treatment Development," *Addiction Biology* 14, no. 1 (2009): 84–98; R. Sinha, "The Role of Stress in Addiction Relapse," *Current Psychiatry Reports* 9, no. 5 (2007): 388–95; R. Sinha, H. C. Fox, K. A. Hong, K. Bergquist, Z. Bhagwagar, and K. M. Siedlarz, "Enhanced Negative Emotion and Alcohol Craving, and Altered Physiological Responses Following Stress and Cue Exposure in Alcohol Dependent Individuals," *Neuropsychopharmacology* (2008).

p. 150. Setting condition: Author correspondence with Charles P. O'Brien, MD, PhD, vice chair, Department of Psychiatry, University of Pennsylvania Health System, December 21, 2006; S. J. Robbins, R. N. Ehrman, A. R. Childress, J. W. Cornish, and C. P. O'Brien, "Mood State and Recent Cocaine Use Are Not Associated with Levels of Cocaine Cue Reactivity," *Drug and Alcohol Dependence* 59, no. 1 (2000): 33–42. For a discussion of emotion as a setting condition, see L. B. Allen, R. K. McHugh, and D. H. Barlow, "Emotional Disorders: A Unified Protocol," in *Clinical Handbook of Psychological Disorders: A Step-by-Step Treatment Manual*, 4th ed., ed. David H. Barlow (New York: Guilford Press, 2008).

p. 151. About to get a milkshake: Author interview with Eric Stice, PhD, research scientist, Oregon Research Institute, February 27, 2007; J. Ng, E. Stice, S. Spoor, and C. Bohon, "A Brain Imaging Study of the Relation of Consummatory and Anticipatory Food Reward to Obesity: Effects of Perceived Caloric Density" (submitted for publication).

p. 151. Emotions amplify reward: A number of theories have been advanced to explain the role of stress in overeating, including the idea that stress leads to a narrowing of attention, reducing inhibitions against food intake. "Eating, however it happens, is a momentary escape," said Todd F. Heatherton, PhD, Champion International Professor, Department of Psychological and Brain Sciences, Dartmouth College. Author interview with Todd Heatherton, February 19, 2007. The argument that overeating is motivated by a desire to escape from self-awareness is developed in T. F. Heatherton and R. F. Baumeister, "Binge Eating as Escape from Self-Awareness," *Psychological Bulletin* 110, no. 1 (1991): 86–108.

Mary F. Dallman, PhD, Faculty, Neurosciences Graduate Program, University of California, San Francisco, has done extensive research on the role of glucocorticoids, a class of steroid hormones. She said, "Glucocorticoids act very rapidly through the endocannabinoid system after stress to increase the intake of highly palatable food or 'comfort food.' They act at the amygdala, nucleus accumbens, hippocampus, prefrontal cortex, and the insular cortex to reinforce the 'want' to eat sugar and fat." If you eat when you are stressed, you form a memory of something pleasurable occurring with stress and learn a behavioral response to future stress. Author interview with Mary Dallman, May 5, 2004.

See also M. F. Dallman, N. Pecoraro, S. F. Akana, S. E. La Fleur, F. Gomez, H. Houshyar, M. E. Bell, S. Bhatnagar, K. D. Laugero, and S. Manalo, "Chronic Stress and Obesity: A New View of 'Comfort Food,'" *Proceedings of the National Academy of Sciences of the United States of America* 100, no. 20 (2003): 11696–701; M. F. Dallman, N. C. Pecoraro, and S. E. La Fleur, "Chronic Stress and Comfort Foods: Self-Medication and Abdominal Obesity," *Brain, Behavior, and Immunity* 19, no. 4 (2005): 275–80; and M. F. Dallman, N. C. Pecoraro, S. E. La Fleur, J. P. Warne, A. B. Ginsberg, S. F. Akana, K. C. Laugero, H. Houshyar, A. M. Strack, S. Bhatnagar, and M. E. Bell, "Glucocorticoids, Chronic Stress, and Obesity," *Progress in Brain Research* 153 (2006): 75–105.

Kent C. Berridge, PhD, professor, Biopsychology Program, University of Michigan, has found evidence that "CRF [a stress hormone] in the nucleus accumbens shell amplifies positive motivation for cued rewards, in particular by magnifying incentive salience that is attributed to Pavlovian cues previously associated with those rewards." S. Pecina, J. Schulkin, and K. C. Berridge,

"Nucleus Accumbens Corticotropin-Releasing Factor Increases Cue-Triggered Motivation for Sucrose Reward: Paradoxical Positive Incentive Effects in Stress?" *BMC Biology* 4 (2006): 8.

Thomas Wadden, PhD, professor of psychology in Psychiatry, University of Pennsylvania Health System, said food can be used to relieve an aversive emotional state, whether it is boredom, mild dysphoria, or more intense distress. "A lot has been written about using food to escape awareness, that you really are trying to get away from yourself, get away from the negative mood that you're experiencing. And it's clear that food is only going to help you escape for a brief period of time, and having terminated the negative feelings, you'll be reinforced to do that in the future. A lot of this is mood regulation by way of food." Author interview with Thomas Wadden, December 24, 2003.

p. 151. Agitated state: Author interview with Bernard Balleine, PhD, associate director for research, Brain Research Institute, University of California, Los Angeles, March 9, 2007.

p. 152. People feel better: Author interview with Loma Flowers, MD, community psychologist and clinical professor, Psychiatry Department, University of California, San Francisco, February 24, 2007.

p. 154. Traces retrieved from memory: M. S. Goldman, F. K. Del Boca, and J. Darkes, "Alcohol Expectancy Theory: The Application of Cognitive Neuroscience," in *Psychological Theories of Drinking and Alcoholism*, 2nd ed., ed. Kenneth E. Leonard and Howard T. Blane, The Guilford Substance Abuse Series (New York: Guilford Press, 1999).

p. 154. Expectancy has powerful effects: Author interview with George F. Koob, PhD, chair of the Committee on the Neurobiology of Addictive Disorders, Scripps Research Institute, March 6, 2007.

p. 154. Food will make us feel better: Irving Kirsch, *How Expectancies Shape Experience* (Washington, DC: American Psychological Association, 1999).

p. 155. Alleviates my negative mood: Author interview with Gregory T. Smith, PhD, professor, Department of Psychology, University of Kentucky, March 27, 2006; S. Fischer, K. G. Anderson, and G. T. Smith, "Coping with Distress by Eating or Drinking: Role of Trait Urgency and Expectancies," *Psychology of Addictive Behaviors* 18, no. 3 (2004): 269–74; G. T. Smith, M. S. Goldman, P. E. Greenbaum, and B. A. Christiansen, "Expectancy for Social Facilitation from Drinking: The Divergent Paths of High-Expectancy and Low-Expectancy Adolescents," *Journal of Abnormal Psychology* 104, no. 1 (1995): 32–40.

p. 155. Cream cakes: Author interview with David Kavanagh, PhD, professor, Clinical Psychology, Department of Psychiatry, University of Queensland, Brisbane, Australia, February 28, 2007.

p. 157. Define it more rigorously: Research strongly suggests that food stimulates the reward circuits of many overweight people, driving them to eat to the point of overconsumption. Nonetheless, we cannot immediately conclude that reward-based eating explains weight gain because not all overweight people demonstrate the associated behaviors, and some lean people do. To learn more, I needed to determine what percentage of the overweight population has the characteristics associated with reward-based eating and whether those characteristics cluster together in overweight people. I was trying to identify a "behavioral phenotype," that is, a package of characteristics that reflects the interaction of genes and the environment.

Timothy Carmody, PhD, clinical professor, Department of Psychiatry, University of California, San Francisco, defines disinhibition as an "absence of the normal range of self-regulation skills in making decisions around health-related and other behaviors." Drawing on his substantial clinical experience, Carmody estimated that about two-thirds of individuals who are at least 50 pounds overweight met that definition. He also made an educated guess that about two-thirds of obese individuals prefer high-fat, high-sugar foods, and lack satiation in the face of them, and that about half that population eats frequent snacks, consumes large portion sizes, and eats at an accelerated pace. Author interview with Timothy Carmody, April 13, 2005.

Other clinicians generally confirmed Carmody's estimates, but everyone emphasized that his or her own anecdotal experiences were only starting places for more research. To find out whether there was a set of characteristics common to the obese, I had to go beyond clinical impressions in search of data.

p. 158. Base on which to build: Dana M. Small, PhD, Associate Fellow, and Jennifer Felsted, research assistant, Affective Sensory Neuroscience, both at the John B. Pierce Laboratory, a Yale University affiliate, helped me understand some of the theories purporting to explain the differences in brain responses between obese and lean individuals.

One theory is that a heightened response to cues increases risk for overeating and obesity. An alternative posits that obese individuals have hypofunctioning reward circuitry, with overeating constituting an effort to compensate (anhedonia hypothesis). K. Blum, P. J. Sheridan, R. C. Wood, E. R. Braverman, T. J. Chen, J. G. Cull, and D. E. Comings, "The D2 Dopamine Receptor Gene as a Determinant of Reward Deficiency Syndrome," *Journal of the Royal Society of Medicine* 89, no. 7 (1996): 396–400; N. D. Volkow, G. J. Wang, F. Telang, J. S. Fowler, P. K. Thanos, J. Logan, D. Alexoff, Y. S. Ding, C. Wong, Y. Ma, and K. Pradhan, "Low Dopamine Striatal D2 Receptors Are Associated with Prefrontal Metabolism in Obese Subjects: Possible Contributing Factors," *Neuroimage* 42, no. 4 (2008): 1537–43.

Still another theory is that both hypo- and hyperactive brain responses are involved. Dana M. Small, "Individual Differences in the Neurophysiology of Food Reward" (presentation at the National Institute of Diabetes and Digestive and Kidney Disorders workshop on "Decision making in eating behavior: Integrating perspectives from the individual, family and environment," April 2008).

Imaging studies show marked contrasts between lean and overweight people. In one such study, twenty-seven adolescent girls, categorized as either lean or overweight based on their body-mass index scores, were shown pictures of appetizing food, unappetizing food, and water and asked to imagine consuming each one. When lean girls looked at those pictures, their brain scans showed that structures geared to optical recognition (visual cortex) were activated, which is what happens when humans look at almost anything. Lean people simply represent food as a visual object. The overweight girls, by contrast, engaged the prefrontal and orbitofrontal cortex when they viewed palatable foods. These are the regions of the brain responsible for pairing emotional reward with learning. Author interview with Eric Stice, research scientist, Oregon Research Institute, University of Texas Clinical Psychology Program, December 22, 2007; E. Stice, "Relation of Food Reward Abnormalities to Obesity: An fMRI Study" (invited presentation at the Seventh Annual Psychology and Health Conference, Netherlands, 2008); E. Stice and S. Spoor, "Relation of Obesity to Disturbances in Anticipatory and Consummatory Food Reward: An fMRI Study" (plenary presentation at the Eating Disorder Research Society Conference, Pittsburgh, Pennsylvania, 2007); E. Stice, "Elevated Reward and Anticipated Reward from Food Intake: Neural Substrates of Obesity?" (presentation at the Academy for Eating Disorders annual meeting, Baltimore, Maryland, 2007).

A study with adults also showed that weight predicted reward system activity in the brain. In particular, the dorsal striatum, anterior insula, hippocampus, and parietal cortex became activated in obese individuals presented with high-calorie foods. Images of high-calorie foods also activated the reward system of obese individuals. "BMI Predicts Striatal Activation in Obese Individuals: An fMRI Study" (poster presentation at Fifth Forum of European Neuroscience, *FENS Forum Abstracts* 3 [2006], A043.15); Y. Rothermund, C. Preuschhof, G. Bohner, H.-C. Bauknecht, R. Klingebiel, H. Flor, and B. F. Klapp, "Differential Activation of the Dorsal Striatum by High-Calorie Visual Food Stimuli in Obese Individuals," *Neuroimage* 37, no. 2 (2007): 410–21.

p. 158. Eating behaviors: Conditioned hypereating differs from the clinically defined eating disorders of binge eating and bulimia, although there are some overlaps. Binge eating involves eating excessively large amounts of food in a short period of time on a regular basis, behavior that people with bulimia follow with self-induced vomiting, excessive exercise, and laxative abuse. People suffering from those eating disorders report feeling "worthless, unlovable, inadequate, powerless, victimized, angry, sad, and numb." One patient declared, "I just wanted to get a knife and cut off my abdomen." K. Proulx, "Experiences of Women with Bulimia Nervosa in a Mindfulness-Based Eating Disorder Treatment Group," *Eating Disorders* 16, no. 1 (2008): 52–72.

Binge eating and bulimia may be extreme adaptations to conditioned and driven eating behavior. Someone who is bulimic, for example, may be a conditioned hypereater who uses a socially maladaptive strategy to compensate for the excessive calories consumed. Binge eaters and people with bulimia have higher-than-average levels of psychopathology, including depression and anxiety. James E. Mitchell, *Binge-Eating Disorder: Clinical Foundations and Treatment* (New York: Guilford Press, 2008).

p. 158. Those who are obese: Barbara Rolls, PhD, Helen A. Guthrie chair and professor, Department of Nutritional Sciences, Penn State University, and Tanja Kral, PhD, Research Assistant Professor, Nutrition in Psychiatry, University of Pennsylvania School of Medicine, shared with me their writings and presentations on differences between lean and obese individuals, including a presentation titled "Eating Behavior as a Phenotype for Obesity," National Institutes of Health, Bethesda, Maryland, 2004.

p. 158. Disinhibited patterns: Disinhibition, the act of losing control in the presence of highly palatable foods, and overeating as a result, is well described in F. Bellisle, K. Clement, M. Le Barzic, A. Le Gall, B. Guy-Grand, and A. Basdevant, "The Eating Inventory and Body Adiposity from Leanness to Massive Obesity: A Study of 2509 Adults," *Obesity Research* 12, no. 12 (2004): 2023–30; and J. Westenhoefer, P. Broeckmann, A. K. Munch, and V. Pudel, "Cognitive Control of Eating Behaviour and the Disinhibition Effect," *Appetite* 23, no. 1 (1994): 27–41.

The classic tool for measuring disinhibited behavior is the Three-Factor

Eating Questionnaire (TFEQ), developed in the 1980s by Albert J. Stunkard, a professor of psychiatry at the University of Pennsylvania School of Medicine, and Samuel Messick, then chief statistician of the Educational Testing Service in Princeton. A disinhibited eater is likely to answer "true" to each of the following statements: "When I smell a sizzling steak or see a juicy piece of meat, I find it very difficult to keep from eating, even if I have just finished a meal." "Sometimes, things just taste so good that I keep on eating even when I am no longer hungry." "When I am with someone who is overeating, I usually overeat, too." "Sometimes when I start eating, I just can't seem to stop." "When I feel lonely, I console myself by eating." A. J. Stunkard and S. Messick, "The Three-Factor Eating Questionnaire to Measure Dietary Restraint, Disinhibition and Hunger," *Journal of Psychosomatic Research* 29, no. 1 (1985): 71–83.

Disinhibition has repeatedly been linked to higher BMI levels and weight gain. N. P. Hays, G. P. Bathalon, M. A. McCrory, R. Roubenoff, R. Lipman, and S. B. Roberts, "Eating Behavior Correlates of Adult Weight Gain and Obesity in Healthy Women Aged 55–65 Y," *American Journal of Clinical Nutrition* 75, no. 3 (2002): 476–83; N. P. Hays and S. B. Roberts, "Aspects of Eating Behaviors 'Disinhibition' and 'Restraint' Are Related to Weight Gain and BMI in Women," *Obesity (Silver Spring)* 16, no. 1 (2008): 52–8; F. Bellisle, K. Clement, M. Le Barzic, A. Le Gall, B. Guy-Grand, and A. Basdevant, "The Eating Inventory and Body Adiposity from Leanness to Massive Obesity: A Study of 2509 Adults," *Obesity Research* 12, no. 12 (2004): 2023–30; V. Hainer, M. Kunesova, F. Bellisle, J. Parizkova, R. Braunerova, M. Wagenknecht, J. Lajka, M. Hill, and A. Stunkard, "The Eating Inventory, Body Adiposity and Prevalence of Diseases in a Quota Sample of Czech Adults," *International Journal of Obesity* 30, no. 5 (2006): 830–6. See also C. Lawton, F. Croden, R. Alam, C. Golding, S. Whybrow, J. Stubbs, and J. Blundell, "Differences between Individuals Resistant and Susceptible to Weight Gain on a High Fat Diet," Abstract T7d:P7d-004, *International Journal of Obesity* 28 Suppl 1 (2004): S218.

Other research has shown the obverse and found that becoming *less* disinhibited predicts successful weight loss. V. Hainer, M. Kunesova, F. Bellisle, M. Hill, R. Braunerova, and M. Wagenknecht, "Psychobehavioral and Nutritional Predictors of Weight Loss in Obese Women Treated with Sibutramine," *International Journal of Obesity* 29, no. 2 (2005): 208–16.

p. 158. Obese group ate more: In studies of meal patterns among groups of obese and nonobese middle-aged Swedish women, scientists at Göteborg University found that obese women consumed significantly more meals and more snacks throughout the day and ate more at nontraditional mealtimes, in the evening, and at night. A. K. Lindroos, L. Lissner, M. E. Mathiassen, J. Karlsson, M. Sullivan, C. Bengtsson, and L. Sjostrom, "Dietary Intake in Relation to Restrained Eating, Disinhibition, and Hunger in Obese and Nonobese Swedish Women," *Obesity Research* 5, no. 3 (1997): 175–82; H. Berteus Forslund, J. S. Torgerson, L. Sjostrom, and A. K. Lindroos, "Snacking Frequency in Relation to Energy Intake and Food Choices in Obese Men and Women Compared to a Reference Population," *International Journal of Obesity* 29, no. 6 (2005): 711–9; H. Berteus Forslund, A. K. Lindroos, L. Sjostrom, and L. Lissner, "Meal Patterns and Obesity in Swedish Women: A Simple Instrument Describing Usual Meal Types, Frequency and Temporal Distribution," *European Journal of Clinical Nutrition* 56, no. 8 (2002): 740–7.

Other research reached similar conclusions about intake among obese women, concluding that they ate more often and later, and consumed more when eating high-fat foods. J. E. Blundell, C. L. Lawton, and A. J. Hill, "Mechanisms of Appetite Control and Their Abnormalities in Obese Patients," *Hormone Research* 39 Suppl 3 (1993): 72–6; C. L. Lawton, V. J. Burley, J. K. Wales, and J. E. Blundell, "Dietary Fat and Appetite Control in Obese Subjects: Weak Effects on Satiation and Satiety," *International Journal of Obesity and Related Metabolic Disorders* 17, no. 7 (1993): 409–16.

p. 158. Beyond the point of hunger: Based on a survey of almost 1,000 women, researchers at the National Institute of Environmental Health Sciences found that Caucasian women who reported that they "eat beyond satiation nearly every day" were six times more likely to be obese than those who rarely or never did so; African American women were fifteen times more likely to be obese than their counterparts who did not report they ate beyond satiation. E. A. Brewer, R. L. Kolotkin, and D. D. Baird, "The Relationship between Eating Behaviors and Obesity in African American and Caucasian Women," *Eating Behaviors* 4, no. 2 (2003): 159–71; B. Barkeling, N. A. King, E. Naslund, and J. E. Blundell, "Characterization of Obese Individuals Who Claim to Detect No Relationship between Their Eating Pattern and Sensations of Hunger or Fullness," *International Journal of Obesity* 31, no. 3 (2006): 435–39; B. Barkeling, E. Naslund, N. King, and J. Blundell, "Correlates with High TFEQ- D and Altered Appetite Control in Obese Subjects," Abstract T7d:P7d-004, *International Journal of Obesity* 28 Suppl 1 (2004): S213.

In a University of Pennsylvania study, researchers studied the influence of a "preload" on appetite—essentially, measuring the impact of "eating before eating" on total caloric consumption. Obese people given a preload, followed by unrestricted access to other foods, consumed more calories than lean people. T. A. Spiegel, E. E. Shrager, and E. Stellar, "Responses of Lean and Obese Subjects to Preloads, Deprivation, and Palatability," *Appetite* 13, no. 1 (1989): 45–69.

p. 158. Work harder for food: Weight was the only variable that influenced the study population's willingness to work for food. Hunger, liking for the snack food, or liking for the other reinforcing activities did not have comparable effects. B. E. Saelens and L. H. Epstein, "Reinforcing Value of Food in Obese and Non-Obese Women," *Appetite* 27, no. 1 (1996): 41–50.

p. 159. Liking and wanting: There is an important distinction between "liking" a food, based on the orosensory pleasure it provides, and "wanting" it, as demonstrated by the motivation to seek it out, according to David J. Mela, PhD, senior scientist, Weight Control and Behavioural Nutrition, Unilever Food and Health Research Institute. People who are overweight do not necessarily enjoy food more than lean people, nor do they experience the taste differently, yet they have more drive to consume. Author interviews with David Mela, December 5, 2006, and October 23, 2006; D. J. Mela, "Eating for Pleasure or Just Wanting to Eat? Reconsidering Sensory Hedonic Responses as a Driver of Obesity," *Appetite* 47, no. 1 (2006): 10–17.

In one study, subjects recorded the foods they chose to eat, rated the predominant taste characteristic as sweet, salty, sour, or bitter, and indicated on a questionnaire how much they liked each one. There were virtually no differences among obese and lean people in "liking" scores. The results were similar when obese and lean people were given a written list of foods and asked to rate how much they liked each one. D. N. Cox, L. Perry, P. B. Moore, L. Vallis, and D. J. Mela, "Sensory and Hedonic Associations with Macronutrient and Energy Intakes of Lean and Obese Consumers," *International Journal of Obesity and Related Metabolic Disorders* 23, no. 4 (1999): 403–10; D. N. Cox, M. van Galen, D. Hedderley, L. Perry, P. B. Moore, and D. J. Mela, "Sensory and Hedonic Judgments of Common Foods by Lean Consumers and Consumers with Obesity," *Obesity Research* 6, no. 6 (1998): 438–47.

Other findings demonstrate that people who are overweight want food more and will work harder to get it, a key characteristic of reward-based eating. University of South Carolina researchers asked study subjects to assess how much they wanted to do a number of different things—including eating, spending time with friends and family, and taking it easy. The data showed clearly that the reinforcement value of eating—that is, the desire to do more of it—was highest for those who were obese. S. B. Jacobs and M. K. Wagner, "Obese and Nonobese Individuals: Behavioral and Personality Characteristics," *Addictive Behaviors* 9, no. 2 (1984): 223–6.

Canadian researchers also demonstrated that obese populations want food more. They gave children a choice of getting a reward immediately, or getting twice the amount of that reward a day later. One of the rewards was edible (a box of candy); the other was not (a playful pen). Both groups of children were equally willing to delay gratification to get more of the nonedible reward the next day. However, they showed significant differences in their willingness to delay gratification for food—nine out of ten obese children (90 percent) chose to have the candy immediately, compared to four out of six (67 percent) normal-weight children. D. P. Bonato and F. J. Boland, "Delay of Gratification in Obese Children," *Addictive Behaviors* 8, no. 1 (1983): 71–4.

See also H. M. Snoek, L. Huntjens, L. J. Van Gemert, C. De Graaf, and H. Weenen, "Sensory-Specific Satiety in Obese and Normal-Weight Women," *American Journal of Clinical Nutrition* 80, no. 4 (2004): 823–31.

p. 159. Reno Diet Heart Study: Sachiko St. Jeor, *Obesity Assessment: Tools, Methods, Interpretations (A Reference Case: The Reno Diet-Heart Study)*, Chapman & Hall Series in Clinical Nutrition (New York: Chapman & Hall, 1997).

p. 159. Three behaviors of interest: My research team at the University of California, San Francisco, focused on three behaviors—loss of control over eating; lack of feeling satisfied by food; and preoccupation with food. To measure loss of control, we used three items from a weight-loss questionnaire that was part of the Reno Diet Heart Study, assessing the extent to which one "feels out of control eating in general," "feels out of control eating on a diet," and "feels out of control eating when not on a diet." To measure lack of satiety, we used three "yes or no" statements from the Three-Factor Eating Questionnaire: "My stomach feels like a bottomless pit," "I am always hungry so can't stop eating before finishing plate," and "I eat if not hungry because things taste good." To measure preoccupation, we used the question from the weight-loss questionnaire that asked, "Are you preoccupied with thinking about food?" and was answered on a scale that ranged from 1 to 5.

p. 160. Latent classification analysis: The most sophisticated approach to classifying participants based on scores on all three behaviors is a latent classification analysis, which is a type of mixture modeling, using Mplus software. This procedure assumes that observed categorical variables are indicators of latent variables. The present analysis specified a single latent variable with two levels (phenotype and nonphenotype). Rather than choosing an arbitrary cutoff on each scale, we wanted to identify people with varying combinations of high scores (such as high scores across three dimensions or a very high score on a single dimension).

p. 160. It turned out: The correlation between loss of control and lack of feeling satisfied was r = .37; the correlation between loss of control and preoccupation with food was r = .52; and the correlation between lack of feeling satisfied and preoccupation was r = .32. These are moderate correlations, and suggest that people who score high on one are likely to score high on the other two, and thus they could comprise part of a phenotype. However, the magnitude of the correlations also shows that there is a great deal of individual variability, in that people may score high on only one or two of these factors.

p. 160. Twice as likely to have been overweight: Among those who exhibited conditioned hypereating, 29 percent were overweight early in life, compared with 17 percent of those who did not exhibit that behavior.

p. 160. A broad swath: As many as 71 million people may exhibit the characteristics of conditioned hypereating, based on the following assumptions: The current US population is 305 million people, including approximately 219 million adults; 50 percent of those who are obese, 30 percent who are overweight, and 17 percent who are lean exhibit conditioned hypereating; and 66 percent of the general population is either obese or overweight.

p. 160. Twice as likely to be obese: Of those who exhibited conditioned hypereating, 42 percent were obese, 37 percent were overweight, and 21 percent were lean. By comparison, of those who did not exhibit conditioned hypereating, 18 percent were obese, 38 percent were overweight, and 44 percent were lean.

p. 161. How humans behave: The Behavioral Activation Scale measures how sensitive an individual is to reward. Researchers interested in determining whether the scale could predict neural activity showed healthy-weight subjects full-color photographs of appetizing food (chocolate cake, ice cream), food that was disgusting (rotten meat, moldy bread), or bland (uncooked rice, potatoes), and photos of neutral nonfood objects (such as a videocassette and an iron). They found that the higher the subjects' behavioral activation scores, the more energetic their responses on MRI scans. J. D. Beaver, A. D. Lawrence, J. van Ditzhuijzen, M. H. Davis, A. Woods, and A. J. Calder, "Individual Differences in Reward Drive Predict Neural Responses to Images of Food," *Journal of Neuroscience* 26, no. 19 (2006): 5160–6.

p. 161. Developed a scale: The eleven questions on the scale assessing conditioned hypereating were: (1) I feel out of control in the presence of delicious food. (2) When I start eating, I just can't seem to stop. (3) It is difficult for me to leave food on my plate. (4) When it comes to foods I love, I have no willpower. (5) I get so hungry that my stomach often seems like a bottomless pit. (6) Others may slow down when eating, but I tend to eat fast until I am done. (7) I don't get full easily. (8) It seems like most of my waking hours are preoccupied by thoughts about eating or not eating. (9) I have days when I can't seem to think about anything else but food. (10) Food is always on my mind. (11) If I didn't worry about what I ate, I would usually choose rich or high-fat foods. In addition to our scale, we asked participants to complete a battery of validated questionnaires assessing various components of eating behavior.

While most studies have examined the differences between obese and lean individuals, we focused on individuals with characteristics of conditioned hypereating, whether they were lean, overweight, or obese. Forty individuals participated in the behavioral and neuroimaging tests: 14 lean (BMI 18.5–24.9), 14 overweight (BMI 25–29.9), 12 obese (BMI 30 and above). Scores on our scale significantly correlated with BMI (p = 0.01; Pearson correlation: 0.391). Furthermore, we observed a significant relationship between waist circumference, a measure of abdominal fat, and our phenotype measure (p = 0.02; Pearson correlation: 0.355).

Our scale was highly correlated with other measures of binge eating behavior, emotional eating, disinhibition, and overall feelings of hunger: Binge Eating Scale: p = 3.2 E-7, Pearson correlation = 0.747; Power of Food Scale: *Food Available* p = 2.2 E-7, Pearson correlation = 0.715, *Food Present* p = 2.4 E-7, Pearson correlation = 0.713, Three-Factor Eating Questionnaire: *Disinhibition* p = 3.4 E-6, Pearson correlation = 0.517, *Hunger* p = 0.0006, Pearson correlation = 0.517; Dutch Eating Behavior Questionnaire: *Emotional Eating Total* p = 0.002, Pearson correlation = 0.471, *Emotional Eating—Diffuse Emotions* p = 0.0002, Pearson correlation = 0.553, *Emotional Eating—Clear Emotions* p = 0.01, Pearson correlation = 0.401, *External Eating* p = 0.001, Pearson correlation = 0.491.

p. 161. Happening in people's brains: Brain scans showed that eating style—including self-reported ratings of cue responsiveness, disinhibition, compulsive eating, and bingeing, as assessed by our eleven-question scale—contributes to obese-specific brain responses, regardless of actual BMI. Lean, overweight, and obese subjects who scored high on our conditioned hypereating scale showed increased response in the amygdala, an area responsive during the anticipatory phase of food reward, and decreased response in the ventral medial prefrontal cortex, a region important for inhibitory control, when ingesting a palatable milkshake, compared with individuals matched for BMI who had scored low on the scale. J. A. Felsted, E. Epel, D. A. Kessler, I. de Araujo, D. M. Small, "Differential Effects of Body Mass Index and Eating Style on Neural Response to Milkshake" (poster presentation at Association for Chemoreception Sciences/International Symposium on Olfaction and Taste 2008 Conference), 184.

p. 161. Anticipatory phase: The differences between the anticipatory and consummatory phases are discussed in D. M. Small, M. G. Veldhuizen, J. Felsted, Y. E. Mak, and F. McGlone, "Separable Substrates for Anticipatory and Consummatory Food Chemosensation," *Neuron* 57 (2008): 786–97. According to the authors, the amygdala encodes the predictive value and relevance of food cues.

p. 161. Cue-induced anticipation: H. P. Weingarten, "Conditioned Cues Elicit Feeding in Sated Rats: A Role for Learning in Meal Initiation," *Science* 220 (1983): 431–33; G. D. Petrovich, B. Setlow, P. C. Holland, and M. Gallagher, "Amygdalo-Hypothalamic Circuit Allows Learned Cues to Override Satiety and Promote Eating," *Journal of Neuroscience* 22 (2002): 8748–53; A. Jansen, "A Learning Model of Binge Eating: Cue Reactivity and Cue Exposure," *Behavioral Research and Therapy* 36 (1998): 257–72.

p. 162. Cluster of symptoms: There is a body of literature that explores the question of what constitutes a condition, a syndrome, and a disease. See E. Robins and S. B. Guze, "Establishment of Diagnostic Validity in Psychiatric Illness: Its Application to Schizophrenia," *American Journal of Psychiatry* 126, no. 7 (1970): 983–7.

Conditioned hypereating might also be a phenotype. See W. L. Nyhan, "Behavioral Phenotypes in Organic Genetic Disease. Presidential Address to the Society for Pediatric Research, May 1, 1971," *Pediatric Research* 6, no. 1 (1972): 1–9; Gregory O'Brien and William Yule, *Behavioural Phenotypes*, Clinics in Developmental Medicine (London: Mac Keith Press, 1995); E. M. Dykens and R. M. Hodapp, "Three Steps toward Improving the Measurement of Behavior in Behavioral Phenotype Research," *Child and Adolescent Psychiatric Clinics of North America* 16, no. 3 (2007): 617–30.

p. 163. Puzzle of conditioned hypereating: For two excellent reviews of the theories advanced to explain why certain people overeat, see J. Wardle, "Eating Behaviour in Obesity," in *The Psychology of Food Choice*, Frontiers in Nutritional Science No. 3., ed. R. Shepherd, Monique Raats, and Nutrition Society (Great Britain) (Wallingford, UK: CABI in association with the Nutrition Society, 2006); and Elena Marie Wood, *Eating Behavior in Men and Women: A Comparison Study* (PhD dissertation, Temple University, 1999).

p. 163. Known as externality: S. Schachter, "Obesity and Eating: Internal and External Cues Differentially Affect the Eating Behavior of Obese and Normal Subjects," *Science* 161, no. 843 (1968): 751–6; Stanley Schachter, *Emotion, Obesity, and Crime*, Social Psychology (New York: Academic Press, 1971).

p. 163. Cracker study: S. Schachter, "Some Extraordinary Facts about Obese Humans and Rats," *American Psychologist* 26, no. 2 (1971): 129–44; William Bennett and Joel Gurin, *The Dieter's Dilemma: Eating Less and Weighing More* (New York: Basic Books, 1982), 38.

p. 164. Roast-beef sandwich experiment: R. E. Nisbett, "Determinants of Food Intake in Obesity," *Science* 159, no. 820 (1968): 1254–5.

p. 164. Too "simplistic": J. Rodin, "Current Status of the Internal-External Hypothesis for Obesity: What Went Wrong?" *American Psychologist* 36, no. 4 (1981): 361–72.

p. 165. Restraint theory: Peter Herman, a Northwestern University faculty member and a former student of Stanley Schachter, and Debbie Mack, who had noticed overeating tendencies among her sorority sisters at Northwestern, long ago helped give credibility to the restraint hypothesis. Their study looked at two groups of people who had been categorized as either restrained or unrestrained eaters. After eating a meal, willing volunteers were divided into three groups—one was given a cup of milkshake to drink; another, two cups; and the third, no milkshake at all—and then offered as much ice cream as they wished. Some followed a predictable pattern—the more milkshake they had consumed, the less ice cream they wanted. But among others, the pattern was just the opposite—the more milkshake, the more ice cream. These turned out to be the people who had been categorized as restrained eaters. C. P. Herman and D. Mack, "Restrained and Unrestrained Eating," *Journal of Personality* 43, no. 4 (1975): 647–60; E. R. Didie, "The Power of Food Scale: Development and Theoretical Evaluation of a Self-Report Measure of the Perceived Influence of Food" (PhD dissertation, Drexel University, June 2003).

Other researchers soon established the same pattern and the restraint theory gained wider acceptance. Many explanations have been offered for the effect of restraint on eating behavior. Herman suggested that once dieters succumb to even the smallest temptation, their determination to limit their food intake may be shattered, at least for a time. That response has been called the "what-the-hell" effect—having lost control, a dieter behaves as if there is no point in trying to reestablish it, at least not immediately. Alcohol and negative emotional states (such as anxiety or depression) have also been implicated in breaking restraint, as has the body's compensatory response to food deprivation.

p. 165. Cracks also appeared: Some recent work on eating behavior has helped swing the pendulum away from restraint and back to externality. One Dutch study, for example, concluded that "overweight children fail to regulate their food intake when they are confronted with temptations like the intense smell and taste of appetizing food. Their overeating is not related to psychological factors, like mood, self-esteem, and a restrained eating style." It is instead related to cues. These youngsters overate because they were more sensitive to cues than their normal-weight peers. A. Jansen, N. Theunissen, K. Slechten, C. Nederkoorn, B. Boon, S. Mulkens, and A. Roefs, "Overweight Children Overeat after Exposure to Food Cues," *Eating Behaviors* 4, no. 2 (2003): 197–209; E. Stice, J. A. Cooper, D. A. Schoeller, K. Tappe, and M. R. Lowe, "Are Dietary Restraint Scales Valid Measures of Moderate- to Long-Term Dietary Restriction? Objective Biological and Behavioral Data Suggest Not," *Psychological Assessment* 19, no. 4 (2007): 449–58; C. P. Herman and J. Polivy, "External Cues in the Control of Food Intake in Humans: The Sensory-Normative Distinction," *Physiology and Behavior* 94, no. 5 (2008): 722–8.

p. 165. Risks of deprivation: "Deprivation sensitizes the neural circuitry that mediates reward-based eating," according to Kenneth Carr, PhD, associate professor of psychiatry and pharmacology, Departments of Psychiatry (Millhauser Labs) and Pharmacology, New York University. Carr also noted that deprivation inhibits other drives that might compete with food-seeking behavior, such as reproductive behavior and pain sensitivity. Author communication with Kenneth Carr, March 5, 2007.

p. 166. Genetic basis of childhood eating: Author interview with Myles Faith, PhD, Center for Weight and Eating Disorders, University of Pennsylvania School of Medicine, January 17, 2007.

p. 167. Five-year-olds: M. S. Faith, R. I. Berkowitz, V. A. Stallings, J. Kerns, M. Storey, and A. J. Stunkard, "Eating in the Absence of Hunger: A Genetic Marker for Childhood Obesity in Prepubertal Boys?" *Obesity (Silver Spring)* 14, no. 1 (2006): 131–8.

p. 167. Studies involving twins: S. Tholin, F. Rasmussen, P. Tynelius, and J. Karlsson, "Genetic and Environmental Influences on Eating Behavior: The Swedish Young Male Twins Study," *American Journal of Clinical Nutrition* 81, no. 3 (2005): 564–9; B. M. Neale, S. E. Mazzeo, and C. M. Bulik, "A Twin Study of Dietary Restraint, Disinhibition and Hunger: An Examination of the Eating Inventory (Three Factor Eating Questionnaire)," *Twin Research* 6, no. 6 (2003): 471–8; author interview with Cynthia Bulik, PhD, professor, Department of Psychiatry, School of Medicine, University of North Carolina–Chapel Hill, January 3, 2007.

p. 167. Eating in the absence of hunger: J. O. Fisher, G. Cai, S. J. Jaramillo, S. A. Cole, A. G. Comuzzie, and N. F. Butte, "Heritability of Hyperphagic Eating Behavior and Appetite-Related Hormones among Hispanic Children," *Obesity (Silver Spring)* 15, no. 6 (2007): 1484–95.

p. 168. Analysis of questionnaires: J. M. de Castro and Lisa R. R. Lilenfeld, "Influence of Heredity on Dietary Restraint, Disinhibition, and Perceived Hunger in Humans," *Nutrition* 21, no. 4 (2005): 446–55.

p. 168. Heritability of disinhibited eating patterns: V. Provencher, L. Perusse, L. Bouchard, V. Drapeau, C. Bouchard, T. Rice, D. C. Rao, A. Tremblay, J.-P. Despres, and S. Lemieux, "Familial Resemblance in Eating Behaviors in Men and Women from the Quebec Family Study," *Obesity* 13, no. 9 (2005): 1624–9.

p. 168. Impulsive: A number of experts have studied the links between impulsivity and the heightened state of arousal that can influence eating behavior. Impulsivity is "acting without thinking," said Chantal Nederkoorn, PhD, assistant professor, Department of Clinical Psychological Science, Maastricht University, Netherlands, who called it a characteristic of people who "prefer immediate, smaller rewards over a delay of reward. . . . We call people impulsive when they don't have the ability to wait for larger goals." People who are impulsive lack what Nederkoorn called "response inhibition . . . that is, they act too soon, they respond too quickly." In their haste, these people may not focus on the most important stimuli, or they may make a less-than-optimal choice among multiple stimuli.

In one study to measure impulsivity, children were instructed to respond to a "go" signal on a computer screen by pressing a button as quickly as possible, and then to inhibit their button-pressing response when an audio "stop" signal sounded. "Stop-signal reaction times are found to differentiate between obese and normal weight children and between restrained and unrestrained eaters," writes Nederkoorn. "Impulsivity was related to overweight at all moments. The most impulsive children were the most overweight ones." C. Nederkoorn, E. Jansen, S. Mulkens, and A. Jansen, "Impulsivity Predicts Treatment Outcome in Obese Children," *Behaviour Research and Therapy* 45, no. 5 (2007): 1071–5.

For related studies, see R. Guerrieri, C. Nederkoorn, and A. Jansen, "The Interaction between Impulsivity and a Varied Food Environment: Its Influence on Food Intake and Overweight," *International Journal of Obesity* 32, no. 4 (2008): 708–14; R. Guerrieri, C. Nederkoorn, K. Stankiewicz, H. Alberts, N. Geschwind, C. Martijn, and A. Jansen, "The Influence of Trait and Induced State Impulsivity on Food Intake in Normal-Weight Healthy Women," *Appetite* 49, no. 1 (2007): 66–73; C. Nederkoorn, C. Braet, Y. Van Eijs, A. Tanghe, and A. Jansen, "Why Obese Children Cannot Resist Food: The Role of Impulsivity," *Eating Behaviors* 7, no. 4 (2006): 315–22; C. Nederkoorn, F. T. Smulders, R. C. Havermans, A. Roefs, and A. Jansen, "Impulsivity in Obese Women," *Appetite* 47, no. 2 (2006): 253–6; D. P. Bonato and F. J. Boland, "Delay of Gratification in Obese Children," *Addictive Behaviors* 8, no. 1 (1983): 71–4.

We also have research that suggests that children who do not delay gratification act more impulsively as adults. Walter Mischel, PhD, the Robert Johnston Niven Professor of Humane Letters in Psychology, Columbia University, gave healthy-weight, four-year-old children a choice between eating one treat (such as a marshmallow or an Oreo cookie) immediately, or waiting until later so that they could eat two. For those who are impulsive, "the value of the delayed reward does not have the salience and the power of the immediate reward," explained Mischel. The stimulus at hand generates the greater arousal. He found a small, but significant, correlation between those who chose the immediate reward as children and their BMI scores three decades later. Those who were impulsive at age four weighed more, proportional to their height, at age 34. Author interview with Walter Mischel, April 4, 2007.

p. 168. Which influence is predominant: At my request, Neil Risch, PhD, professor of human genetics at the University of California, San Francisco, summarized the heritabilities of disinhibition and restraint in four key studies. The heritabilities of "disinhibition" were .44, .52, .00, and .25. The heritabilities of "restraint" were .00, .82, .44, and .05. B. M. Neale, S. E. Mazzeo, and C. M. Bulik, "A Twin Study of Dietary Restraint, Disinhibition and Hunger: An Examination of the Eating Inventory (Three Factor Eating Questionnaire)," *Twin Research* 6, no. 6 (2003): 471–8; S. Tholin, F. Rasmussen, P. Tynelius, and J. Karlsson, "Genetic and Environmental Influences on Eating Behavior: The Swedish Young Male Twins Study," *American Journal of Clinical Nutrition* 81, no. 3 (2005): 564–9; J. M. de Castro and L. R. R. Lilenfeld, "Influence of Heredity on Dietary Restraint, Disinhibition, and Perceived Hunger in Humans," *Nutrition* 21, no. 4 (2005): 446–55; V. Provencher, L. Perusse, L. Bouchard, V. Drapeau, C. Bouchard, T. Rice, D. C. Rao, A. Tremblay, J.-P. Despres, and S. Lemieux, "Familial Resemblance in Eating Behaviors in Men and Women from the Quebec Family Study," *Obesity* 13, no. 9 (2005): 1624–9.

p. 169. Population-wide shift: Author interview with Susan Johnson, PhD, director, the Children's Eating Laboratory, University of Colorado Health Sciences Center, January 3, 2007.

p. 170. Slightly older population: S. L. Johnson and L. A. Taylor-Holloway, "Non-Hispanic White and Hispanic Elementary School Children's Self-Regulation of Energy Intake," *American Journal of Clinical Nutrition* 83, no. 6 (2006): 1276–82.

p. 171. Jennifer Fisher: J. O. Fisher, B. J. Rolls, and L. L. Birch, "Children's Bite Size and Intake of an Entree Are Greater with Large Portions Than with Age-Appropriate or Self-Selected Portions," *American Journal of Clinical Nutrition* 77, no. 5 (2003): 1164–70. Barbara J. Rolls showed slightly different results in a study that suggested younger children (mean age, 3.6) did not eat significantly different amounts whether they were given small, medium, or large portions of macaroni and cheese, while older children (mean age, 5) did eat more. That work suggests a window of time in which children stop eating solely in response to hunger and satiety and begin to respond to other cues. B. J. Rolls, D. Engell, and L. L. Birch, "Serving Portion Size Influences 5-Year-Old but Not 3-Year-Old Children's Food Intakes," *Journal of the American Dietetic Association* 100, no. 2 (2000): 232–4.

p. 171. Large entrée portions: "There is something fundamental about the visual cues provided by portion size that are altering the microstructures of eating. When you double the entrée size, you see increased food consumption and you see increased energy intake at the meal. . . . You don't see really large changes in the number of bites children take, but you see the average bite size increase," said Jennifer Fisher, PhD, researcher, the Center for Obesity Research and Education, Temple University. Author interview with Jennifer Fisher, February 13, 2007.

p. 173. Neighborhood food stores: M. C. Wang, C. Cubbin, D. Ahn, and M. A. Winkleby, "Changes in Neighbourhood Food Store Environment, Food Behaviour and Body Mass Index, 1981–1990," *Public Health Nutrition* 11, no. 9 (2008): 963–7.

p. 174. Barriers have been lowered: Author interviews with David J. Mela, PhD, senior scientist, Weight Control and Behavioural Nutrition, Unilever Food and Health Research Institute, November 2005, October 23, 2006, and January 17, 2007.

p. 174. People ate meals: Meredith Luce, dietitian in private practice, Orlando, Florida, presentation at the American Society of Bariatric Physicians annual meeting, Orlando, 2004.

p. 174. Snacking is now the norm: L. Jahns, A. M. Siega-Riz, and B. M. Popkin, "The Increasing Prevalence of Snacking among US Children from 1977 to 1996," *Journal of Pediatrics* 138, no. 4 (2001): 493–8; L. S. Adair and B. M. Popkin, "Are Child Eating Patterns Being Transformed Globally?" *Obesity Research* 13, no. 7 (2005): 1281–99; C. Zizza, A. M. Siega-Riz, and B. M. Popkin, "Significant Increase in Young Adults' Snacking between 1977–1978 and 1994–1996 Represents a Cause for Concern!" *Preventive Medicine* 32, no. 4 (2001): 303–10.

p. 175. Several kinds of analysis: P. Rozin, K. Kabnick, E. Pete, C. Fischler, and C. Shields, "The Ecology of Eating: Smaller Portion Sizes in France Than in the United States Help Explain the French Paradox," *Psychological Science* 14, no. 5 (2003): 450–4.

p. 176. Strong meal structure: Author interview with France Bellisle, PhD, head researcher, Diabetes Department, Hotel Dieu Hospital, Paris, February 28, 2007.

p. 176. Vagabond feeding: J. P. Poulain, "The Contemporary Diet in France: 'De-Structuration' or From Commensalism to 'Vagabond Feeding,'" *Appetite* 39, no. 1 (2002): 43–55.

p. 177. Trend is unmistakable: The prevalence of obesity in the adult French population rose from just over 8 percent in 1997 to 11.3 percent in 2003. Over the same six-year period, the percentage of overweight adults (BMI between 25 and 30) rose from 36.7 percent to 41.6 percent. F. Bellisle, "Nutrition and Health in France: Dissecting a Paradox," *Journal of the American Dietetic Association* 105, no. 12 (2005): 1870–3; J. L. Volatier and P. Verger, "Recent National French Food and Nutrient Intake Data," *British Journal of Nutrition* 81 Suppl 2 (1999): S57–9; M. F. Rolland-Cachera, K. Castetbon, N. Arnault, F. Bellisle, M. C. Romano, Y. Lehingue, M. L. Frelut, and S. Hercberg, "Body Mass Index in 7–9-Y-Old French Children: Frequency of Obesity, Overweight and Thinness," *International Journal of Obesity and Related Metabolic Disorders* 26, no. 12 (2002): 1610–6; M. A. Charles, A. Basdevant, and E. Eschwege, "[Prevalence of Obesity in Adults in France: The Situation in 2000 Established from the OBEPI Study]," *Annales d'Endocrinologie* 63, no. 2, pt. 1 (2002): 154–8.

p. 181. Invitations to the brain: Author interview with James Leckman, MD, director of research, Neison Harris Professor of Child Psychiatry and Pediatrics, Child Study Center, Yale University School of Medicine, April 29, 2007.

p. 182. Compulsive hair pulling: Author interview with Raymond G. Miltenberger, PhD, director, Applied Behavior Analysis Masters Program, Department of Child and Family Studies, University of South Florida, May 10, 2007; R. G. Miltenberger, D. W. Woods, and M. Himle, "Tic Disorders and Trichotillomania," in *Handbook of Functional Analysis and Clinical Psychology*, ed. P. Sturmey, 151–70 (Burlington, MA: Elsevier, 2007); C. Deaver, R. G. Miltenberger, and J. Stricker, "Functional Analysis and Treatment of Hair Twirling in a Young Child," *Journal of Applied Behavior Analysis* 34 (2001): 535–38; D. Woods and R. G. Miltenberger, eds., *Tic Disorders, Trichotillomania, and Repetitive Behavior Disorders: Behavioral Approaches to Analysis and Treatment* (Norwell, MA: Kluwer, 2001).

p. 182. Old habit is still there: Author interview with Mark E. Bouton, PhD, professor of psychology, University of Vermont, March 2, 2007; M. E. Bouton and A. M. Woods, "Extinction: Behavioral Mechanisms and Their Implications," in *Learning and Memory: A Comprehensive Reference (Vol. 1, Learning The-*

ory and Behaviour), ed. J. H. Byrne, D. Sweatt, R. Menzel, H. Eichenbaum, and H. Roediger, 151–71 (Oxford: Elsevier, 2008).

p. 182. Context, conditioning, and memory: M. E. Bouton, "The Concept in the Human and Animal Memory Domains," in *Science of Memory: Concepts*, ed. H. L. Roediger, Y. Dudai, and S. M. Fitzpatrick, 115–19 (Oxford: Oxford University Press, 2007); M. E. Bouton, *Learning and Behavior: A Contemporary Synthesis* (Sunderland, MA: Sinauer Associates, 2007); M. E. Bouton, A. M. Woods, E. W. Moody, C. Sunsay, and A. García-Gutiérrez, "Counteracting the Context-Dependence of Extinction: Relapse and Tests of Some Relapse Prevention Methods," in *Fear and Learning: From Basic Processes to Clinical Implications*, ed. M. G. Craske, D. Hermans, and D. Vansteenwegen, 175–96 (Washington, DC: American Psychological Association, 2006).

p. 184. Reversing longstanding habits: R. G. Miltenberger, "Habit Reversal," in *Encyclopedia of Behavior Modification and Cognitive Behavior Therapy Vol. II*, ed. A. Gross and R. Drabman, 873–77 (Thousand Oaks, CA: Sage, 2005); C. Romaniuk, R. G. Miltenberger, and C. Deaver, "Long Term Maintenance Following Habit Reversal and Adjunct Treatment for Trichotillomania," *Child and Family Behavior Therapy* 25, no. 2 (2003): 45–59; R. G. Miltenberger, "Habit Reversal Treatment Manual for Trichotillomania," in *Tic Disorders, Trichotillomania, and Repetitive Behavior Disorders: Behavioral Approaches to Analysis and Treatment*, ed. D. Woods and R. Miltenberger, 171–95 (Norwell, MA: Kluwer, 2001); N. H. Azrin and R. G. Nunn, "Habit-Reversal: A Method of Eliminating Nervous Habits and Tics," *Behaviour Research and Therapy* 11, no. 4 (1973): 619–28; R. G. Miltenberger, R. W. Fuqua, and D. W. Woods, "Applying Behavior Analysis to Clinical Problems: Review and Analysis of Habit Reversal," *Journal of Applied Behavior Analysis* 31, no. 3 (1998): 447–69.

p. 184. Very difficult to do: Author interview with James Leckman, MD, director of Research, Neison Harris Professor of Child Psychiatry and Pediatrics, Child Study Center, Yale University School of Medicine, April 29, 2007.

p. 185. Leads you to eat: Author interview with Raymond G. Miltenberger, PhD, director, Applied Behavior Analysis Masters Program, Department of Child and Family Studies, University of South Florida, May 10, 2007.

p. 186. Begin to self-monitor: Author interview with Matthew W. State, MD, PhD, director, Program of Neurogenetics, Yale School of Medicine, April 2, 2007.

p. 187. Verbally mediated: Author interview with Philip D. Zelazo, PhD, professor and Canada Research Chair in Developmental Neuroscience, Department of Psychology, University of Toronto, April 6, 2007; P. D. Zelazo and W. Cunningham, "Executive Function: Mechanisms Underlying Emotion Regulation," in *Handbook of Emotion Regulation*, ed. J. Gross, 135–58 (New York: Guilford Press, 2007); W. Cunningham and P. D. Zelazo, "Attitudes and Evaluation: A Social Cognitive Neuroscience Perspective," *Trends in Cognitive Sciences* 11 (2007): 97–104; C. Lamm, P. D. Zelazo, and M. D. Lewis, "Neural Correlates of Cognitive Control in Childhood and Adolescence: Disentangling the Contributions of Age and Executive Function," *Neuropsychologia* 44 (2006): 2139–48.

p. 188. Changing the way you think: Author interview with Kevin N. Ochsner, PhD, assistant professor, Department of Psychology, Columbia University, April 5, 2007; K. N. Ochsner and J. J. Gross, "The Neural Architecture of Emotion Regulation," in *The Handbook of Emotion Regulation*, ed. J. J. Gross and R. Thompson, 87–109 (New York: Guilford Press, 2007); K. N. Ochsner, "How Thinking Controls Feeling: A Social Cognitive Neuroscience Approach," in *Social Neuroscience: Integrating Biological and Psychological Explanations of Behavior*, ed. E. H. Jones and P. Winkielman, 106–36 (New York: Guilford Press, 2007); K. N. Ochsner and J. J. Gross, "Cognitive Emotion Regulation: Insights from Social, Cognitive and Affective Neuroscience," *Current Directions in Psychological Science* 17, no. 1 (2007): 153–8.

p. 189. Social networks: N. A. Christakis and J. H. Fowler, "The Spread of Obesity in a Large Social Network over 32 Years," *New England Journal of Medicine* 357, no. 4 (2007): 370–79.

p. 191. Automatic contingencies: Author interview with Walter Mischel, PhD, the Robert Johnston Niven Professor of Humane Letters in Psychology, Columbia University, April 4, 2007; J. Metcalfe and W. Mischel, "A Hot/Cool-System Analysis of Delay of Gratification: Dynamics of Willpower," *Psychological Review* 106, no. 1 (1999): 3–19.

p. 191. Rules in mind: Author interview with Kevin N. Ochsner, PhD, assistant professor, Department of Psychology, Columbia University, April 5, 2007.

p. 191. Engage in contrary behavior: Author interview with Matthew W. State, MD, PhD, director, Program of Neurogenetics, Yale School of Medicine, April 2, 2007.

p. 191. Did not develop cravings: Cravings for fats, sweets, carbohydrates, and fast-food fats were measured among participants on either a low-calorie, low-fat diet, or a low-carbohydrate diet, over a period ranging from 12 to 104 weeks. The authors concluded that restricting "certain types of foods results in decreased cravings and preferences for those foods while dieting. These results provide empirical data to address dieters' concerns that food restriction/dieting will increase cravings." C. K. Martin, D. Rosenbaum, P. Geiselman, H. Wyatt, S. Klein, J. Hill, and G. Foster, "Low Carbohydrate and Low Calorie/Low Fat Diets Decrease Cravings and Preferences for Restricted Foods Over Two Years," abstract, *Obesity* 16, Supp 1 (2008).

p. 192. Inhibit the behavior: Author interview with Silvia Bunge, PhD, head, Cognitive Control and Development Laboratory, University of California, Berkeley, April 12, 2007. Silvia A. Bunge and Jonathan D. Wallis, *Neuroscience of Rule-Guided Behavior* (Oxford: Oxford University Press, 2008).

p. 194. Study of smokers: Author interview with Alain Dagher, PhD, associate professor, Montreal Neurological Institute, McGill University, March 20, 2007; D. McBride, S. P. Barrett, J. T. Kelly, A. Aw, and A. Dagher, "Effects of Expectancy and Abstinence on the Neural Response to Smoking Cues in Cigarette Smokers: An fMRI Study," *Neuropsychopharmacology* 31, no. 12 (2006): 2728–38.

p. 196. Positive associations: Author interview with Philip D. Zelazo, PhD, professor and Canada Research Chair in Developmental Neuroscience, Department of Psychology, University of Toronto, April 6, 2007. P. D. Zelazo, M. Moscovitch, and E. Thompson, *The Cambridge Handbook of Consciousness* (Cambridge: Cambridge University Press, 2007).

p. 197. Emotional underpinnings: Author interview with Arnold M. Washton, PhD, addiction psychologist, director, Recovery Options, May 9, 2007; Arnold M. Washton, *Willpower's Not Enough: Understanding and Recovering from Addic-*

tions of Every Kind (New York: Harper & Row, 1989); Arnold M. Washton and Joan E. Zweben, *Treating Alcohol and Drug Problems in Psychotherapy Practice: Doing What Works* (New York: Guilford Press, 2006).

p. 198. Cigarette is aversive: Author interview with Walter Mischel, PhD, the Robert Johnston Niven Professor of Humane Letters in Psychology, Columbia University, April 4, 2007. For more about emotional regulation, see O. Ayduk, R. Mendoza-Denton, W. Mischel, G. Downey, P. K. Peake, and M. Rodriguez, "Regulating the Interpersonal Self: Strategic Self-Regulation for Coping with Rejection Sensitivity," *Journal of Personality and Social Psychology* 79, no. 5 (2000): 776–92; I. M. Eigsti, V. Zayas, W. Mischel, Y. Shoda, O. Ayduk, M. B. Dadlani, M. C. Davidson, J. Lawrence Aber, and B. J. Casey, "Predicting Cognitive Control from Preschool to Late Adolescence and Young Adulthood," *Psychological Science* 17, no. 6 (2006): 478–84; and W. Mischel, "Toward an Integrative Science of the Person," *Annual Review of Psychology* 55 (2004): 1–22.

p. 199. Activate a positive memory: Author interview with Russell H. Fazio, PhD, Harold E. Burtt Professor, Department of Psychology, Ohio State University, June 19, 2007. Russell H. Fazio and Richard E. Petty, *Attitudes: Their Structure, Function, and Consequences*, Key Readings in Social Psychology (New York: Psychology Press, 2007); Richard E. Petty, Russell H. Fazio, and Pablo Brinol, *Attitudes: Insights from the New Implicit Measures* (New York: Psychology Press, 2008).

p. 200. Automatic behavior: Frank Ryan, "Appetite Lost and Found: Cognitive Psychology in the Addiction Clinic," and C. McCusker, "Towards Understanding Loss of Control: An Automatic Network Theory of Addictive Behavior," in *Cognition and Addiction*, ed. M. Munafò and I. Albery (Oxford: Oxford University Press, 2006); J. A. Bargh, ed., *Social Psychology and the Unconscious: The Automaticity of Higher Mental Processes* (Philadelphia, PA: Psychology Press, 2007); R. Hassin, J. Uleman, and J. Bargh, eds., *The New Unconscious* (New York: Oxford University Press, 2005); J. A. Bargh, "What Have We Been Priming All These Years? On the Development, Mechanisms, and Ecology of Nonconscious Social Behavior," *European Journal of Social Psychology* 36 (2006): 147–68; K. L. Duckworth, J. A. Bargh, M. Garcia, and S. Chaiken, "The Automatic Evaluation of Novel Stimuli," *Psychological Science* 6 (2001): 515–9; J. A. Bargh and T. L. Chartrand, "The Unbearable Automaticity of Being," *American Psychologist* 54 (1999): 462–79; J. A. Bargh and M. L. Ferguson, "Beyond Behaviorism: On the Automaticity of Higher Mental Processes," *Psychological Bulletin* 126 (2000): 925–45.

p. 207. Change the way you eat: Gary D. Foster, PhD, director, Center for Obesity Research and Education, Temple University, summarized the evidence that behavioral modification works over the long term in a presentation at the annual meeting of the North American Association for the Study of Obesity, Boston, 2006. Foster said behavior change must be concrete and specific, with patients "trained to be students of their own behavior." Typically, cognitive behavioral therapy achieves about a 10 percent weight loss over twenty to twenty-four weeks, with patients regaining one-third of their weight at the one-year mark. T. A. Wadden, M. L. Butryn, and K. J. Byrne, "Efficacy of Lifestyle Modification for Long-Term Weight Control," *Obesity Research* 12 (2004): 151S–162S.

Because obesity is a chronic disorder, short-term behavioral therapy is inadequate to keep weight off. See T. A. Wadden and M. L. Butryn, "Behavioral Treatment of Obesity," *Endocrinology Metabolism Clinics of North America* 32

(2003): 981–1003; M. G. Perri and J. A. Corsica, "Improving the Maintenance of Weight Lost in Behavioral Treatment of Obesity," in *Handbook of Obesity Treatment*, ed. T. A. Wadden and A. J. Stunkard, 357–79 (New York: Guilford Press, 2002).

p. 209. Replace chaos with structure: Many clinicians who have devoted their careers to caring for patients who overeat emphasize the importance of structure, as does an extensive body of research literature. For example: "When you go into a day that's unplanned, then you're just faced with whatever hits you. If you have a plan and you know what you're going to be eating that day, then you don't let the unplanned things get in your way." Author interview with David Besio, MS, RD, clinical dietitian, Department of Nutrition and Food Services, University of California, San Francisco, June 28, 2007. "My suspicion is that, over a number of years, as one loses control and one loses the proper behavioral cues, it spirals out of control. I think that's why you have to reinstitute structure." Author interview with Paul Lemanski, MD, MS, director, Center for Preventive Medicine and Cardiovascular Health, Albany, New York, July 5, 2007. "Giving people specific rules and telling them that they are required to follow them as part of this treatment is better than telling them about principles of energy balance," said Robert W. Jeffery, PhD, professor of epidemiology, University of Minnesota. However, Jeffery also warns that people tend to abandon structure over time. "Rule violation is very common and very early and very frequent." Author interview with Robert Jeffery, June 15, 2007. See also R. R. Wing, R. W. Jeffery, L. R. Burton, C. Thorson, K. S. Nissinoff, and J. E. Baxter, "Food Provision Vs Structured Meal Plans in the Behavioral Treatment of Obesity," *International Journal of Obesity and Related Metabolic Disorders* 20, no. 1 (1996): 56–62; R. W. Jeffery and R. R. Wing, "Long-Term Effects of Interventions for Weight Loss Using Food Provision and Monetary Incentives," *Journal of Consulting and Clinical Psychology* 63, no. 5 (1995): 793–6. "Repetitiveness and repeatability" is key, according to Cathy Nonas, MS, RD, a clinical dietitian with the New York City Department of Health. That strategy explained the success of the Subway diet, in which a man managed to lose 245 pounds by eating only two Subway sandwiches a day. Cathy Nonas, "Meal Replacements" (presentation at North American Association for the Study of Obesity annual meeting, 2007).

p. 210. Rules that support your structure: Investigators who have pioneered treatment programs for eating disorders such as binge eating and bulimia have a great deal to teach us about treatment for conditioned hypereating. See, for example, Zafra Cooper, Christopher G. Fairburn, and Deborah M. Hawker, *Cognitive-Behavioral Treatment of Obesity: A Clinician's Guide* (New York: Guilford Press, 2003); Christopher G. Fairburn, *Cognitive Behavior Therapy and Eating Disorders* (New York: Guilford Press, 2008); Christopher G. Fairburn, *Overcoming Binge Eating* (New York: Guilford Press, 1995): W. Stewart Agras and Robin F. Apple, *Overcoming Eating Disorders: A Cognitive-Behavioral Therapy Approach for Bulimia Nervosa and Binge-Eating Disorders: Therapist Guide*, 2nd ed., Treatments That Work (Oxford: Oxford University Press, 2008); W. Stewart Agras and Robin F. Apple, *Overcoming Your Eating Disorder: A Cognitive-Behavioral Treatment for Bulimia Nervosa and Binge-Eating Disorder, Guided Self-Help Workbook*, Treatments That Work (New York: Oxford University Press, 2008); and the series of manuals from the Neuropsychiatric Research

Institute (Fargo, ND), including *Professional's Guide to Bulimia Nervosa; Individual Treatment Workbook for Bulimia Nervosa; Group Treatment Workbook for Bulimia Nervosa; Group Treatment for Binge Eating Disorder; Self-Help Manual for Bulimia Nervosa; Healthy Eating: A Professional's Guide; Healthy Eating: A Meal Planning System; Healthy Eating Manual: 2.1 (Simplified System); Healthy Eating: Meal Planning & Food List (Pocket Guide).*

p. 210. Secret behind meal replacements: Meal replacements promote weight loss because they provide structure. See S. B. Heymsfield, C. A. van Mierlo, H. C. van der Knaap, M. Heo, and H. I. Frier, "Weight Management Using a Meal Replacement Strategy: Meta and Pooling Analysis from Six Studies," *International Journal of Obesity and Related Metabolic Disorders* 27, no. 5 (2003): 537–49; M. Noakes, P. R. Foster, J. B. Keogh, and P. M. Clifton, "Meal Replacements Are as Effective as Structured Weight-Loss Diets for Treating Obesity in Adults with Features of Metabolic Syndrome," *J. Nutr.* 134, no. 8 (2004): 1894–9.

Further data support meal structure as an important element of eating and weight control. J. Westenhoefer, B. von Falck, A. Stellfeldt, and S. Fintelmann, "Behavioural Correlates of Successful Weight Reduction over 3 Y. Results from the Lean Habits Study," *International Journal of Obesity and Related Metabolic Disorders* 28, no. 2 (2004): 334–5.

p. 212. Strong cognitive element: Author interview with Jeffrey M. Brunstrom, PhD, senior lecturer, Department of Experimental Psychology, University of Bristol, England, July 30, 2007. J. M. Brunstrom, N. G. Shakeshaft, and N. E. Scott-Samuel, "Measuring 'Expected Satiety' in a Range of Common Foods Using a Method of Constant Stimuli," *Appetite* 51, no. 3 (2008): 604–14.

p. 212. Served a meal: P. Pliner and D. Zec, "Meal Schemas During a Preload Decrease Subsequent Eating," *Appetite* 48, no. 3 (2007): 278–88.

p. 213. Protein the most satiating: M. Veldhorst, A. Smeets, S. Soenen, A. Hochstenbach-Waelen, R. Hursel, K. Diepvens, M. Lejeune, N. Luscombe-Marsh, and M. Westerterp-Plantenga, "Protein-Induced Satiety: Effects and Mechanisms of Different Proteins," *Physiology and Behavior* 94, no. 2 (2008): 300–7; D. Paddon-Jones, E. Westman, R. D. Mattes, R. R. Wolfe, A. Astrup, and M. Westerterp-Plantenga, "Protein, Weight Management, and Satiety," *American Journal of Clinical Nutrition* 87, no. 5 (2008): 1558S–61S; S. Oesch, L. Degen, and C. Beglinger, "Effect of a Protein Preload on Food Intake and Satiety Feelings in Response to Duodenal Fat Perfusions in Healthy Male Subjects," *American Journal of Physiology—Regulatory, Integrative and Comparative Physiology* 289, no. 4 (2005): R1042–7.

p. 213. Simple sugars: Author interview with Martin S. Wickham, PhD, chief designer of the world's first artificial stomach, and Richard Faulks, a member of his research team, Institute of Food Research, Norwich, England, October 2, 2007; author interview with David Ludwig, MD, PhD, director, Obesity Program, Children's Hospital, Boston, June 26, 2004.

p. 213. Fat is somewhat: I. Welch, K. Saunders, and N. W. Read, "Effect of Ileal and Intravenous Infusions of Fat Emulsions on Feeding and Satiety in Human Volunteers," *Gastroenterology* 89, no. 6 (1985): 1293–7.

p. 213. Fat paradox: J. E. Blundell, J. R. Cotton, H. Delargy, S. Green, A. Greenough, N. A. King, and C. L. Lawton, "The Fat Paradox: Fat-Induced Satiety Signals Versus High Fat Overconsumption," *International Journal of Obesity and Related Metabolic Disorders* 19, no. 11 (1995): 832–5.

p. 215. Mental rehearsal: Jim Taylor and Gregory S. Wilson, *Applying Sport Psychology: Four Perspectives* (Champaign, IL: Human Kinetics, 2005); N. Zinssers, L. K. Bunker, and J. M. Williams, "Cognitive Techniques for Improving Performance and Building Confidence," in *Applied Sport Psychology: Personal Growth to Peak Performance*, 3rd ed., ed. J. M. Williams, 219–36 (Mountain View, CA: May Field, 2001).

p. 216. Implantation intentions: P. M. Gollwitzer, U. Bayer, and K. McCullouch, "The Control of the Unwanted," in *The New Unconscious*, ed. R. Hassin, J. Uleman, and J.A. Bargh, 485–515 (Oxford: Oxford University Press, 2005); P. M. Gollwitzer, K. Fujita, and G. Oettingen, "Planning and the Implementation of Goals," in *Handbook of Self-Regulation: Research, Theory and Applications*, ed. R. F. Baumeister and K. D. Vohs, 211–28 (New York: Guilford Press, 2004); P. M. Gollwitzer and U. Bayer, "Deliberative Versus Implemental Mindsets in the Control of Action," in *Dual-Process Theories in Social Psychology*, ed. S. Chaiken & Y. Trope, 403–22 (New York: Guilford Press, 1999).

p. 218. Emotional stressors: Paul M. Lehrer, Robert L. Woolfolk, and Wesley E. Sime, *Principles and Practice of Stress Management*, 3rd ed. (New York: Guilford Press, 2007).

p. 219. Frontal cortex active: Author interview with Rajita Sinha, PhD, director, Research Program on Stress, Addiction and Psychopathology, Yale University School of Medicine, September 5, 2007.

p. 219. Learned to manage risk: There is an extensive literature on techniques that are effective in managing cue-triggered responses. Richard A. Rawson, *The Matrix Model: Intensive Outpatient Alcohol & Drug Treatment: A 16-Week Individualized Program: Therapist's Manual* (Center City, MN: Hazelden, 2005); Dennis C. Daley and G. Alan Marlatt, *Overcoming Your Alcohol or Drug Problem: Effective Recovery Strategies: Workbook*, 2nd ed., Treatments That Work (New York: Oxford University Press, 2006); Dennis M. Donovan and G. Alan Marlatt, *Assessment of Addictive Behaviors*, 2nd ed. (New York: Guilford Press, 2005); G. Alan Marlatt and Dennis M. Donovan, *Relapse Prevention: Maintenance Strategies in the Treatment of Addictive Behaviors*, 2nd ed. (New York: Guilford Press, 2005); G. Alan Marlatt and Gary R. VandenBos, *Addictive Behaviors: Readings on Etiology, Prevention, and Treatment* (Washington, DC: American Psychological Association, 1997); A. Thomas Horvath, *Sex, Drugs, Gambling, & Chocolate: A Workbook for Overcoming Addictions* (San Luis Obispo, CA: Impact Publishers, 1998); Dennis C. Daley and G. Alan Marlatt, *Overcoming Your Alcohol or Drug Problem: Effective Recovery Strategies Workbook*, 2nd ed., Treatments that Work (Oxford: Oxford University Press, 2006); Gail Steketee, *Overcoming Obsessive-Compulsive Disorder: A Behavioral and Cognitive Protocol for the Treatment of OCD: Client Manual*, Best Practices for Therapy (Oakland, CA: New Harbinger, 1999); Gail Steketee, Teresa A. Pigott, and Todd Schemmel, *Obsessive Compulsive Disorder: The Latest Assessment and Treatment Strategies*, 3rd ed. (Kansas City, MO: Compact Clinicals, 2006); Mary Marden Velasquez, *Group Treatment for Substance Abuse: A Stages-of-Change Therapy Manual* (New York: Guilford Press, 2001); Peter M. Monti, *Treating Alcohol Dependence: A Coping Skills Training Guide*, 2nd ed. (New York: Guilford Press, 2002).

p. 221. Learn active resistance: Richard Maisel, David Epston, and Ali Borden, *Biting the Hand That Starves You: Inspiring Resistance to Anorexia/Bulimia* (New York: W.W. Norton, 2004).

p. 221. Thought stopping: Author interview with Richard Rawson, PhD, associate director, UCLA Integrated Substance Abuse Programs, University of California, Los Angeles, August 9, 2007.

p. 222. Total reversal: Author interview with Arnold M. Ludwig, MD, Emeritus Professor of Psychiatry, University of Kentucky Medical School, Adjunct Professor of Psychiatry and Human Behavior, Brown University School of Medicine, August 9, 2007.

p. 223. History of shoplifting: Author interview with Jon E. Grant, MD, JD, Department of Psychiatry, University of Minnesota Medical School, August 14, 2007. Jon E. Grant, *Impulse Control Disorders: A Clinician's Guide to Understanding and Treating Behavioral Addictions* (New York: W.W. Norton, 2008).

p. 224. Exercise: S. Brené, A. Bjørnebekk, E. Åberg, A. A. Mathé, L. Olson, and M. Werme, "Running Is Rewarding and Antidepressive," *Physiology and Behavior* 92, nos. 1–2 (2007): 136–40; A. R. Ozburn, A. Harris, and Y. A. Blednov, "Wheel Running, Voluntary Ethanol Consumption, and Hedonic Substitution," *Alcohol* 42, no. 5 (2008): 417–24; H. Vargas-Perez, J. Mena-Segovia, M. Giordano, and J. L. Diaz, "Induction of C-Fos in Nucleus Accumbens in Naive Male Balb/C Mice after Wheel Running," *Neuroscience Letters* 352, no. 2 (2003): 81–4; R. E. Andersen, T. A. Wadden, S. J. Bartlett, B. Zemel, T. J. Verde, and S. C. Franckowiak, "Effects of Lifestyle Activity Vs Structured Aerobic Exercise in Obese Women: A Randomized Trial," *JAMA* 281, no. 4 (1999): 335–40.

p. 228. Weight loss consultant: Author interview with Jordon Carroll, weight loss consultant in private practice, New York City, July 5, 2007.

p. 231. Childhood finger cuffs: The childhood finger cuffs are a metaphor for the therapeutic technique of paradoxical behavior to treat anxiety to help break the vicious cycle that ensues when someone tries harder and harder to stop a behavior, only to see the anxiety increase. L. Michael Ascher, *Therapeutic Paradox* (New York: Guilford Press, 1989).

p. 231. Internal policing process: George Ainslie, MD, is chief of psychiatry at the Veterans Affairs Medical Center, Coatesville, Pennsylvania. G. Ainslie and J. R. Monterosso, "A Marketplace in the Brain?" *Science* 306, no. 5695 (2004): 421–3; G. Ainslie and J. R. Monterosso, "Building Blocks of Self-Control: Increased Tolerance for Delay with Bundled Rewards," *Journal of the Experimental Analysis of Behavior* 79 (2003): 37–48; G. Ainslie and J. R. Monterosso, "Hyperbolic Discounting as a Factor in Addiction: A Critical Analysis," in *Choice, Behavioural Economics and Addiction*, ed. Rudy Vuchinich and Nick Heather (Amsterdam: Pergamon, 2003).

p. 232. Highly restrictive rules: John Foreyt, PhD, professor, Department of Psychiatry and Behavioral Sciences and Department of Medicine, Baylor College of Medicine, presentation at the American Dietetic Association Certificate of Training in Adult Weight Management Program, 2004.

p. 235. Critical perceptual shift: Author interview with Arnold M. Ludwig, MD, Emeritus Professor of Psychiatry, University of Kentucky Medical School, Adjunct Professor of Psychiatry and Human Behavior, Brown University School of Medicine, September 7, 2007; Arnold M. Ludwig, *Understanding the Alcoholic's Mind: The Nature of Craving and How to Control It* (New York: Oxford University Press, 1988). Ludwig credits Gloria Litman for the concept of critical perceptual shift. See G. Litman, "Personal Meanings and Alcoholism Survival: Translating Subjective Experience into Empirical Data," in *Personal Meaning: The First Guy's Hospital Symposium on the Individual Frame of Reference*, ed. Eric Shepherd and J. P.

Watson (Chichester, UK: Wiley, 1982). Ludwig and Litman use the term "critical perceptual shift" to mean a person coming to see "himself and the world about him in an entirely new light." I focus here primarily on a shift in the way we come to view the food we eat, and how that perception affects us.

p. 242. Jacked up what works: Author interview with Joseph Stiglitz, PhD, professor, Columbia University, July 14, 2007.

p. 243. Research chef at Chili's: Author interview with Stephen Kalil, executive chef at the Culinary Innovations Center at Frito-Lay and president of the Research Chefs Association, October 6, 2008. In an earlier capacity, Kalil was director of innovation at Chili's Grill & Bar.

p. 243. Marketers of good times: Heath McDonald, "Marketing to Children: Tactics, Impacts and Controls" (presentation at International Society for Behavioral Nutrition and Physical Activity, Sixth Annual Meeting, June 20–23, 2007, Oslo, Norway). See also Max Sutherland and Alice K. Sylvester, *Advertising and the Mind of the Consumer: What Works, What Doesn't, and Why*, 2nd ed. (St. Leonards, Australia: Allen & Unwin, 2000).

p. 247. List the calorie counts: New York City's Health Code §81.50 now requires that chain restaurants serving standardized meals "prominently display publicly available information about the calorie content of such items on menu boards and menus in an effort to facilitate patrons' nutritional choices at time of purchase." I joined the American Medical Association, Trust for America's Health, Congressman Henry Waxman, and others in filing an *amici curiae* brief supporting the New York City Board of Health's action in *New York State Restaurant Association v. New York City Board of Health*, United States District Court for the Southern District of New York, Case No. 1:07-cv-05710 [RJH]. California has taken similar steps, becoming the first state in the union to require nutrition labels on restaurant menus, effective 2011.

For more about the influence of caloric information on restaurant menus, see Keystone Forum, *The Keystone Forum on Away-from-Home Foods: Opportunities for Preventing Weight Gain and Obesity*, 2006, http://www.cfsan.fda.gov/~dms/nutrcal.html; US Food and Drug Administration, *Calories Count: Report of the Working Group on Obesity*, 2004, http://www.cfsan.fda.gov/~dms/owg-toc.html; J. L. Pomeranz and K. D. Brownell, "Legal and Public Health Considerations Affecting the Success, Reach, and Impact of Menu-Labeling Laws," *American Journal of Public Health* 98, no. 9 (2008): 1578–83; M. T. Bassett, T. Dumanovsky, C. Huang, L. D. Silver, C. Young, C. Nonas, T. D. Matte, S. Chideya, and T. R. Frieden, "Purchasing Behavior and Calorie Information at Fast-Food Chains in New York City, 2007," *American Journal of Public Health* 98, no. 8 (2008): 1457–9; M. Berman and R. Lavizzo-Mourey, "Obesity Prevention in the Information Age: Caloric Information at the Point of Purchase," *JAMA* 300, no. 4 (2008): 433–5.

p. 247. By mandate: To ensure a nationwide standard, Congress should amend the Labeling and Education Act of 1990 to require chain restaurants to provide nutritional information, including calorie counts, on all menus and menu boards. During my tenure as commissioner of the US Food and Drug Administration, the FDA attempted to require some nutrition information in restaurants in the early 1990s. Under the Nutrition Labeling and Education Act, our proposals for regulations to enforce the labeling law would have required restaurants making claims about a product's health benefits or nutrition content to display the same kind of Nutrition Facts label that we mandated on virtually all packaged foods (FDA press release, June 10, 1993).

We lost the battle to clear that regulation with the White House (see David A. Kessler, *A Question of Intent: A Great American Battle with a Deadly Industry* [New York: Public Affairs, 2001]), but its importance has become even greater in recent years. My anonymous industry source, called "the food consultant" in this book, believes that in the absence of labeling requirements, the restaurant industry has felt free to develop new offerings without concern for their caloric, fat, or sugar content and consumers are more likely to indulge.

He said that customers go right to the food label, particularly when a new product arrives on grocery-store shelves, and that it "tends to put a lid on the degree to which people will tolerate high-fat, high-carbohydrate food." But they still have a desire for "cheap thrills . . . some form of entertainment . . . and they get it at the restaurant level where there is a suspension of disbelief." People know they shouldn't be eating French fries or doughnuts, but because the nutrition information is not "rubbed in their faces . . . they don't have to look; therefore they don't look; and they indulge. If they had the label on that, people would right away jump to it, and they wouldn't order it."

As of December 2008, two restaurant labeling bills had been introduced in Congress. The better of them is the Menu Education and Labeling (MEAL) Act, which would require caloric and nutrient labeling on both the menu boards of fast-food restaurants and the printed menus of table-service restaurants. The MEAL Act was introduced by Senator Tom Harkin (D-Iowa) (S. 274) and by Rep. Rosa DeLauro (D-Connecticut) (H.R. 3895). An alternative, the Labeling Education and Nutrition (LEAN) Act, is substantially weaker because it would allow restaurants to post information less prominently. The LEAN Act was introduced by Senators Thomas Carper (D-Delaware) and Lisa Murkowski (R-Alaska) (S. 355) and by Rep. Jim Matheson (D-Utah) (H.R. 7187) and is supported by the National Restaurant Association.

p. 248. **Redefining norms:** A substantial body of literature documents the value of countermarketing and efforts to "demonize" tobacco. W. L. Hamilton, L. Biener, and R. T. Brennan, "Do Local Tobacco Regulations Influence Perceived Smoking Norms? Evidence from Adult and Youth Surveys in Massachusetts," *Health Education Research* 23, no. 4 (2008): 709–22; B. Alamar and S. A. Glantz, "Effect of Increased Social Unacceptability of Cigarette Smoking on Reduction in Cigarette Consumption," *American Journal of Public Health* 96, no. 8 (2006): 1359–63; S. H. Kim and J. Shanahan, "Stigmatizing Smokers: Public Sentiment toward Cigarette Smoking and Its Relationship to Smoking Behaviors," *Journal of Health Communication* 8, no. 4 (2003): 343–67; E. A. Gilpin, L. Lee, and J. P. Pierce, "Changes in Population Attitudes about Where Smoking Should Not Be Allowed: California Versus the Rest of the USA," *Tobacco Control* 13, no. 1 (2004): 38–44; R. Murphy-Hoefer, A. Hyland, and C. Higbee, "Perceived Effectiveness of Tobacco Countermarketing Advertisements among Young Adults," *American Journal of Health Behavior* 32, no. 6 (2008): 725–34; M. C. Farrelly, C. G. Healton, K. C. Davis, P. Messeri, J. C. Hersey, and M. L. Haviland, "Getting to the Truth: Evaluating National Tobacco Countermarketing Campaigns," *American Journal of Public Health* 92, no. 6 (2002): 901–7; C. Pechmann, G. Zhao, M. E. Goldberg, and E. T. Reibling, "What to Convey in Antismoking Advertisements for Adolescents? The

Use of Protection Motivation Theory to Identify Effective Message Themes," *Journal of Marketing* 67 (2004): 1–18.

p. 251. Philosophers, theologians, and scientists: Paul and Augustine: Christopher C. Cook, *Alcohol, Addiction and Christian Ethics*, New Studies in Christian Ethics 27 (Cambridge: Cambridge University Press, 2006). Siddhartha: William Braxton Irvine, *On Desire: Why We Want What We Want* (Oxford: Oxford University Press, 2006). Freud: *Freud: A Collection of Critical Essays*, Modern Studies in Philosophy (Garden City, NY: Anchor Books, 1974). Jung: C. G. Jung, Herbert Edward Read, Michael Fordham, and Gerhard Adler, *The Collected Works of C. G. Jung*, Bollingen Series 20 (New York: Pantheon Books, 1953); James Hollis, *Why Good People Do Bad Things: Understanding Our Darker Selves* (New York: Gotham, 2007). Assagioli: Roberto Assagioli, *The Act of Will*, An Esalen Book (New York: Viking Press, 1973). Bishop: F. Michler Bishop, *Managing Addictions: Cognitive, Emotive, and Behavioral Techniques* (Northvale, NJ: Jason Aronson, 2001). Schwartz: Richard C. Schwartz, *Internal Family Systems Therapy*, The Guilford Family Therapy Series (New York: Guilford Press, 1995).

LIST OF AUTHOR INTERVIEWS

Julie Adams, Kellogg Company

Michael Arbib, PhD, Fletcher Jones Professor of Computer Science; director, USC Brain Project, University of Southern California

Louis Aronne, MD, clinical professor of medicine, Weill Cornell Medical College, Cornell University

Richard Atkinson, MD, clinical professor of pathology, Virginia Commonwealth University, and director, Obetech Obesity Research Center

Samuel A. Ball, PhD, associate professor of psychiatry, Yale University School of Medicine; director of research, The APT Foundation, Inc.

Bernard Balleine, PhD, associate director for research, Brain Research Institute, University of California, Los Angeles

Samuel Barondes, MD, professor, Jeanne and Sanford Robertson Endowed Chair in Neurobiology and Psychiatry, Department of Psychiatry, University of California, San Francisco

Linda Bartoshuk, PhD, professor, Community Dentistry and Behavioral Science, College of Dentistry, University of Florida

Michael Baumann, PhD, research biologist, Clinical Psychopharmacology Section, Intramural Research Program, National Institute on Drug Abuse, National Institutes of Heath

Jacqueline Beckley, president, The Understanding and Insights Group

France Bellisle, PhD, head researcher, Diabetes Department, Hôtel-Dieu Hospital, Paris

Joshua Berke, PhD, assistant professor and neuroscience scholar, Department of Psychology, University of Michigan, Ann Arbor

Kent Berridge, PhD, professor, Biopsychology Program, University of Michigan

David Besio, MS, RD, clinical dietitian, Department of Nutrition and Food Services, University of California, San Francisco

Daniel H. Bessesen, MD, professor, Health Sciences Center, University of Colorado, Denver

George L. Blackburn, MD, PhD, S. Daniel Abraham Chair, Nutrition Medicine, Harvard Medical School; director, Center for the Study of Nutrition Medicine, Beth Israel Deaconess Medical Center

Mark Bouton, PhD, professor of psychology, University of Vermont

Jeffrey Brunstrom, PhD, senior lecturer, Department of Experimental Psychology, University of Bristol, England

Jerilyn Brusseau, founder of Cinnabon

Cynthia M. Bulik, PhD, William R. and Jeanne H. Jordan Distinguished Professor of Eating Disorders, Department of Psychiatry, School of Medicine, University of North Carolina, Chapel Hill

Silvia A. Bunge, PhD, head, Cognitive Control and Development Laboratory, University of California, Berkeley

Nancy F. Butte, PhD, professor of pediatrics, Baylor College of Medicine

Michel Cabanac, MD, professor, Department of Anatomy and Physiology, University Laval, Quebec, Canada

Anthony Caggiula, PhD, professor and departmental chair, Department of Psychology, University of Pittsburgh

Regina Carelli, PhD, director of Behavioral Neuroscience Program, University of North Carolina, Chapel Hill

Timothy Carmody, PhD, clinical professor, Department of Psychiatry, University of California, San Francisco

Kenneth D. Carr, PhD, associate professor of psychiatry and pharmacology, Departments of Psychiatry (Millhauser Labs) and Pharmacology, New York University

Jordon Carroll, weight-loss consultant in private practice, New York City

Kathleen Carroll, PhD, professor, Yale University

Regina Casper, MD, Emeritus Professor, Psychiatry and Behavioral Science, Stanford University, Palo Alto, California

Gail Vance Civille, president, Sensory Spectrum

Cynthia A. Conklin, PhD, assistant professor of psychiatry, University of Pittsburgh Medical Center

Rebecca Corwin, PhD, associate professor, Department of Nutritional Sciences, Penn State University

Alain Dagher, PhD, associate professor, Montreal Neurological Institute, McGill University

Mary Dallman, PhD, professor, Neurosciences Graduate Program, University of California, San Francisco

John Davis, PhD, E. W. Bourne Behavioral Research Laboratory, New York Hospital, Cornell Medical Center

Kathryn Deibler, director of Flavor Product Development, Ungerer and Company

Robert De Niro, actor

Harriet de Wit, PhD, director of the Human Behavioral Pharmacology Laboratory, Department of Psychiatry, University of Chicago

Gaetano Di Chiara, MD, Department of Toxicology and Centre for Neuropharmacology, University of Cagliari, Italy

Adam Drewnowski, PhD, director, Nutritional Sciences Program, University of Washington

Elissa Epel, PhD, associate professor, Department of Psychiatry, and codirector, Center for Obesity Assessment, Study and Treatment, University of California, San Francisco

Myles Faith, PhD, Center for Weight and Eating Disorders, University of Pennsylvania School of Medicine

Mathea Falco, JD, president, Drug Strategies, Inc.

Richard Faulks, science director, Model Gut, Institute of Food Research, Norwich, England

Russell Fazio, PhD, Harold E. Burtt Professor, Department of Psychology, Ohio State University

Howard Fields, MD, PhD, director, Wheeler Center for the Neurobiology of Addiction, University of California, San Francisco

Jennifer Fisher, PhD, researcher, The Center for Obesity Research and Education, Temple University

Katherine Flegal, PhD, senior research scientist, National Center for Health Statistics, Centers for Disease Control and Prevention

Food industry consultant

Eleftheria Maratos-Flier, MD, associate professor, Endocrinology, Harvard Medical School; investigator, Joslin Diabetes Center

Loma Flowers, MD, community psychologist and clinical professor, Psychiatry Department, University of California, San Francisco

Michele Foley, research manager, Frito-Lay and PepsiCo

Wai-Tat Fu, PhD, assistant professor, Applied Cognitive Science Lab, University of Illinois at Urbana-Champaign

Yoshiyuki Fujishima, DPhil, chemist and executive, Ajinomoto USA, Inc.

Lisa Giannetto, MD, internist, University of California, San Francisco

Peter Gillat, Kettlefoods, UK

Jon E. Grant, MD, JD, Department of Psychiatry, University of Minnesota

Jeff Grimm, PhD, associate professor, Department of Psychology and Program in Behavioral Neuroscience, Western Washington University

Evette M. Hackman, PhD, RD, retired, Emeritus Professor, Seattle Pacific University

Andras Hajnal, MD, PhD, associate professor, Neural and Behavioral Sciences, Penn State Milton S. Hershey Medical Center

John Haywood, restaurant industry expert consultant

Todd F. Heatherton, PhD, Champion International Professor, Department of Psychological and Brain Sciences, Dartmouth College

David Heber, MD, PhD, founding chief, Division of Clinical Nutrition, David Geffen School of Medicine, University of California, Los Angeles, and University of California, Los Angeles School of Public Health

James O. Hill, PhD, professor of pediatrics, and director, Center for Human Nutrition, University of Colorado, Denver

Bart Hoebel, PhD, professor, Department of Psychology, Princeton University

Peter Holland, PhD, Krieger-Eisenhower Professor of Psychology, Johns Hopkins University

David Huron, PhD, professor, School of Music & Center for Cognitive Science, Ohio State University

Robert W. Jeffery, PhD, professor of epidemiology, University of Minnesota

Susan L. Johnson, PhD, director, The Children's Eating Laboratory, University of Colorado Health Sciences Center

Stephen Kalil, executive chef at the Culinary Innovations Center, Frito-Lay, and president, Research Chefs Association

John Kane, MD, PhD, professor of medicine, University of California, San Francisco, School of Medicine

Jerome Kagan, PhD, Daniel and Amy Starch Research Professor of Psychology, emeritus, Harvard University

Leonard D. Katz, PhD, Visiting Scholar of Philosophy, Department of Linguistics and Philosophy, Massachusetts Institute of Technology

David Kavanagh, PhD, professor, Clinical Psychology, Department of Psychiatry, University of Queensland, Brisbane, Australia

Ann Kelley, PhD, Distinguished Neuroscience Professor, Department of Psychiatry, University of Wisconsin

George F. Koob, PhD, chair, Committee on the Neurobiology of Addictive Disorders, Scripps Research Institute

Thomas R. Kosten, MD, Waggoner Professor of Psychiatry and Neuroscience, and director, Division of Alcohol and Addictive Disorders, Baylor College of Medicine

E. P. Köster, PhD, advisor, European Sensory Network, Unilever Research Laboratories, Vlaardingen, the Netherlands

Diane Lattemann, PhD, research professor, Department of Psychiatry and Behavioral Sciences, University of Washington School of Medicine

James F. Leckman, MD, director of research, Neison Harris Professor of Child Psychiatry and Pediatrics, Child Study Center, Yale University School of Medicine

Paul Lemanski, MD, director, Center for Preventive Medicine and Cardiovascular Health, Albany, New York

Barry Levin, MD, clinical professor, Pharmacology and Physiology, Department of Neurology and Neurosciences, New Jersey Medical School

Allen S. Levine, PhD, professor and dean, College of Food, Agricultural and Natural Resource Sciences, University of Minnesota, and director, Minnesota Obesity Center

David A. Levitsky, PhD, professor of psychology and nutritional services, Cornell University

Bonnie Lieberman, nutrition director, Center for Science in the Public Interest, Washington, DC

Walter Ling, MD, professor-in-residence of psychiatry and director of the Integrated Substance Abuse Programs, University of California, Los Angeles

Arnold Ludwig, MD, professor of psychiatry, University of Kentucky

David Ludwig, MD, PhD, director, Obesity Program, Children's Hospital, Boston

Michael C. McCloud, owner, Uptown Bakers

Frances McSweeney, PhD, Regents professor, Department of Psychology, Washington State University

Ron Mehiel, PhD, professor, Department of Psychology, Shippensburg University

Herbert L. Meiselman, PhD, senior research scientist, retired, United States Department of Defense Food Research Program

David J. Mela, PhD, senior scientist, Weight Control and Behavioural Nutrition, Unilever Food and Health Research Institute, Vlaardingen, the Netherlands

Raymond G. Miltenberger, PhD, director, Applied Behavior Analysis Masters Program, Department of Child and Family Studies, University of South Florida

Walter Mischel, PhD, Robert Johnston Niven Professor of Humane Letters in Psychology, Columbia University

Thomas Najarian, MD, director, The Najarian Center, Inc.

Chantal Nederkoorn, PhD, assistant professor, Department of Clinical Psychological Science, Maastricht University, Netherlands

Eric Nestler, MD, PhD, chairman of neuroscience, Mt. Sinai Medical Center

Raymond Niaura, PhD, professor of psychiatry and human behavior, Brown University Medical School

Ranzell "Nick" Nickelson, PhD, chief scientist, Standard Meat

Martha S. Nolte, MD, associate clinical professor of medicine, endocrinology, University of California, San Francisco

Cathy Nonas, MS, RD, clinical dietitian, New York City Department of Health

Frank Q. Nuttall, MD, PhD, professor of medicine, University of Minnesota, Minneapolis

Charles O'Brien, MD, PhD, vice chair, Department of Psychiatry, University of Pennsylvania

Kevin Ochsner, PhD, assistant professor, Department of Psychology, Columbia University

Marcia Pelchat, PhD, associate member, Monell Chemical Senses Center

Harold Pincus, MD, professor of psychiatry, Columbia University

Gloria Pink, Pink's Hot Dogs

Patricia Pliner, PhD, professor, Department of Psychology, University of Toronto, Mississauga

Susan Pockett, PhD, Physics Department, University of Auckland, Australia

Wolfgang Puck, chef

Howard Rachlin, PhD, research professor, Emeritus Distinguished Professor, Psychology Department, State University of New York, Stony Brook

Eric Ravussin, PhD, Douglas L. Gordon Chair in Diabetes and Metabolism and professor, Department of Human Physiology, Pennington Biomedical Research Center

Richard Rawson, PhD, associate director, UCLA Integrated Substance Abuse Programs, University of California, Los Angeles

Nick Read, MD, university chair, retired, Gastrointestinal Physiology, Human Nutrition, Integrated Medicine, University of Sheffield, England

Neil Risch, PhD, professor of human genetics, University of California, San Francisco

Dwight Riskey, former Frito-Lay executive

Robert C. Ritter, VMD, PhD, professor, Physiology and Neuroscience, Department of Veterinary and Comparative Anatomy, Pharmacology and Physiology, College of Veterinary Medicine, Washington State University, Pullman

Nancy Rodriguez, president, Food Marketing Support Services

Peter Rogers, PhD, professor of Biological Psychology, University of Bristol, England

Barbara J. Rolls, PhD, Helen A. Guthrie chair and professor, Department of Nutritional Sciences, Penn State University

Edmund Rolls, professor, Experimental Psychology, University of Oxford, England

Billy Rosenthal, former president, Standard Meat

John Salamone, PhD, professor, Division of Behavioral Neuroscience, Department of Psychology, University of Connecticut

Arline Salbe, PhD, research nutritionist, Scientific Advisory Board Member, and senior clinical research fellow, Kronos Longevity Research Institute

Cary R. Savage, PhD, associate professor, Department of Psychiatry and Behavioral Sciences, Kansas University Medical Center

Craig Schiltz, PhD, Department of the Neuroscience Training Program, University of Wisconsin-Madison

Dale A. Schoeller, PhD, professor, Department of Nutritional Sciences, University of Wisconsin-Madison

Anthony Sclafani, PhD, Distinguished Professor, Department of Psychology, Brooklyn College, City University of New York

Gordon Shepherd, MD, PhD, professor of neuroscience and neurobiology, Yale School of Medicine

Rajita Sinha, PhD, director, Research Program on Stress, Addiction and Psychopathology, Yale University School of Medicine

Dana Small, PhD, associate fellow, John B. Pierce Laboratory, a Yale University affiliate

Gerard Smith, MD, Professor Emeritus of Psychiatry, Department of Psychiatry, Joan and Sanford I. Weill Medical College of Cornell University

Gregory Smith, PhD, professor, director of Clinical Training, Department of Psychology, University of Kentucky

Robert Smith, former vice president, Research and Development, Nabisco

John R. Speakman, director, Institute of Biological and Environmental Sciences, School of Biological Sciences, University of Aberdeen, King's College, Scotland

Sonja Spoor, PhD, Oregon Research Institute

Sachiko St. Jeor, PhD, professor and chief, Division of Medical Nutrition, and director, Center for Nutrition and Metabolic Disorders, Department of Internal Medicine, University of Nevada School of Medicine

John Staddon, PhD, James B. Duke Professor of Psychological and Brain Sciences and professor of biology and neurobiology, Duke University

Matthew W. State, MD, PhD, Harris Associate Professor of Child Psychiatry and Genetics, Department of Genetics, Yale Medical School

Eric Stice, PhD, research scientist, Oregon Research Institute

Joseph Stiglitz, PhD, University Professor, Economics, Columbia University

Herb Stone, PhD, senior advisor and cofounder, Tragon, and former president, Institute of Food Technologists

James Stubbs, PhD, obesity and research specialist at Slimming World UK

Albert J. "Mickey" Stunkard, MD, Professor Emeritus of Psychiatry, University of Pennsylvania

P. Antonio Tataranni, MD, investigator head at the Obesity, Diabetes and Energy Metabolism Unit, Department of Health and Human Services, Phoenix

Andy Taylor, PhD, professor of flavour technology, School of Biosciences, University of Nottingham, England

Laurence H. Tecott, MD, PhD, associate professor in residence of psychiatry, Department of Biopharmaceutical Sciences, University of California, San Francisco

Scott A. Teitelbaum, MD, associate professor, Department of Psychiatry, University of Florida College of Medicine

Peter M. Todd, PhD, professor, Cognitive Science, Informatics, and Psychology, Indiana University, Bloomington

Craig Van Dyke, MD, professor, Department of Psychiatry, University of California, San Francisco School of Medicine

Nora D. Volkow, MD, director, National Institute of Drug Abuse

Thomas Wadden, PhD, professor, Psychology and Psychiatry, University of Pennsylvania

Gene-Jack Wang, MD, scientist, Medical Department, Brookhaven National Laboratory

Sara Jane Ward, PhD, postdoctoral research fellow, University of North Carolina at Chapel Hill

Jane Wardle, PhD, researcher, Health Behavior Unit, Department of Epidemiol-
   ogy and Public Health, University College London, England
Arnold Washton, PhD, addiction psychologist, Director, Recovery Options
David Scott Weigle, MD, professor of medicine, Division of Metabolism, Endocri-
   nology and Nutrition, University of Washington
Michael Weintraub, MD, president, Weintraub Pharmaceutical Consulting; previ-
   ously head, Clinical Pharmacology Unit, University of Rochester School of
   Medicine; and director, Office of Drug Evaluation 5, US Food and Drug
   Administration
Robert West, PhD, professor of health psychology, Department of Epidemiology
   and Public Health, Health Behaviour Research Centre, University College
   London
Martin S. Wickham, PhD, platform leader, chief executive, Model Gut, Institute
   of Food Research, Norwich, England
Josh Wooley, MD, PhD, Center for Obesity Assessment, Study and Treatment,
   University of California, San Francisco
Holly Wyatt, MD, assistant professor of medicine, Department of Medicine, Divi-
   sion of Endocrinology, Metabolism and Diabetes, Center for Human Nutrition,
   University of Colorado Health Sciences Center
Martin R. Yeomans, PhD, CPsychol AFBPsS, reader in Experimental Psychology
   Department of Psychology, School of Life Sciences, University of Sussex,
   Brighton, England
Philip David Zelazo, PhD, professor and Canada Research Chair in Developmen-
   tal Neuroscience, Department of Psychology, University of Toronto

ACKNOWLEDGMENTS

The End of Overeating is the work of many years. Without the efforts of Karyn Feiden, I would be at it still and this book would not exist. Her writing skills and her ability to decipher my meaning are unmatched. Karyn brought dedication, intelligence, and insight to this book, as she has to our many other projects together over the past two decades. Through too many shared meals of layered and loaded food and too many late-night phone calls, she understood the public health importance of this project and the meaning of friendship. I am deeply appreciative.

Thank you to Dick Todd for his editing genius, his critical eye, and for always pointing me in the right direction. Jeff Goldberg, too, provided invaluable advice on how to take this book to another level.

Al Gore introduced me and this book to Steven Murphy, the president of Rodale, who was enthusiastic as soon as he read the manuscript and instantly understood what I was trying to accomplish. Joe Klein sent me to my agent, Kathy Robbins, who has been a discerning and enthusiastic advocate. I am grateful to them all.

My association with Rodale has been a pleasure. Karen Rinaldi's commitment to *The End of Overeating* is unstinting. She cares about this book as much as I do. Julie Will's editing has been pitch perfect. Thanks also to Nancy N. Bailey, Beth Davey, Christina Gaugler, and Beth Lamb.

I was ably assisted in everything from tracking down journal articles, to scheduling and transcribing interviews, to fact-checking and copyediting by Chris Jerome, Richard Alwyn Fisher, Cal Johnson, Harry Slomovitz, Josh Marx, Bob Marsh, Megan O'Neill, Jennifer Hornsby, Erana Bumbardatore, Nancy Rutman, and the incomparable Deb Taylor.

My gratitude also goes to Chip Kidd, who understood my message and used his ability to turn a concept into the art for this book's cover.

I am most appreciative of Jerry Mande's and Elizabeth Drye's early research in the literature.

Nick Gimbel's legal brilliance allowed me to concentrate on the task at hand and for that, and so much else, I thank him.

My sincere thanks go to Brooke Shearer, Mathea Falco, and Joel Ehrenkranz, who read and provided cogent comments on earlier versions of the manuscript and to my friends Connie Casey, Lynn Gryll, Ruth Katz, and Nina Questal, who hunted for typos. I always enjoyed talking about children and food with the late Ann Litt. Marci Robinson, Jeff Nesbit, Jim O'Hara, Sharan Jayne, Drew Altman, Tina Hoff, and Doug Levy have helped me communicate the public health messages in this book.

The annual conference of the Society for the Study of Ingestive Behavior brings together scientists whose work focuses on the biology of eating. I have benefitted enormously from their collegiality and perceptive analyses. To the hundreds of scientists who have taught me so much and especially to my collaborators and colleagues Elissa Epel, Dana Small, Andras Hajnal, Jeffrey Grimm, Dianne Figlewicz, Jennifer Felsted, Gaetano Di Chiara, Michael Acree, Dina Halme, and Tanya Adams, I hope I have accurately captured the state of our knowledge.

Over the years of extensive research, I received financial support from Stewart and Lynda Resnick, Marc and Lynne Benioff, and Lionel Pincus. Their belief in my work and in me has meant a great deal to me and I thank them. I have served as an adviser to and on the advisory boards of a few companies in the food industry. I know I haven't pulled any punches, but I hope we have learned from each other.

I am honored to call Keith Yamamoto my friend and am continually inspired by his calm and principled approach to life. Thank you, Keith.

My thanks to my mother and father, Roz and Irv Kessler, who taught me to enjoy food and much more.

My children, Elise and Ben, are unceasing sources of pleasure and pride. I am in awe of the people they have become. I thank them for so much, including their always candid views on the subject of this book.

And—Paulette, wise counsel and wife, whom I've loved since Amherst snack bar days, I'll be downstairs in a minute.

He just wanted a decent book to read ...

Not too much to ask, is it? It was in 1935 when Allen Lane, Managing Director of Bodley Head Publishers, stood on a platform at Exeter railway station looking for something good to read on his journey back to London. His choice was limited to popular magazines and poor-quality paperbacks – the same choice faced every day by the vast majority of readers, few of whom could afford hardbacks. Lane's disappointment and subsequent anger at the range of books generally available led him to found a company – and change the world.

'We believed in the existence in this country of a vast reading public for intelligent books at a low price, and staked everything on it'
Sir Allen Lane, 1902–1970, founder of Penguin Books

The quality paperback had arrived – and not just in bookshops. Lane was adamant that his Penguins should appear in chain stores and tobacconists, and should cost no more than a packet of cigarettes.

Reading habits (and cigarette prices) have changed since 1935, but Penguin still believes in publishing the best books for everybody to enjoy. We still believe that good design costs no more than bad design, and we still believe that quality books published passionately and responsibly make the world a better place.

So wherever you see the little bird – whether it's on a piece of prize-winning literary fiction or a celebrity autobiography, political tour de force or historical masterpiece, a serial-killer thriller, reference book, world classic or a piece of pure escapism – you can bet that it represents the very best that the genre has to offer.

Whatever you like to read – trust Penguin.